MARKETING WITH E-MAIL

Third Edition

Other Titles of Interest From Maximum Press

101 Ways to Promote Your Web Site, Third Edition: Sweeney,
1-885068-57-3

Business-to-Business Internet Marketing, Fourth Edition: Silverstein,
1-885068-72-7

Marketing on the Internet, Fifth Edition: Zimmerman, 1-885068-49-2

101 Internet Businesses You Can Start From Home: Sweeney,
1-885068-59-X

The e-Business Formula for Success: Sweeney, 1-885068-60-3

Internet Marketing for Your Tourism Business: Sweeney,
1-885068-47-6

*Internet Marketing for Information Technology Companies, Second
Edition:* Silverstein, 1-885068-67-0

Internet Marketing for Less Than $500/Year, Second Edition:
Yudkin, 1-885068-68-9

The Business Guide to Selling Through Internet Auctions: Hix,
1-885068-73-5

For more information, visit our Web site at *www.maxpress.com*
or e-mail us at *moreinfo@maxpress.com*

MARKETING WITH E-MAIL

Third Edition

A spam-free guide to increasing sales, building loyalty, and increasing awareness

Shannon Kinnard

MAXIMUM PRESS
605 Silverthorn Road
Gulf Breeze, FL 32561
(850) 934-0819
www.maxpress.com

Publisher: Jim Hoskins

Manager of Finance/Administration: Joyce Reedy

Production Manager: ReNae Grant

Cover Design: Lauren Smith Design

Compositor: PageCrafters Inc.

Copyeditor: Andrew Potter

Proofreader: Jacquie Wallace

Indexer: Susan Olason

Printer: P.A. Hutchison

This publication is designed to provide accurate and authoritative information in regard to the subject matter covered. It is sold with the understanding that the publisher is not engaged in rendering professional services. If legal, accounting, medical, psychological, or any other expert assistance is required, the services of a competent professional person should be sought. ADAPTED FROM A DECLARATION OF PRINCIPLES OF A JOINT COMMITTEE OF THE AMERICAN BAR ASSOCIATION AND PUBLISHERS.

Recognizing the importance of preserving what has been written, it is a policy of Maximum Press to have books of enduring value published in the United States printed on acid-free paper, and we exert our best efforts to that end.

Library of Congress Cataloging-in-Publication Data

Kinnard, Shannon, 1972-
Marketing with e-mail : a Spam-free guide to increasing sales,
building loyalty, and increasing awareness / Shannon Kinnard.— 3rd ed.
p. cm.
"Published simultaneously in Canada."
Includes index.
ISBN 1-885068-68-9
1. Internet marketing. 2. Internet. I. Title.
HF5415.1265 .K565 2002
658.8'4—dc21
2001004117

Acknowledgments

This book is dedicated to Steve Hansen, for your unwavering support and belief in my abilities. Thank you for being next to me from the very beginning, telling me: "Well, *of course* you can do it!" I honestly couldn't have done it without you.

I wish I had more room to thank, individually, the colleagues, clients, family members and friends who have helped me over the past two years, contributing ideas and money toward my business and supporting my efforts to put together this book. While there are too many to thank individually, a few really stand out, especially my agent Alan Kellock, who helped turn this idea into a book proposal, and author Gerri Detweiler, who introduced me to Alan and encouraged me every step of the way.

On both a professional and a personal level, I want to thank Elecia Osadchuk, a good friend and talented writer who worked on many of the resources sections of *Marketing With E-Mail*, as well as providing top-notch service to Idea Station's clients while I was working on the original manuscript.

I am grateful for all the e-mail marketing expertise I've received since opening the doors of Idea Station. Most of that advice I've tried to funnel into this book. All of the following people were so generous in answering e-mail and spending time on the phone sharing their expertise with me: Sharon Tucci, Nancy Roebke, Rosalind Resnick, Andy Bourland, Stuart Obermann, Lisa Bryan, Christopher Knight, George Matyjewicz, Gary Foote, John Audette and Kate Schultz.

The members of the discussion list Online Publishers provided much of the groundwork for this book through their energetic and resource-filled discussions. They helped me focus on which topics to cover and what to skip. Readers are encouraged to join this ongoing discussion by sending an e-mail to *op-request@listhost.net* with the word "subscribe" (without the quotes) in the body of the message.

Personally, I want to thank my family. My incredible mother, Sheila Kinnard, has always, magically, known when to let me lean on her and when to make me lean on myself. My grandmother, Evelyn Acheson, is a constant inspiration for being independent and keeping an optimistic attitude. My grandfather, Austin Kinnard, helps me keep things in perspective by reminding me of the importance of stopping to smell the roses. My sister, Debra Fisher, and my brother-in-law, Greg Fisher, are a team who, through their incredible journey of recovery over the past two years have given me strength to fight my own little battles along the way. My brother, David Kinnard, lets me pick at his great business mind for free, perhaps the best investment of all for Idea Station.

My father, Fred Kinnard, a small-business owner, also gets credit for teaching me about having my own business, because he taught me a lesson that comes out as my philosophy of e-mail marketing. Dad has operated a little pharmacy in my hometown for over 30 years. When I was growing up in Sarasota, people tended to know my dad. I remember one teacher in high school who, when she read my name, exclaimed, "Kinnard? Are you Fred Kinnard's daughter? Your dad saved my cat Fluffy's life two years ago by crushing up her pills and just yesterday I was in the pharmacy and he asked about Fluffy! I can't believe he remembers Fluffy's name!" I later found out that my dad, standing behind that pharmacy counter, takes notes on his repeat customers (feeding a database) and then reviews these notes when the customer next comes into the store. He then asks the appropriate follow-up questions, so that he can be a better pharmacist to them. I tell this story because I think it exemplifies the true potential of e-mail marketing: It's not about tricking your customer into giving you information that serves your purposes. It's about finding out more about them so that you can build relationships that best serve their needs.

Lastly, I am so very grateful to my wonderful roommates Nicole Lessard and Stacey Allen. Their friendship, encouragement and devotion to their own difficult nursing careers kept me from becoming burned out after my own marathon days working on this book. I can't remember how many times one of them would poke their head around a corner and say, "are you *still* writing?" followed by a glass of wine or mug of coffee, depending on the hour of the day.

Disclaimer

The purchase of computer software or hardware is an important and costly business decision. Although the author and publisher of this book have made reasonable efforts to ensure the accuracy and timeliness of the information contained herein, the author and publisher assume no liability with respect to loss or damage caused or alleged to be caused by reliance on any information contained herein and disclaim any and all warranties, expressed or implied, as to the accuracy or reliability of said information.

This book is not intended to replace the manufacturer's product documentation or personnel in determining the specifications and capabilities of the products mentioned in this book. The manufacturer's product documentation should always be consulted, because the specifications and capabilities of computer hardware and software products are subject to frequent modification. The reader is solely responsible for the choice of computer hardware and software. All configurations and applications of computer hardware and software should be reviewed with manufacturer's representatives prior to choosing or using any computer hardware and software.

Trademarks

The words contained in this text that are believed to be trademarked, service marked, or otherwise to hold proprietary rights have been designated as such by use of initial capitalization. No attempt has been made to designate as trademarked or service marked any personal computer words or terms in which proprietary rights might exist. Inclusion, exclusion, or definition of a word or term is not intended to affect, or to express judgment upon, the validity of legal status of any proprietary right that may be claimed for a specific word or term.

Table of Contents

Part One: The Tools

Chapter 1:
E-Mail Newsletters   2

Chapter 2:
Discussion Lists   26

Chapter 3:
Online Networking   46

Chapter 4:
Signature Files   64

Chapter 7:
Promotions and Direct E-Mail 123

Chapter 8:
Online Public Relations 140

Chapter 9:
Advertising in E-Publications 157

Part Two: The Process

Chapter 10:
The E-Mail Marketing Rulebook   177

Chapter 11:
Technical Know-How   194

Chapter 12:
Measuring Results   220

Introduction

Your "Members Only" Companion Web site

The companion Web site for Marketing With E-mail, at *http:// www.marketingwithemail.com*, is your current source of information, resources and next steps. This site will have the latest news about e-mail marketing, book updates, expanded information, and other e-mail marketing-related resources. The site is open only to members, which are the savvy marketers who own this book. To access the companion Web site, visit the password protected Web site at *http://www.MarketingWithEmail.com* and follow the links to the Marketing With E-mail site. To enter, you'll be prompted to enter the following username and password:

> User ID: *mktemail2e*

> Password: *wall*

You will then have full access to the members-only site. If you bookmark the page once you enter, you'll never have to enter the user ID and password again. Please enjoy the site as our thanks to you for buying the book. We ask that you not share the user ID and password for the site with anyone else.

What Is E-Mail Marketing?

I once spoke at a conference with about 1,000 people in the audience. I described a typical spam message: the type of unsolicited commercial e-mail that advertises some get-rich-quick business venture, salacious promise or irresistible product offer. I asked members of the audience to raise their hand if they'd ever received one of these messages. Just about every person groaned and raised a hand. I then asked the members of my audience to keep those hands up if they'd ever responded to one of these messages, built a relationship with the sender, and bought the product or service being offered. Guess what? Not a single hand stayed up. You could have heard a pin drop.

I'll tell you why not one single person kept a hand up. Because what I described was spam: unsolicited, untargeted, unwanted, and ineffective e-mail. Spam doesn't work. But this book will tell you what does work: legitimate strategic marketing tactics applied to e-mail. E-mail is a communications tool and marketing is about communications. This book will also tell you exactly how to launch an e-mail marketing program, which will not only put you in touch with your target market, but will also help you (if you listen to your audience) build strong relationships with those markets (and perhaps even discover markets that you didn't even know existed).

E-mail is a popular commercial advertising medium. It is a powerful marketing tool—but only if used correctly. This book is going to teach you how to make sure that your e-mail publication is the cream of the crop in the eyes of your audience. The pervasiveness in e-mail is a double-edged sword to Internet marketers. The bad side is that we're reaching critical mass. Everyone is inundated with e-mail that is of both a personal and a business nature. The good side is that it's an easy way to reach a large audience. It's a preferred method of communication for many people. The number of active e-mail users in the United States over 13 years of age is expected to jump from 78 million at year-end 1999 (accounting for 35% of the population) to 135 million users (59% of the population) by year-end 2002. The number of e-mail boxes worldwide went from 234 million in 1998 to 409 million only one year later. The implication is that we must respect this medium and its users—making efficient and effective use of time spent building relationships. Forrester Research predicted that the e-mail marketing industry will soar to a $4.8 billion industry by 2004. They also predict that U.S. marketers will be sending 200 billion e-mail messages, more than twice the 79 billion pieces of bulk mail delivered by the U.S. Postal Service in 1998.

E-mail marketing, the act of sending marketing communications via e-mail to recipients who first request it, is just one tool at your disposal for reaching consumers on the Internet. Other Internet marketing options might include building and hosting your own company's Web site, placing ads on advertising networks, on niche sites and on popular portals and search engines such as Yahoo!.

The most popular pathway (Web sites) that online marketers use to reach this online audience has a fatal flaw: It's passive. With this approach, Web sites languish on the Internet and require consumers to find their own way to them. If you take this approach, you're asking consumers to find you, and then for them to find their way *back* to you for subsequent visits. The major flaw with this logic is that Web sites require the consumer to take action. This results in one-time visits that are not very productive. It's a big waste of resources and a wasted opportunity to gather consumer data.

The majority of sites, too, are the same for each person that visits, meaning the content that person A sees is exactly what person B sees, even when these two visitors are coming from different market segments for different reasons, looking for different information. Some sites (such as My Yahoo! or My Excite) are making strides to customize content to the individual as a way to give each visitor a unique experience and thus, a reason for returning to the site. But this demands an army of technical resources. An easier way to customize the experience of your online presence for your site visitors is through e-mail.

E-mail offers a magic combination of lower cost and faster service when compared with traditional marketing methods, or even when compared with using Web sites to market your company. E-mail marketing, when used to its full potential, offers everything that marketers dream about: It's cost-effective, personal, individualized, popular, interactive, measurable and convenient. eMarketer reports that the cost for traditional direct mail is between $1 and $2 per piece. But e-mail is a mere $0.01 to $0.25 per piece. Due to e-mail's omnipresence across business and personal demographics, it offers an incredible reach. Due to technology's innovative abilities to use databases to customize each outgoing message to each recipient, e-mail is customizable on a massive scale. Finally, with tracking ability enabled by codes imbedded into e-mail messages or with unique URLs or other tracking mechanisms, e-mail marketers can measure the response (on individual and aggregate levels) to outgoing campaigns.

But the practice is changing rapidly, as more and more marketers discover e-mail. Sharon Tucci is the CEO of Slingshot Media, which runs a division called Listhost.net. With this division devoted solely to hosting discussion lists and e-mail newsletters, Tucci refers to "the battle of the inbox" in a recent issue of Listhost News. She lists all the advantages of e-mail as a marketing medium: speed, low cost, convenience, personalization, and tracking. However, she cautions, "as more advertisers become enamored with e-mail as a marketing tool, the quantity of even opt-in messages is growing exponentially. The harder it is for people to cope with the flood, the less receptive they'll be even to communications they agreed to receive."

Because subscribers don't always realize the volume of e-mail they'll receive when they opt-in for a publication, they may ignore your legitimate efforts instead of taking the time to unsubscribe. Tucci's advice is to change your thinking from permission marketing to "want" marketing by focusing on valuable content and keeping your marketing message small ("incidental" she says), in the readers' eyes.

Banner ads and similar Internet marketing options pale in comparison to e-mail marketing. These other options are limited and expensive when placed side by side with e-mail's fast and flexible production cycle, fast and inexpensive delivery to consumers and fast and measurable response from recipients. Mass distributed, automatically customized and personalized e-mail messages sent to self-selected recipients are an emerging and proven marketing tool.

There's a huge misperception, however, about the phrase "e-mail marketing." On the surface, it's often mistaken for a nasty little practice called spam. So it's important to understand, right up front, what e-mail marketing *is not*. It is not a get-rich-quick scheme. It is not guaranteed to have instant success. It is not a stand-alone marketing tactic. Most important, it is not to be sent uninvited or unsolicited by the recipient.

With the commercialization of the Internet comes a wealth of possibilities for savvy and creative marketers. It also brings a wealth of possibilities for people to misuse and abuse the system. Make the decision right now to conduct an e-mail marketing program that is legitimate, honorable and methodical. It's the only way to guarantee success...not instant success, but there are some tricks in this book to help you jump start your e-mail marketing campaign.

At another conference, a panel discussion hosted in January 2001 by the National Retail Federation, luxury goods marketers talked about e-mail's ability to build relationships. At this conference, Henry Nasella, chairman and co-founder of Online Retail Partners, moderated a session that included Paul Blum, executive vice president and COO of Kenneth Cole Productions; Denise Incandela, COO of Saks Direct; Gregg Renfrew, CEO of The Wedding List; Rochelle Udell, president of the Internet Division for Fairchild Publications; and Gregory Furman, formerly of Bergdorf-Goodman and now chairman of The Luxury Marketing Council. One of the conclusions reached by the group was that e-mail has become the most effective marketing tool for luxury marketing, but that brands need to constantly pack entertainment and fun into their info-offerings.

E-mail marketing is the Web's true killer application. The term encompasses everything from building your own database of e-mail addresses to renting third-party lists. It is the online equivalent of an offline direct mail campaign, with more bang for your buck than any traditional direct marketer ever dreamed. Andy Bourland, with the ClickZ network, an online-marketing-information supersite, calls e-mail marketing the most important tool that online business owners and marketers can develop to give people a reason to visit a Web site at least every week, if not every day. The bottom line, he says, is to give them new, personalized, customized, compelling information.

Who Should Use This Book?

Gus Venditto, editor-in-chief of Internet.com, Mecklermedia's Web service, recently wrote, "E-mail lists are maturing into a serious business tool that has only begun to scratch the surface of its full potential." To keep on top of this growing marketing opportunity, this book will be of value to the following audiences:

- Businesses already engaged in e-commerce that want to expand and improve marketing communications efforts.

- Politicians interested in the legislation issues surrounding unsolicited commercial e-mail (UCE), anonymous bulk e-mail (SPAM) and the valid commercial applications of e-mail.

- Advertising, public relations, and marketing executives and consultants who need to have online marketing knowledge to stay current.

- Small business owners who are catching on to the exciting prospect that e-mail marketing can help level the playing field versus larger competitors, and are desperate for guidance about how to exploit this huge new opportunity.

- Business consultants and business writers who need an expert resource.

How To Use This Book

Marketing communications, delivered via e-mail, to willing and interested recipients, present an ideal opportunity for personal dialogue. They allow a one-to-one relationship between you, the marketer, and your target audience. This book will outline all the tools at your disposal and then will give you an outline to use to build your own e-mail marketing plan that suits your business.

This book is divided into two sections. Part I outlines each of the tools that you can use to build your e-mail marketing plan. Use this section of the book to make notes as you discover applications for your own business. Chapter 1 discusses e-mail newsletters, how they work to reach your audience and how they can be scaled to fit any size budget and any size audience. They are the number one e-mail marketing tool at your disposal. Chapter 2 will turn you on to discussion lists: both participating in them and hosting your own. Both will dramatically increase awareness of you and your business and will establish your expertise in your industry. Chapter 3 outlines online networking, which is a combination of several online activities that will personally introduce your company to thousands of prospects.

Chapter 4 explains the importance and the logistics of using a signature file as your electronic business card. Signature files are integral to just about every other e-mail marketing effort. Chapter 5 explains how autoresponders can simplify your life by automating the process of sending information out to clients, customers, prospects, and the media. Chapter 6 goes over the essential online customer service component of your e-mail marketing plan. Chapter 7 talks about promotions and direct e-mail, which let you test out the e-mail marketing waters or run a full-scale campaign. Chapter 8 discusses how members of the press who are online will appreciate and reward you for using the Internet smartly and efficiently. Public relations has made a significant transition into the online realm. Chapter 9 talks about advertising in e-mail publications, both how other e-mail publications can work for you, by allowing you to reach their niche audience and how you, as an online publisher, can make nominal (or substantial) money by selling ads in your e-mail publication. This practice is predicted, by eMarketer, to grow substantially. They report that U.S. firms will increase their spending on e-mail ads from $97 million in 1999 to $2 billion in 2003.

Part II guides you through the technical aspects of the e-mail marketing process. If Part I is the "what to do," then Part II is the "how to do." Chapter 10 goes over the rules associated with e-mail marketing, namely "don't spam!" Chapter 11 gives some of the technical instructions for different e-mail marketing programs. In Chapter 12, you'll read about the importance of testing and measuring results and you'll learn about some of the tools that allow you to make the most of your e-mail marketing dollars. Chapter 13 goes over opt-in list brokers, which are the only reputable alternative to building your own e-mail marketing database of names.

It doesn't end when you finish the book. This book includes, of course, a companion e-mail newsletter, the Marketing With E-mail Idea Feed. To subscribe, visit *http://www.ideastation.com/feed.html.*

A History of E-Mail-Based Publications

E-mail-based communication has been around for a long time, but has only recently started becoming recognized for its marketing capabilities. The main use of e-mail as a vehicle for marketing use had always been opt-in e-mail newsletters and special product promotions. Early efforts consisted of simple software tools and programs that at a maximum inserted the first name of the recipient in the e-mail message at some appropriate point.

Even these early and basic campaigns with little or no personalization could be effective. According to a report by the research firm Forrester, "Opt-In E-mail Gets Personal," e-mail marketers using relatively simplistic campaigns to drive traffic to their site report click-through rates of 14% to 22% (1998). Messages that had the objective of driving sales report a conversion rate of 4%. Compared to direct marketing offline, these are phenomenally successful rates. However, given that some e-mail marketing campaigns can yield results as high as 30%, these campaigns can be improved. The report also showed that e-mail marketing is more cost effective than traditional marketing by mail because e-mail eliminates the paper, postage and printing that accounts for 60% of the cost of direct mail. The trick is knowing how to make sure that your e-mail marketing pieces are anticipated and enjoyed by the recipient...that means you have to think in terms of giving the recipient excellent information to build trust, not a sales pitch to build profits.

There are some different terms being thrown around related to subscriber-based e-mail publications. Here's a definition:

> *An e-zine is a non-commercial, hobby-focused e-mail newsletter. It is derived from* zine *(rhymes with "nine") not* magazine. *A "zine" is an underground print publication, generally alternative and extremely niche focused. An e-zine is the electronic version of a zine. E-mail newsletters are often miscalled e-zines. This happens so frequently that the two phrases have become synonymous.*

An e-mail newsletter is, in content, basically the electronic equivalent of a print newsletter. Generally, it is a subscriber-based marketing tool for a business or association. Content may include topics ranging from business happenings to industry happenings to feedback mechanisms. While it doesn't have to be totally marketing-free, the key word in *newsletter* is news, so it's important to deliver valuable content, not lengthy ads. E-mail newsletters can come in three formats: HTML (like a Web page), plain text (like you're reading right now), and more current proprietary technology designed to encapsulate and send detailed graphic images as tiny files.

E-mail discussion lists are a many-to-many form of communication. These are either filtered through a moderator (an actual person who decides which messages to approve) or hosted without a moderator (so every member can send whatever and however much they want). Subscribers or members are encouraged to submit their own posts, which make up the bulk of content. A "post" is an e-mail message, sent to a central address and then distributed to all the members. Posts that contribute to existing discussions are collectively referred to as "threads."

Why E-Mail?

Immediacy is one of the most compelling reasons to use e-mail as a marketing vehicle. It works for the sender and for the recipient. The e-mail publisher also enjoys immediate measurement with the ability to track delivery, response, action, and purchase for each and every message sent. The flip side is pretty attractive as well. Consumers are able to receive an offer and act immediately. For example, let's say you're a software publisher and you offer a free software demo. When your message is sent, the recipient downloads your software. Or let's say you're a major online retailer like RedEnvelope.com. You can send a message to your audience one week before Father's Day reminding your audience that all dads like to eat cookies. You also let them know that you're offering a discount on your own brand of gourmet cookies. Finally, you include in your message a quick link that let's them easily send a gourmet batch right to dad. A couple days later, you can generate a quick report letting you know how many sons and daughters on your list took you up on your offer and you can measure the effectiveness of your campaign.

E-mail is quickly growing in acceptance, evidenced by the fact that there are more than 90,000 different e-mail newsletters and discussion lists. Subjects range from academic to commercial to pure fun, from moderated discussion to unmoderated discussion to one-way announcement.

Christopher "Sparky" Knight says that he has made millions of dollars with his e-mail lists. The secret, he says, is using them in non-spam, innovative, and creative ways. Through his company, SparkNET, which offers list management technology and expertise, Knight currently manages more than 216 lists, with around 100,000 subscribers and about 8 million outgoing e-mails per month in volume. These are just the lists related to SparkNET, not their clients. Factor in the client services offered through SparkLIST.com, and he's got millions of list members and 60+ million e-mails delivered each month.

Knight defines e-mail marketing as "creating demand for yourself and your business by delivering value to others, via e-mail, with lists that you give to the marketplace to opt-into." He believes that lists are the best way to support any new Web site business. E-mail marketing publications are great for a variety of things, including increasing sales, delivering value, keeping top of mind awareness, improving customer confidence, and pulling clients back to a site, instead of having to wait for them to get around to visiting a site.

There are many more reasons why e-mail is working for so many marketers:

- You can reach a super-targeted niche! There's so much potential for reaching a very specific segment. Perhaps thirty-year-old unmarried Jewish men in the United States with annual incomes above $80k who drink coffee, own Springer Spaniels, and are in the market for a new pair of running shoes aren't your target market, but they're someone's, and a list of them either exists or can be built.

- You can build a one-to-one relationship with a large group. No other medium, not direct mail, television, telemarketing, not any other targeted tool, can ensure the same reach and pull as e-mail marketing. A customized direct mail piece, for example, even addressed to a specific recipient, doesn't tell the marketer if the person opened or even received it.

- Your recipients pick YOU! By definition, opt-in means that the consumer wants to receive your information and they tell you so themselves. They come to you because they want you, so they're qualified.

- Measurability can be built in using a variety of low-tech (like discount codes with purchase) or high-tech (like trackable URLs) mechanisms.

- There's the potential for higher response rates. Because measurability is so high, accountability is high. Thus, responsible marketers tailor their campaign based on what testing and measuring indicates they should do are sure to see higher response rates.

- Existing e-mail newsletters are highly targeted. This gives you the opportunity to place ads that guarantee a specific and targeted audience from a range of demographics. Special interest newsletters attract the type of audience that you want to reach.

- You can create a campaign for any budget! Because you can do it yourself, you can work on a shoestring. But if you've got a big budget, you'll still get your money's worth with this measurable and cost-effective medium.

- Consider all the things you're *not* paying for—printing, postage, long distance. Cost is lowered by orders of magnitude when you compare direct mail to direct e-mail.

- E-mail campaigns create an opportunity for long-term relationships. It's more cost-effective to keep a customer than to acquire a new one, so take advantage of e-mail's ability to turn prospects into repeat buyers.

Take advantage of the convenience of e-mail. E-mail can sit in your in-box for a little while, but the phone can't keep ringing endlessly and you can't leave a customer fuming on hold for very long. E-mail can replace the phone for customer interactions in a variety of situations. Encouraging this will reduce actual cost and cost spent on time for customer service.

Opt-in e-mail marketing, combined with a database that recipients fill in themselves, increases the accuracy of demographics about your recipients, increasing the effectiveness of your messages to them, assuming that they truthfully reveal their tastes and interests to you, which they will do if you promise to meet those interests.

Your creativity is appreciated with e-mail marketing! Recipients of personalized, informative and entertaining e-mails are very responsive.

There's potential for building loyalty to your brand. E-mail marketing that rewards customers (with appreciation, specials, etc.) will see that customers return the favor with continued patronage. You can track users from signup to purchase to repeat purchase, and then match these buyers to related products or customers-only special offers.

It's easy for prospects and customers to respond by e-mail. If a direct mail piece comes to consumers and they want to respond, they have to respond by phone or mail. But via e-mail, it's a simple click of the Reply button to deal with an offer.

E-Mail and the Right to Privacy

Spam violates recipients for a dozen reasons, but the most infuriating is the trespass on privacy. This book outlines an entire chapter on the ways to avoid becoming a spammer and to respect an online consumer's right to privacy. The big distinction here is the term *opt-in*. The crucial element of any e-mail marketing campaign is the recipient and their choice to receive your e-mail message. They must choose to receive your message; they should not be tricked into having to choose *not to* receive your message. If you make them choose not to receive your message, it is called "opt-out" and it is the same thing as spam.

Christopher Knight, "Sparky" of Sparky's List-Tips advises designing a privacy statement in order to reassure your list subscribers that you care about their privacy, which will raise their trust in you and encourage them to become your customers. Because the members of your list need to be able to trust you to protect their identity, not having this public statement that you will comply may keep them from joining your list community. One of the most important roles in marketing is to increase customer confidence and trust in you, your product, your brand name and your list.

The privacy statement on SparkList's site reads as follows:

> *We respect your privacy! Any and all information collected at this site will be kept strictly confidential and will not be sold, reused, rented, loaned, or otherwise disclosed. Any information you give to SparkNET Interactive will be held with the utmost care, and will not be used in ways that you have not consented to. A more detailed explanation about how we safeguard your personal information is described below. If you have any questions, please don't hesitate to let us know.*
>
> *Resale or disclosure of information to third parties:*
>
> *SparkNET Interactive does not sell, rent, loan, trade, or lease any personal information collected at our site, including membership forms or email lists.*
>
> *Browser information collected on the website:*
>
> *SparkNET Interactive analyzes our website logs to constantly improve the value of the materials available on our website. Our website logs are not personally identifiable, and we make no attempt to link them with the individuals that actually browse the site.*

Use of cookies:

We do not use cookies on this site.

Privacy of our email lists:

SparkNET Interactive maintains several email lists to keep SparkLIST/SparkNet members, the press, and interested members of the general public informed about breaking events. Individuals must affirmatively request to join our mailing lists by signing up through a form on our web site. We do not sell, rent, loan, trade, or lease the addresses on our list to anyone. In addition, we configure our list server software to refuse to divulge the email addresses of our list subscribers to anyone but authorized SparkNET Interactive staff, including other list subscribers.

If you have comments about our privacy policy, send them to: privacy@list-tips.com."

This privacy statement assures all potential list members and visitors to the site that their information will be respected. In addition, it serves as an excellent example to the rest of the Internet community for creating a statement that encompasses a broad range of situations.

Your Database

The heart and soul of e-mail marketing is the database. This plan focuses on a robust and clean collection of information about your audience. The progression of work is as follows:

- Create a list of details that you'd like to know about your audience.

- Establish a welcome message that includes instructions for joining and unjoining your database.

Industry Uses of E-Mail Marketing

In WebPromote's excellent guide to permission marketing on the Web, Deena Flammang, co-founder of marketing and business development consultancy Net StrategEase and Harvey John Morris, WebPromote's Director of Corporate Branding, outline how different industries can take advantage of e-mail marketing. (This excerpt is reprinted with permission from Ken Wruk at WebPromote).

Travel Industry

A major airline uses opt-in e-mail to alert its clients to last-minute fares that are priced at a special low rate for online purchase. This information gets to prospects and clients much quicker—and more cost-effectively—than a newspaper or radio ad. The airline reaches its target audience more effectively and has a quicker turn-around time to fill the airplane seats vs. waiting till people respond to print or broadcast advertisements.

Software Industry

A premier method of getting a prospect's attention is offering free trial software via the Web. A leading software reseller that exists only in cyberspace and employs the Internet as its primary marketing channel has grown its database of clients exponentially by adapting this approach and by lowering the inherent overhead costs associated with a bricks-and-mortar store.

Financial Services

Another effective means a leading financial institution utilized to attract new clients was offering special low-interest credit cards to a select demographic. Their response rate using qualified third-party opt-in e-mail lists was a whopping 32%. This shows what can happen when you direct a great offer to the right target audience.

Industrial Products

A European industrial company decided to test opt-in e-mail to offer a print catalog to prospects in specific geographic areas throughout the European Union. The response rate was 10% higher than their past direct mail efforts. They calculated that they saved over $30,000 which they would have incurred using traditional direct mail and they would not have achieved such a high response rate. As a result, they could use the dollars they saved to do additional marketing to their target audience online.

Medical Industry

A pharmaceutical corporation sends medical news updates monthly to its entire opt-in database of doctors and hospitals which includes current information about new drugs, their benefits, and their side effects. Providing value-added information is one of the surest ways to attract and maintain new clients through doctor referrals. An added benefit that the pharmaceutical company receives is a tremendous amount of feedback that helps them know their end-client better, what they are thinking and what other information doctors are interested in receiving.

- Estimate how much time you will put into maintenance of your plan. Devote the personal time it takes to construct online relationships.

- Allocate a budget for various in-house costs such as hosting and software; for outsource costs, such as writers and programmers; and for purchases, such as opt-in lists and advertising.

- Have a clear sense of your objectives. Make them known to your company and your audience.

- Identify and implement tactics to achieve your objectives.

Your plan will allow you to think holistically, across all media, not just e-mail, not just the Internet...but print, outdoor, in-store and broadcast as well.

A Word About Viruses

In the Spring of 2000, a virus known as the ILOVEYOU virus crippled e-mail servers worldwide. Nagaraja Srivatsan, vice president, Digital Vision Labs at SeraNova, Inc., explained how this virus worked: "Someone sent this file as an attachment to an e-mail user. The user thinks that the message and attachment are from a friend. User opens the attachment. The attachment is actually a Visual Basic (VB) script that installs itself as a VB application. This VB application scans the Microsoft Outlook address book and looks for contacts and then starts to e-mail those in the address book with a copy of itself." He further explained that this particular virus only worked on people who opened the attachment using Microsoft Outlook under Microsoft Windows. His advice: "do not open attachments from unknown people." People start viruses to be malicious, vindictive or for recognition.

Srivatsan says that the threat of viruses can impact legitimate e-mail marketing efforts. "Everyone is now going to set up rules that will delete e-mail automatically if it is not from a known source. Legitimate e-mail efforts have to have a clear Opt In/Opt out strategy."

With this in mind, remember that a good e-mail marketing plan is about the human element. Make sure that there's a real person behind your e-mail marketing program, and that person is devoted to communicating individually with subscribers.

Make a Plan!

The guidelines in this book aren't hard and fast rules; they're idea starters! Use them as a way to get started on your own plan. Chapter 14 offers worksheets and charts that can be used to create a plan of your own.

The plan that you create is the essential first step for creating your list. You don't have to put together a full-blown hundred-page e-mail marketing document complete with graphs and footnotes in order for it to be effective. But you do have to define some of the following essentials before you get started:

- Who is your audience? What do you want them to do? What tools will you use?

- For each tool, outline the executional details: tactics, policies, responsibilities.

- Establish the benchmarks against which you will measure success. Be prepared to tailor your campaign (and this document along with it) to improve your success ratio.

- Before you start any program involving subscribers (including discussion lists, e-mail newsletters and promotional announcements), establish a welcome message that includes subscribe and unsubscribe instructions, rules for subscribers, and a description of what your list is about.

- Estimate how much time you will put into maintenance of your plan. Devote the personal time it takes to construct online relationships.

- Allocate a budget for various in-house costs such as hosting and software; for outsource costs, like writers and programmers; and for purchases, such as opt-in lists and advertising.

While it's not necessary to have a formal plan, you do have to have a clear sense of your objectives. The bulk of your e-mail marketing plan is to outline how you will achieve your objective. Each tool you implement is a tactic; the plan will connect how each tactic delivers on each objective.

Your plan will allow you to think holistically, which is important, because cross-media campaigns are shown to be the most effective. In conjunction with a cross-media approach, creating a plan and sharing it with your entire organization allows you to get buy-in across company departments. If your campaign will require the support of other departments, such as sales, customer service and technical support, the plan is essential.

The table shown in Figure I-1 is an example of a simple, yet effective, plan run by the United Way and the Technology Association of Georgia. The program, called Web Challenge, used a simple e-mail marketing program to remind high school students to work on Web sites that they were creating and posting to be judged as part of a competition for scholarship money.

Your plan can be as simple as the one shown in the example. The point is just to touch base often enough to build a relationship. A simple spreadsheet lets you view distribution dates, subject lines and content of each e-mail that goes out.

Resources

- "Engaging Customers in E-Business; How to Build Sales, Relationships and Results with Email" by Jeffrey L. Farris and Laura Langendorf. Available from e2Communications by e-mailing *sales@e2communications.com* or calling 888-883-2542 (toll free).

- "One to One Email" by Darren Bosik and Tony Kubrin. Sponsored by MessageMedia and available from the Peppers & Rogers Group by calling 203-316-5121 or visiting *http://www.1to1.com.*

Date	Subject Line	Content
1/20/00	FTP Early & FTP Happy!	Hey Web Challenge Teams! It's getting close to the deadline for uploading your sites for review by the Web Challenge judging panel. Don't wait until the last minute to get your files uploaded to the servers. Transferring files can get a bit tricky, and this email is designed to help. Included with your MindSpring hosting account should be files and instructions on how to FTP. You can also find information at the Software Depot, located at *download.mindspring.com*. Insert information from the Users Guide, on the MindSpring site, if you can find it. Make sure that your permissions are set correctly if you're using scripts. Scripts must be kept in the CGI-Bin directory. Good luck. Don't forget the deadline is 2/5/2000 at 5 pm.
1/24/00	Don't Wait Until Later, Navigator	With the deadline for entries looming, make sure your site navigation is thoroughly tested. Now that you've got your site transferred to your account (right?), you should take the time to check each link from an outside computer, such as a library, not a computer on which the site was built (called the 'client side'). This allows you to locate missing links and find deadends on your site.
1/31/00	A Picture Is Worth How Many Points?	Graphics can be tricky on the Web because they display differently on different computers—and that includes the judges' computers! So make sure that you look at your pictures from several computers. Make sure pictures work at the two most popular resolutions: 640 x 480 and 800 x 600. Also, make sure your pictures display correctly on the two most popular browsers: Internet Explorer and Netscape.
2/2/2000	Don't Use No Grammar or Spelling Misteaks	You should have cringed when you saw that subject line! If not, get someone else on your team to run through your text with an English teacher's eye. Check out your grammar, spelling

Figure I.1. The Web Challenge program, run by the United Way and the Technology Association of Georgia. *(continued on next page).*

Date	Subject Line	Content
		and readability of the content on your site. Attention to detail is a major part of this competition, and now's the time to be running this type of final check.
2/4/2000	10...9...8...7... 6....5....4....3.... 2...1 day left until your site is due!	Here is a recap of what we hope were motivational and helpful tips. These final checks should ensure that your site has a fighting chance: - Make sure your permissions are set to run scripts properly. - Make sure all your links land on an active page. - Proofread, proofread, proofread! - Test your graphics.
2/5/2000	Today's the Day!	Just a final note that today is the deadline. By close of business today...that's 5 PM... your site must be up in its final, final form. Passwords will be changed at that point and you will no longer have access to your site. Good luck!
2/6/2000	Congrats! You're Done!	Thanks for playing! Here's the information that you need for the next step (could it be winning the big prize?). Details/dates/etc. about final event.

Figure I.1. The Web Challenge program, run by the United Way and the Technology Association of Georgia. *(continued from previous page)*.

- The PriceWaterhouseCoopers, *http://www.pwcglobal.com*, 1999 Technology Forecast is available for US$450 by calling 1-800-654-3387.

- WebPromote's Practical Guide to Permission Marketing on the Web, *http://www.webpromote.com/pmguide*, is a white paper that covers the applications of e-mail marketing to different industries.

- *Permission Marketing: Turning Strangers into Friends, and Friends into Customers,* by Seth Godin, Founder, Yoyodyne, now part of Yahoo! ($24, Simon & Schuster) is about how traditional "interruptive" advertising techniques are wasteful and ineffective by themselves, but when a consumer volunteers to receive marketing messages, it's effective. Get four free chapters via e-mail by submitting your e-mail address to *http://www.permission.com*.

- Web Marketing Today newsletter, *http://www.wilsonweb.com/wmt*, is a free e-mail newsletter published twice monthly, with a large subscriber base.

- The Privacy Alliance offers guidelines online to help you write a privacy statement to post to your site or in conjunction with your e-mail newsletter. Visit *http://www.privacyalliance.org/resources/ppguidelines.shtml* for details.

- WebCMO Surveys, *http://www.WebCMO.com/mis/survey.htm*, is a partnership between WebCMO and the LinkExchange Daily Digest to explore Web business practices and offer reports to the public. Topics include e-mail marketing strategy, Web marketing performance, privacy issues, online promotion strategy and customer satisfaction.

- The Email Place, *http://www.theemailplace.com*, sponsored by Brooklyn North Software, is a resource for e-mail marketers, with a wealth of articles on a variety of aspects of this industry.

- Ezine Seek, *http://www.ezineseek.com/*, is an e-zine directory that offers a free biweekly e-zine with articles and tips for publishers, as well as reviews and site updates. Subscribers can participate in ePub, a moderated online discussion about publishing online. To subscribe to ePub via e-mail, send a blank message to *epub-subscribe@onelist.com*.

- EMarketer, *http://www.emarketer.com*, is a resource for updates on what is happening in all facets of the Web, including statistics, advertising, and a free weekly newsletter that reports on all new Web marketers.

- ChannelSeven, *http://www.channelseven.com*, is another resource for news and information on marketing and advertising on the Web. Features are the Daily NarrowCast newsletter and research and case studies on specific firms and agencies.

- Promotion World, *http://www.promotionworld.com*, offers tutorials, articles and interviews on promoting Web sites.

Cheat Sheet: What To Take Away From This Book

1. Make a plan that defines your audience. State your objectives and goals first. Then lay the groundwork for each step that you'll have to take to reach those objectives.

2. Start building your "house list" (a list of e-mail addresses that you keep in your own company database) this minute! Each consumer that visits your site for the first time and leaves without sharing their contact information and personal preferences is a *completely wasted opportunity!*

3. There's a 99.9% chance that an e-mail newsletter is the right marketing move for your business. Even if it's the ONLY thing you do.

4. Follow this cycle: Plan your e-mail marketing campaign carefully and against set objectives. Measure how the actual response compares to the planned response by watching recipients and tracking respondents. Tailor the next outgoing e-mail message to incorporate all the feedback you receive. This cycle ensures that your campaign will continually improve.

5. Learn exactly what activity constitutes opt-out e-mail, unsolicited commercial e-mail and spam. Vow to never, ever incorporate these dastardly evils into your e-mail marketing plan.

6. Be different in voice, tone, content, style, or subject. You've got a lot of competition out there. Make your e-mail publication one of the best online.

7. Become a part of the online community, through discussion lists and one-to-one networking.

8. Design your e-mail marketing plan around an e-mail publication that has value to the consumer. Make it clear that there will be a sweet reward for those consumers who become members (through opt-in) of your e-mail database.

9. Do a good job. Yes, that seems obvious or easy, but it's not. Even when you're writing about your most favorite topic ever and you're the world's leading expert, the process simply takes time to ensure quality, informative, unique, and non-salesy content. The easiest way to ensure this is to pay attention to what is relevant for *your audience*. Members should feel like they have the pull to influence editorial decisions and offers. They should feel respected.

10. Be creative: the rules aren't set in stone. Your house list is your own personal focus group. Try lots of different approaches and use the one that is the most effective.

11. Promote it! Take the time to trade advertising, to purchase advertising, to use your signature file well, to get in discussion groups, to use banner ads, to add an announcement of your e-mail publication to all your print advertising, billing, in-store literature and other offline forums. Build your user base!

12. Last, understand that this is a growing, changing industry. If you're reading this book, chances are that you're already one of the people who is shaping the outcome of the practices of e-mail marketing. If not, this book is your ticket to become a part of history by participating, learning, perfecting and instructing others!

The bottom line is this: the market for your product either exists online today or it will tomorrow. According to the *Computer Industry Almanac*, the number of people with Internet e-mail access worldwide will grow 800 percent to 450 million in the next three years, up from 60 million today.

What portion of those people will you reach?

Part One:

The Tools

1

E-Mail Newsletters

The first chapter of this book is devoted to e-mail newsletters for one reason: They work. They are effective at achieving your number one goal, which is to build a relationship with subscribers. An offer, from your Web site, of a regularly delivered e-mail newsletter full of helpful tips and articles serves a specific function. You, the publisher, are making a promise to your subscribers. In return for their attention and permission, you reward them by delivering valuable content. Forget trying to sell to them. Simply focus on servicing them. While your end goal could be sales, that isn't the first step. At a minimum, they give you permission to deliver your information to them. As you build trust or as you offer more valuable information, you can begin to delve deeper into demographics and psychographics about your subscribers. You can trade this valuable content for valuable details about their interests, demographics, and lifestyles.

Your newsletter might be as simple as a one-paragraph tip each week related to your industry. By relating such a tip to your product, you will build the important relationship between you and your subscriber. You might consider making a discount offer just to turn readers into buying customers, but in the early stages consider their attention and permission just as important as their purchase. Of course, you can publish a newsletter that is as complex as a full editorial schedule of columns and articles in return for the reader's e-mail address plus first name, date of birth, occupation, and favorite dessert (or whatever juicy pieces of data serve your marketing purposes).

Building these levels of permission allows you to use data that your subscribers volunteer to give you in return for whatever information you're offering as the content of your e-mail marketing program. Once you capture their data, you can send them the promised information, which builds the relationship between you and them—it's the first step of trust. Potential customers might come to your site only one time but never return. However, if you offer them the option of signing up to automatically receive information from you (such as an e-mail newsletter), they become a part of your database of subscribers. From this point forward, they don't have to make the effort or remember to visit your site again, but they still receive regular, useful pieces of information from you, reminding them to purchase your products and services.

E-mail newsletters are the oldest and, in the opinion of some, best weapon in your e-mail marketing arsenal. It's simple, really: You make the promise to regularly deliver an informative, value-added e-mail newsletter to a self-selected group of prospects who have visited your site. All that you ask of them is their e-mail address, possibly some other pieces of information, and permission to send them the e-mail publication described on your site. They think, "okay, I want to hear more from this company." This is when the fun begins....

What Is an E-Mail Newsletter?

An e-mail newsletter is just like a regular newsletter. It is a collection of articles, commentary, special offers, tips, quotes and other pieces of information. The only difference is that it is delivered to subscribers via e-mail. There are two main reasons why these newsletters are important to your business and vital to your e-mail marketing endeavors. Marketing messages are everywhere, so recipients are becoming *increasingly savvy about*, *rather distrusting of*, and *remarkably unaffected by* the overwhelming amounts of sales pitches and marketing messages thrown at them through television, print, Internet, and outdoor advertising. Because of the mass of e-mail that every consumer deals with—both personal and commercial, the same thing is happening with e-mail: We're reaching critical mass.

E-mail is not only ubiquitous, it is preferred over voice and face-to-face communications, according to Ernst & Young and the American Management Association. It is available everywhere—home, office, and cybercafes worldwide. It's also an important tool that must be correctly implemented in order to brand your company the way you want outsiders to see you. "Think of your newsletter as the windows and door of a brick and mortar business. It is the first thing people see before visiting your company," warns Robert M. Caruso, CEO of OnMercial *(http://www.MercialXpress.com)*, which sells an innovative software program for distributing graphic e-mails to a subscriber base. "If it does not look good or is unprofessionally presented, you will make a poor impression on your recipient."

There are several required elements for an e-mail newsletter. First, recipients must "subscribe," meaning *they* contact *you* and ask to be added to your list of subscribers. Second, the content that you send must be useful: news, instructions, and announcements, not sales—unless you've specifically indicated that your newsletter will consist of sales specials or straight advertising material. The differences between a print newsletter and an e-mail newsletter lie in both the medium and the delivery mechanism. While both reach a niche target audience with valuable, newsy, informative articles, traditional newsletters are printed on paper and e-mail newsletters are delivered as an e-mail message.

You're probably already familiar with print newsletters, distributed via postal mail or as take-one displays in places like the waiting rooms of doctors' offices, the check-out counter of stores, and on newsstands alongside magazines and newspapers. E-mail newsletters are delivered via e-mail over the Internet. For companies that offer both print and e-mail newsletters, sometimes there's a charge for subscription (one example is the *Wall Street Journal*), but most often, subscription is free. Print newsletters almost always have some type of artwork (drawings, clip art, or photographs), but e-mail newsletters started off as simply text. As the technology advances, more and more publishers include graphic images in their newsletter.

The most popular way to create an e-mail newsletter with graphics is to use HTML (hypertext markup language). Other ways include rich media, an attached file, or special software that is written for the specific purpose of sending graphic images, such as OnMercial, mentioned earlier. HTML is the same coding used to create Web pages. With a graphical e-mail newsletter, subscribers have to use an e-mail program that reads HTML, a browser (such as Netscape Navigator and Microsoft Internet Explorer), or a graphics reader (such as Adobe Acrobat). Figure 1.1 shows the difference in appearance between an e-mail newsletter created as ASCII text and one created using HTML. This book

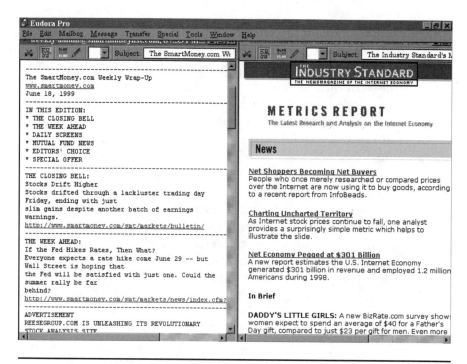

Figure 1.1.   Text (left) vs. HTML (right) e-mail.

does not cover the process of creating HTML documents, however, there are plenty of available resources on- and offline for coding HTML.

Subscribers normally find an e-mail newsletter on the Internet while searching through different Web sites for other purposes. In fact, the number one reason most Web site owners launch an e-mail newsletter is to encourage prospects to keep in touch after that initial visit. A link that says, "Subscribe to Our FREE Newsletter!" (like the example shown in Figure 1.2) is one of the best ways to make sure that you get prospects' e-mail addresses and their permission to use that address to send them information about your company. While you can't expect all visitors to bookmark your site and return regularly, you can expect almost all of them to request your e-mail newsletter when they drop by and to accept that e-mail newsletter on a regular basis.

It's important that you be aware of the deal that you are making when you accept a new subscriber. You're making a promise to each and every subscriber that your newsletters will contain news. Too many e-mail newsletter publishers waste thousands of opportunities to sell more when they build up a valuable list of subscribers and then insult

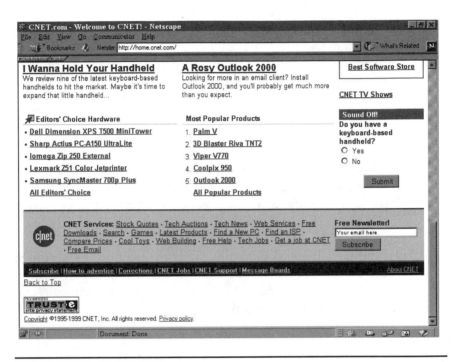

Figure 1.2.   CNET's Web site home page (*http://home.cnet.com*). Reprinted with permission from CNET, Inc., © copyright 1995–1999.

them with a newsletter that is just a thinly veiled self-promotion. It's a surefire way to send subscribers scrambling for the delete key.

Now that you understand what does and doesn't belong in your e-mail newsletter, how are you going to design the perfect e-mail newsletter for your business? First, determine your goals. What benefit are you trying to get from your e-mail marketing program? What do you want to accomplish? If your goals are met by one of the key benefits discussed in the following pages, then we've got plenty of suggestions on the perfect e-mail newsletter for your business.

Key Benefits: Building Relationships, Branding, Added Sales, Market Research

If you are proactive with your e-mail marketing program, you will be able to build relationships with your subscribers. An excellent way to build these relationships is to promise and deliver an excellent e-mail newsletter. The promise is that you will publish the targeted, valuable information described at the point of signup and that you will publish it on a regular basis. If your goal is to build a relationship that promotes your expertise and credibility, punctuality is important. When you deliver on your promise, you will build trust with your readers.

It's quite simple: The larger your subscriber numbers become, the more chances you have to publicize your business. CNET, located at *http://www.cnet.com*, sends more than 40 newsletters either weekly or bimonthly to more than 3 million readers. CNET consistently pulls readers back into their site by offering education, news, and updated features. They also promote their site partners and advertisers. Topics cover everything from computer industry news to product reviews to commentary to resources. To subscribe, visit the site and click on the Subscribe radio button next to the publications you would like to receive.

As you brainstorm over the possible topics that an e-mail newsletter from your company could cover, go further than just your company's product or service. This way, you can reach a broader, yet still targeted audience. For example, let's say you sell cigars and a correlation has been shown between cigar smokers and wine drinkers. In each issue of your cigar newsletter, why not highlight an excellent bottle of wine? (This example is real, by the way: go to *http://www.paylesscigars.com* and sign up for "The Lector" to learn more about excellent cigars and the libations that accompany them.) Include a tag line with your newsletter title that says something to the effect of "brought to you by X Corporation, makers of XYZ." When your readers decide that they are in the market for your product or service (and you probably helped them come to this conclusion) the trust-based relationship that you have built will prove to be valuable.

E-mail newsletters also give you the opportunity to position yourself on a regular basis in front of an online audience that increases daily. As your newsletter's subscriber base grows, so does your credibility and expert status. For this reason, it is important to report the information from an impartial standpoint. You can inject your honest opinion, but don't let that opinion be swayed by the almighty dollar (such as advertising revenue) or you'll lose much of your credibility.

Each issue is a sales opportunity. Focus your editorial content on the problems that the reader is having that you can solve. Write in depth about those problems. What causes the problem? What widespread effects does the problem have that your industry addresses?

Then it's easy for you to insert specifics about your product, perhaps linking that advertisement to the article.

For example, if you sell Web site development services, your newsletter would focus on building and promoting a better Web site and different online resources. A specific article might be, "How to Reassure Consumers That Shopping on Your Site Is Secure." Coinciding with the article might be a special offer on firewall software installation.

Another benefit to having an e-mail newsletter is that your subscribers become a ready-made focus group. Through reader surveys and polls, as well as interactive question and answer sections, you can discover your target market's interests and what will influence their purchase decisions.

Where Will You Get Ideas for Content? Start With an Objective!

Start with a mission or guiding statement that summarizes your editorial strategy. Your strategy must focus on the goal. What is your goal? A bit of advance research will help you discover what your competition is doing, what your target audience is looking for, and how you will determine your success. Set up goals that position you uniquely in the market.

To write a statement of purpose or mission statement, think about what information you often have to give prospects during sales (in a proposal or on the phone during a sales call) to help them make a purchase decision. What benefit are you offering them over the competition, or over not purchasing from you? Sum this up in a three-line paragraph.

In spite of your marketing and self-promotion goals, your e-mail newsletter doesn't have to be specifically about your business. Instead, it should be about your business's customers and their big picture perspective. They may be looking for more than a place to buy, they may be looking specifically for research, support, or expertise.

Richard Hawk is an expert in communications skills, and founder of Time Well Spent Seminars *(http://www.timewellspent.com)*. In a recent issue of ListHost News, he offered some tips for writing an e-mail newsletter. First, he says, keep your writing concise and to the point, with a very brief introduction about what's in the current issue. Second, try different things in each issue to discover what works and update that, too, after a few issues. Third, keep your personality shining in every issue. Fourth, use few advertisements so that readers get your valuable content.

The Internet company NETrageous offers two e-mail publications: Internet ScamBusters and NETrageous SITEings. The first is sent to over 30,000 subscribers, with the goal of helping recipients avoid getting ripped off by Internet scams. NETrageous founder Audri Lanford considers the monthly publication a public service. The second, "NETrageous SITEings," is simply a review of what the publisher considers truly useful Internet marketing sites.

Without promoting their site guide newsletter, they already boast over 3,000 subscribers. As a testament to the information overload that consumers receive, the popular newsletter does half the work for recipients by ferreting out and reviewing one excellent site every week. People actually get mad at the publishers if they miss a week, according to Lanford.

Your mission statement might include one or more of the following (Figure 1.3):

- *To Educate My Prospects.* Your goal is to inform the members of your target audience so that they can make purchase decisions. They must first know about your product to see how it makes them smarter, faster, or more profitable. To educate them, keep them informed about your industry. Tell them about your products or services, but don't make a hard pitch. Instead, use your product or service to illustrate points that you're making. The BizWeb E-Gazette by JDD Publishing Company reaches over 25,000 subscribers. Their mission statement is to help people make money online. The publisher, Jim Daniels, says that his newsletter builds relationships with customers and prospects by educating them so that they can achieve their goals. He says that the weekly help that he offers to his prospects is how he builds their confidence in his abilities. As the methods he recommends work, readers are reassured of his expertise. In the end, when they're ready to outsource, they put their money with Daniels. He makes it a point to educate his readers every week, because it doesn't just help them out, it also helps form lasting relationships.

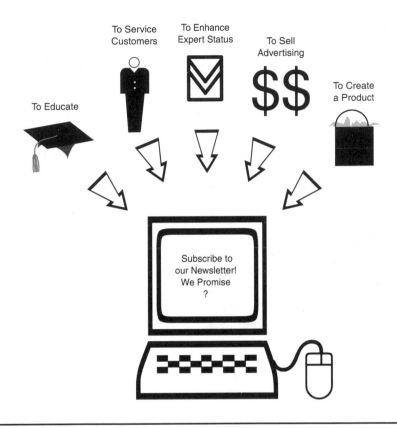

To Service Customers

To Enhance Expert Status

To Sell Advertising

To Create a Product

To Educate

Subscribe to our Newsletter! We Promise ?

Figure 1.3.   What is your mission statement?

- *To Service My Customers.* Your goal is to keep your customers happy. E-mail newsletters are a value-added service that shows your appreciation for the people that make up your company's support network. Create one with existing clients, vendors, stockholders, or members in mind. Include profiles and case studies about your readers, and invite them to guest write articles. Address frequently asked questions and reinforce customers' decision to do business with your company.

- *To Enhance My Expert Image.* Your goal is to position your organization as a source of expertise in your field. Do this by providing deeply researched and well-written articles that address issues in your industry. Include client success stories and announce company developments and press mentions. Encourage readers to print and save your e-mail newsletters in a reference binder. Publish yearly indices and archive issues in a searchable online database.

- *To Sell Advertising.* At some point, if you are consistently publishing quality content to a large (and growing) audience, you will have justification to charge others to advertise. Advertising sales for e-mail newsletters are normally based on subscriber numbers and require a more detailed level of commitment to your newsletter and demographic profile of your audience.

- *To Create a Product.* Your e-mail newsletter, quite simply, might be your product in and of itself. Beyond advertising, you might want to create something that you charge subscribers, print publishers, or content resellers for. Randy Cassingham, of Freelance Communications, created the e-mail newsletter This is True in June 1994. He describes it as a "weekly compilation of bizarre-but-TRUE news stories with running smart-ass commentary." By November 1998, he was up to 156,000 subscribers and working on the fourth volume of the version printed as a book collection. This is True came out of several desires, according to Cassingham. First, he wanted to create intellectual property, something with a long shelf life that would give him residual income over many years. The publication was designed to be timeless, so that book collections could sell for years and years (the fourth volume is on the press right now). Also, he was looking for some fame after writing his first "esoteric" technical book, which drew a very limited audience.

How To Create Content

The first step in creating content is to decide what departments, columns, or sections you can make regular and deliver consistently in each issue. Figure 1.4 shows how these building blocks are compiled. Start with a header that names your publication "as presented by" your business. Follow with your name and contact information. Then cover each of your departments in the same order with roughly the same length articles each issue. Think about how your favorite maga-

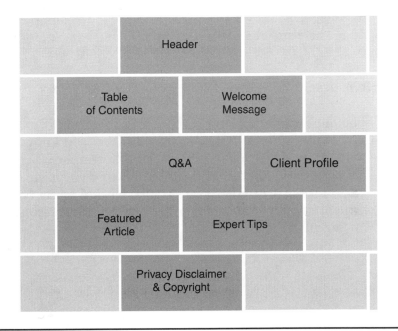

Figure 1.4. The building blocks of an e-mail newsletter.

zine always includes the same type of information up front, feature articles, and regular columns, such as your monthly horoscope.

Departments make reading your publication easier for your subscribers because they'll know what to expect and where to find their favorite sections. Each department must promise a gem that gives subscribers valuable information that will make their lives easier, their businesses more profitable, or both. Never hype your product (meaning don't go overboard about yourself and your capabilities). It's tacky, it turns readers off, and it's not necessary. You're already building credibility by publishing the e-mail newsletter. A standard template will make it easier for you, too. Regular sections speed up the writing process.

Copywriting Tips: Pick One or Use a Combination

The tedious job of creating content for your e-mail marketing program can be made simpler by following some simple writing tricks and getting help from the outside. Experiment with the different options presented here and keep your content fresh and relevant for your readers.

Write It Yourself

The most economical approach, in the long run, is to write it yourself. Is this the best method for you? Only you know. If you enjoy writing, if you have lots of ideas for different articles, if you have a firm grasp of grammar and spelling, then you can probably put together an e-mail newsletter on a regular basis. A recent Network World (*http://www.nwfusion.com*) article by writer Drew Robb lists the following rules for effective writing:

1. Get to the point

2. Integrate text and graphics

3. Know your audience

4. Define your terms

5. Put yourself in their shoes (referring to the recipient)

The secret to good writing is twofold: Write as if you are holding a conversation with your audience and keep it simple. Robb's excellent guidelines focus on simply communicating important (as deemed by the receiver) information to your audience. Write to communicate with them, not to sell to them.

Solicit Material from Clients and Vendors

It's like free advertising for them. You've set up the infrastructure; they just insert content. The same rules apply to them, though: Articles must be informative, valuable, and in line with your publication's mission statement. Vendors can be expected to write about how to use their product, seasonal uses of their product, or events and issues in their industry. Clients can be expected to write about how their experience with your company was successful (so that others can learn from them) or another issue of importance to their industry.

Find Other Mutually Beneficial Partnership Opportunities

Producing valuable articles for your readers week after week or month after month is no minor task. Because e-mail publications are increasing in popularity and in number, it's harder than ever to get your audience's undivided attention. Consider the benefits of partnering for content and sharing an audience with a complementary business. You'll have your audience's attention for less effort. An example of partnering is the contract signed between the comparison shopping network iBuyer.net *(http://www.ibuyer.net)* and Demonews.com *(http://www.demonews.com)*, a media site with the latest news, reviews, and previews about gaming and computers. Users of Demonews.com are interested in news about products from gaming and computer manufacturers. By partnering with iBuyer.net, Demonews.com can provide the latest product pricing news to their users. The reverse is that iBuyer.net can provide their shoppers with Demonews' informative content. "We are very optimistic about the new content keeping our users entertained and informed at the same time. Our new section should be able to help our viewers who shop online," said Johnny Cedergren, owner and writer of Demonews.com.

Another example of this was a March 2000 announcement from Morningstar and CNNfn.com. These two leading investment information companies signed an agreement to provide CNNfn.com with data and editorial content from Morningstar, from proprietary fund information to analyst commentary. Allen Wastler, managing editor of CNNfn.com said, "Our goal continues to be to provide the most comprehensive financial information available on the Web, and Morningstar helps us achieve that goal." The deal also provided Morningstar with exposure to CNNfn.com's extensive audience.

Ask Your Readers To Write

The people who subscribe to your newsletter are probably in your industry, right? So they will have their own perspective on what kind of content should be included in your newsletter. Ask them to submit their own articles. Be sure to outline the rewards for them: They'll get the chance to be published, which can be a credibility booster. You can offer them a free ad or simply add an extended byline to their article.

Hire Freelance Writers

Having developed a mission statement, you've done the hard part. If you disagree, because you find writing to be the hardest part, you probably aren't a writer and would waste considerable time and effort on each issue. It's more cost-effective for non-writers to simply hire a professional copywriter who can work within the confines of your mission statement and budget. One low-cost option is the E-ZineZ (*http://www.e-zinez.com*) E-zine News and Content Service, which sends subscribers copyright-free articles for general business and general living audiences (see Figure 1.5). Customers can add their own name as a byline and have the articles to publish in their own newsletters.

Run a Sister Discussion List

In Chapter 2 you'll learn about running a discussion list. Whereas discussion lists are informal and often full of chatter (back-and-forth

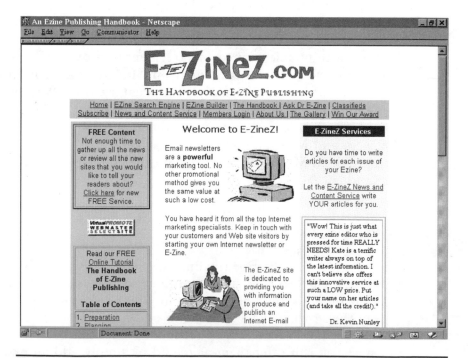

Figure 1.5.   E-ZineZ.com's home page.

conversation that strays off topic), newsletters are more organized. If you run a discussion list in conjunction with your e-mail newsletter, you could simply tag interesting posts and use them to form articles in your newsletter. You could also create an article based on an entire conversation as it takes place virtually via your e-mail discussion list.

Point Elsewhere

NETrageous SITEings is an example of one great, easy way to get content. Just use what's out there and link to it, making your own commentary on why you're sending readers there. Hyperlinks are what the Web was built on, after all. Hyperlinks connect to a Web site's address, or Universal Resource Locator (URL). Today, if a browser doesn't automatically recognize *http://* as the beginning of a URL and turn it into a clickable link automatically, it at least displays a URL that can be cut and pasted into a browser window.

Design a Template

To make each issue easier to put together and distribute, design a template that can be customized (with the issue number and date, for example) and filled in with articles for each issue. A standard template includes a header that has your newsletter name and your business name (for example, Gorgeous Gardens, published by Silver's Landscaping Service). Follow this information with your name and contact information. Include a reminder that the recipients requested the information right up front (sometimes people forget!), along with unsubscribe instructions in case they've changed their mind.

Present a consistent format to your readers in each issue so that they know what to expect. Think about how your favorite magazine includes the same regular columns each month so that you know where to go to find them. Dividing your newsletter into regular sections also makes writing easier. Some sections that might work could be "Expert Tips" (perhaps written by a vendor), "Success Stories" (telling how a customer used your product or service), and "How To..." (explaining a useful skill).

If you distribute your newsletter weekly, include no more than five sections with three or fewer paragraphs each. If you're distributing less often, you can double or triple that length. Online newsletters can be delivered as often as every day or as infrequently as once a month. Plan yours according to how much time you have to spend.

Include a copyright notice indicating that because you own the publication it may only be forwarded in its entirety and a privacy statement promising you will keep subscribers' e-mail addresses private.

If your newsletter will be a plain ASCII-text document, put a hard return at the end of each line at 65 or fewer characters wide.

You're Ready and Set To GO!

You've done all the hard work for developing an e-mail newsletter: You've picked a topic, determined your goals, developed sections, secured content sources, and should be able to put each issue together, from a content standpoint, on schedule.

The other component of your e-mail newsletter is covered in the rest of the book. You've got to have someone to send it to. Your subscriber base is actually a database of self-selected prospects: people who have seen your publication's name somewhere online, offline, or on your Web site and come to you with their hand raised, volunteering and consenting that they want to be included in your database. The process of signing up these people and getting your e-mail newsletter mass delivered to them is covered in the rest of the book.

Case Study: What's Up @ E-Greetings

The E-Greetings Network recently presented their case for e-mail as a powerful promotional tool. The company produces digital postcards and animations as a free service to consumers. An example e-greeting is shown in Figure 1.6. Totally advertising supported, the company offers more than 2,500 e-greetings to a total database of 1.9+ million registered users—a number they managed to reach in only a couple months!

Their goals with their e-mail promotion campaign were to bring value to their customers, drive site traffic and transactions, stimulate more involvement with the site, expand their relationship with customers, provide additional sponsorship vehicles, and support brand affinity. The tools they used were their newsletter and event-specific mailings. Their newsletter, What's Up @ E-greetings!, is their main

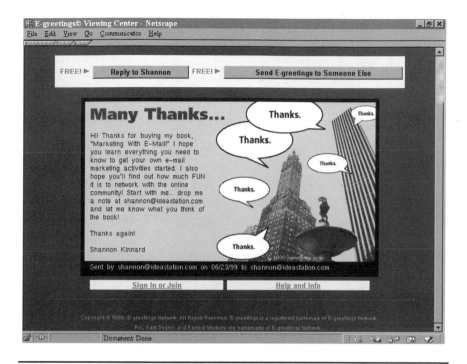

Figure 1.6. A sample e-greeting.

relationship-building tool. Delivered biweekly, the newsletter is a combination of in-house and external resources and is currently being migrated from text to HTML.

Their tongue-in-cheek creative execution is very important to building their brand identity of being a fun company. They contribute their success to the importance they place on their brand and personality, both of which come through in every issue. Each newsletter is made up of three parts, the introduction, the body highlighting new offerings, and a friendly sign off. The following samples are taken from the pre-Valentine's Day issue. A sample introduction includes their unsubscribe instructions:

BREAKING UP IS HARD TO DO. UNSUBSCRIBING IS EASY

Okay, you want to unsubscribe. We'll take you off our list if you Reply to this newsletter with "Unsubscribe" in the subject line.

Can we still be friends?

Here are samples of body content:

*NO, MOM, I'M NOT GETTING MARRIED ANYTIME
SOON.*

HEY, BACHELORS AND BACHELORETTES...

*Celebrate the fact you're able to eat dinner straight out of
the can, throw your underwear on the floor and dodge your
mother's nosy questions. We have E-greetings that express
every sentiment from "Get over him" to "Getting it?"...
and we won't ask when you plan on settling down.*

Check out our Living Single collection:

http://fan2.egreetings.com/m/whatsup

Here's a sample log off:

*ATTENTION HOPELESS ROMANTICS. KEEP HOPE
ALIVE!*

*LOG-ON, LOVE-IN SWEEPSTAKES IS COMING THIS
FEBRUARY!*

*The countdown to Valentine's Day has begun and the roman-
tic devils at E-greetings have another great sweepstakes
planned for you! All you have to do is send E-greetings and
you could win the "Most Romantic Vacation on Earth." So,
stop staring starry-eyed at your beloved, send Valentine's
Day E-greetings!*

Until we *greet* again,

The E-greetings Gang

The result of their e-mail newsletter campaign is remarkable. Each
issue produces an immediate 8% to 15% increase in site traffic, resulting in an average conversion rate of 45%. The average attrition
rate is a mere 1%.

The key factors that contribute to their success, according to the company, are these:

- The list is totally opt-in.

- Their biweekly schedule has been shown to be the most effective frequency.

- They reach their subscribers on a consistent basis.

- They are relevant with their content.

- They handle unsubscribe problems and customer service immediately.

Another example is Delta Airlines, with their Web Fares and Fan Fares programs. When potential passengers sign up at *http:// www.delta-air.com*, they give the airline their name, zip code, and some preferred destinations. Every week, Delta sends out e-mails, addressing recipients by name (using a personalization program) and giving the best rates for flights leaving the hometown airport, plus the cost of the preferred destination flights. Delta is experiencing an average click-through rate of 10%. They're projecting increased online ticket sales of 400% next year and are currently sending 1 million messages a month. They also expect to see the number of customers using this program to grow by 900% this year. Overall, they credit their e-mail marketing program with significantly reducing marketing costs and improving customer service.

Resources for Learning about E-Mail Newsletters

- David Hallum's *Newbie's Guide to Publishing an Ezine*, which can be downloaded at *http://www.mbn-businesscomplex.net/ NewbieGuide.html*, is a free guide, filled with information and tools.

- The U.S. Copyright Office Home Page, at *http://www.lcweb. loc.gov/copyright*, will help you comply with copyright laws when you use freelancers' work and free articles, as well as when you decide your own copyright rules for outgoing information.

- Mershon Shrigley (*shrigley85@aol.com*) is a coach, author, and teacher specializing in e-mail newsletters. She offers frequent tele-classes on the subject of publishing e-mail newsletters.

- NETrageous SITEings, at *http://www.netrageous.com*, is a free, weekly publication geared toward small and medium-size businesses. It presents names of both new and established sites that are worth visiting.

- E-Scribe—The Mailing List Archive, at *http://www.escribe.com,* is a free service for list owners to provide their subscribers with the ability to search for past messages online. Visitors to the site may search by mailing list or category.

Resources for Finding Other E-Mail Newsletters and Listing Yours

- Infojump's database at *http://www.infojump.com* is a great place to list your publication so that potential subscribers can find you.

- A directory of e-zines can be found at *http://www.meer.net/~johnl/e-zine-list*, which has a collection of 3,715 lists assembled by John Labovitz in which users can browse by keyword or e-zine title.

- List-Archives.com (send e-mail to *info@list-archives.com* at *http://www.list-archives.com*) is a searchable Web-based archival service for e-mail list owners. Services range in price from $75 to $99 annually, with no monthly fee for archiving.

- The Internet Scout Project, at *http://www.scout.cs.wisc.edu/scout/caservices/new-list/subscribe.html*, provides notification of the creation of a new list on any topic. The list is updated daily. To subscribe, send an e-mail to *listserv@cs.wisc.edu*. In the body of the message, type *subscribe new-list YourFirstName YourLastName*.

- New-List, at *http://New-List.com*, is a service that announces new lists in up to twenty different categories of special interests: Arts–Entertainment, Humor, Books–Publishing, Inspirational, Business, Finance, Internet, Computers, Kids, Education, News–Media, Fashion, Regional, Science, Foods, Social Sciences, General, Sports, Health–Fitness, and Travel.

Resources for Finding Content

- Inscriptions, at *http://Inscriptionsmagazine.com*, is a weekly e-zine for professional writers. Over 1,500 professional writers and editors are on the list, and they will run a free listing for you if you are willing to pay writers. To list your newsletter, send writing guidelines, current needs, and payment rates to *MaidenFate@aol.com* with the subject heading *Inscriptions*.

- Idea Marketers, at *http://www.ideamarketers.com/publish/*, is a writer/publisher/media matching service that will, for free, actually create your Web-based and e-mail newsletters for you. Using a searchable database of articles from writers, publishers can search for articles appropriate for their publication, add them, compile the document and send. For a free test drive, use the username *demo* and password *demo*.

- CONTENTIOUS, at *http://www.contentious.com*, was developed for writers and editors who create content for online media. It offers a monthly publication that is distributed in two parts (beginning and middle of the month) and includes site reviews and discussions of issues relevant to the industry of online publication.

Cheat Sheet: Steps to Build Your E-Mail Newsletter

1. Research your online market. Make a list of the types of people you want to influence and what you want them to do as a response to your e-mail newsletter.

2. Create a mission statement by determining what type of content you will need to promise to subscribers to lure them into your subscriber base. Base this on the information that you

will need to send to convince your audience to act on your call to action.

3. Plan your editorial calendar and the length of each issue.

4. Determine how you will evaluate the e-mail newsletter's success. Set up measurable feedback systems.

5. Tell the world about yourself to find subscribers. List your newsletter in directories and announce it in your signature file (see Chapter 4 for details on setting up a signature file).

6. Start writing content. If you need help, find sources who can write for you. Consider using freelancers, customers, experts, and the public relations departments of companies in your industry. These sources can feed you information to include in the publication.

7. Design a template that includes header, footer, departments, and a copyright notice. Figure out the width of each line and how you will indicate section dividers.

8. Carefully proofread your newsletter, checking spelling and grammar.

9. Distribute it to your subscribers using a basic e-mail program, a Web-based distribution program or service, or a custom list software product (more information about distribution is in Chapter 11).

10. Continue marketing and monitoring feedback from subscribers to improve with each issue and to gauge your success.

Easy, Guaranteed, Proven Advice for You!

In the April 2, 1999, issue of Sparky's List Tips, published by SparkLIST, publisher Christopher Knight listed the 39 most effective words in the English language for writing effective headlines, recommending that you use them in your e-mail newsletter headlines:

• Free	• Trustworthy
• Guaranteed	• Good Looking
• New	• Comfortable
• Your	• Proud
• You	• Healthy
• Introducing	• Safe
• Easy	• Value
• Money	• Right
• Discover	• Why
• Results	• Winnings
• Proven	• Fun
• Love	• Advice
• Benefits	• Wanted
• Save	• Announcing
• Alternative	• People
• Now	• Most
• Sale	• Effective
• Win	• Strategy
• Gain	• Happy

Knight also recommends using these words when you create e-mail ads for placement in other publications (see Chapter 9), and you might want to try them in your signature file (see Chapter 4).

2

Discussion Lists

More and more people are using discussion lists to learn, to make contacts and to pass the time. The number of subscribers to these lists, which cover just about every topic imaginable, is growing quickly. There are two reasons to use these e-mail-based lists: to learn more about your industry and to market yourself and your business. Most e-mail marketers will tell you that discussion lists are an indispensable part of their e-mail marketing endeavors, but not just because of the ability to publicize yourself instantly to a larger Internet audience. These lists can help you in many other ways, such as continuing education. In the beginning of the commercialization of the Internet, sometime in 1994 or 1995, there was no textbook on how to use the Internet for business. Internet advertising and Internet marketing were not yet a significant part of the integrated marketing mix, so professionals were left floundering, without guidelines to follow, but with a serious desire to take advantage of the network.

As these professionals in advertising, marketing, and other industries started to realize the potential of the Internet, articles started appearing in various trade publications. There was a shortage of market research on this new tool. Everyone wanted to know what worked, what failed, and what others were doing. Slowly, these early adapters started forming groups. Being online, they formed online discussion groups. These online groups were centered on specific topics, such as advertising and marketing. The early groups formed on a system known as Usenet (more in Chapter 3). Then other groups started forming through e-mail. They've been getting stronger and more popular with more robust software to automate them ever since.

You can use these lists in three major ways:

1. *Education.* You can learn a great deal from the archived and current discussions that take place on these lists. Not only can you ask specific questions, those questions will be answered by people in your target market, by peers who have the same responsibilities as you, and by professionals with years of hands-on experience.

2. *Publicity.* Your participation on these lists is great publicity for you, primarily, and for your company, secondarily. The more you ask questions, answer others' questions, and let people know who you are and what you do, the more you'll find that prospects come to you to learn more. In the next chapter, we'll go into detail about how to get involved for publicity purposes.

3. *Community.* There's a great online community of professionals who are willing to share information, pass along leads for new business, and give you advice on your practices. Becoming a part of this community provides you with a safety net in case you stumble. In the true spirit of community, discussion lists are there for support as well.

How will you use these lists to your advantage? The possibilities are endless. Says one active participant, Tom Geller of *SueSpammers.org*, "I've gotten jobs, friends, and dates through opt-in mailing lists. I've learned about resources, bought and sold products, and, on the more human side, have seen suicides prevented. As a population we really are greater than the sum of our members."

But What Exactly *Is* a Discussion List?

A discussion list is simply a redistribution tool, as shown in Figure 2.1, through which an e-mail message is sent to one address and then is automatically forwarded, via e-mail, to all the people who are sub-

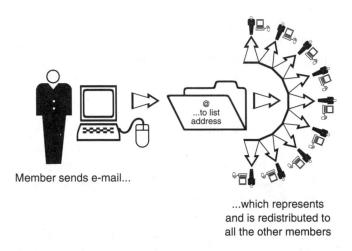

Member sends e-mail...

...which represents
and is redistributed to
all the other members

Figure 2.1. A discussion list is a series of e-mails sent to a large group of subscribers. Every message is distributed to the whole group.

scribed to that address. This is done in one of two ways: post-by-post or digest. Post-by-post, as the name indicates, means that recipients get each e-mail from the other members individually. Digest means that they are all compiled, one after another, and sent out according to a schedule, such as once per day or once per week. Discussion list digests tend to look like a note that is passed from person to person, with each person adding his or her two cents' worth at the end. Conceptually, what is taking place is like a virtual forum for conversation.

The following example is taken from an actual discussion list, We Are Business Women Connected. This particular issue has six active participants and three topics. The current discussions (called "threads") are about a member's new product called Angel Babies, merchant accounts in the United Kingdom, and a request for help finding an old post. While the conversation goes back and forth via post-by-post e-mail for some members, those posts are compiled into a digest at once for other members. What results, for digest members, is an actual conversation going back and forth or a question that is asked and answered by the time the digest version is created. A ">" character indicates a message from a previous day that is being responded to by the current message. The digest ended up looking like this (notice the helpful table of contents):

To: we-are-bwconnected-digest@thewebdepot.com

Subject: BWC Digest PM 13 May 99

Message 1: BWC: Angel Babies from Phyllis Schockner

Message 2: BWC: Angel Babies from Debbie Randolph

Message 3: Re: BWC: Merchant accounts for the UK? from Yvette Hernandez

Message 4: BWC: Angel Babies from Phyllis Schockner

Message 5: RE: BWC: Merchant accounts for the UK? from Ruth Michunovich

Message 6: Re: BWC: Merchant accounts for the UK? from Ann Zustak

Message 7: BWC: can't find from Kaci Dunham

Message 1: Subject: BWC: Angel Babies

From: Phyllis Schockner

Hi everyone, I just wanted to let you know that our new project is off the ground, it's called Sweet Dreams from Angel Babies. Through a remarkable new photo-imaging process, your photo keepsakes can be put into fantasy environments that exist nowhere else and are but one of the many innovations that make Sweet Dreams so unforgettable.

Take a look at our Web site to see what it's all about; you won't believe your eyes. We're at http://www.angelbabies.com.

Message 2: Subject: Re: BWC: Angel Babies

From: Debbie Randolph

*We do the Debbie's Round-Up Mall and would be
interested in listing your site, check us out at http://
www.western2.com/mall. We are always open to suggestions.*

*Message 3: Subject: Re: BWC: Merchant accounts for
the UK?*

From: Yvette Hernandez

*Does anyone know whether I can get a merchant
account in the UK?*

>>Thanks

*What about CC Now? They take 9.5% off every order
with no minimum monthly orders and no monthly
service charges, no leasing of equipment. They handle
the charges under their name and send the funds to you.
They're at http://www.ccnow.com/. I don't use them but
probably will someday as to me they have a great deal!*

Message 4: Subject: BWC: Angel Babies

From: Phyllis Schockner

*I just checked with my brother, and he said that the site
won't be up for another few weeks. I thought it was
finished. If you are interested you can still call him for
any info that you need. I'll let everyone know when it
will be up. Sorry about the mistake.*

*Message 5: Subject: RE: BWC: Merchant accounts for
the UK?*

From: Ruth Michunovich

*I've watched the thread on this, and am I the only one
who is concerned with the illegal implications of using
someone else's merchant account? My merchant account*

agreement emphatically states that it is unlawful for me to accept a credit card purchase on behalf of someone else. This is called "Factoring." When I was searching for a merchant account and processing software, I talked to a ton of companies. One of the things I learned was that if someone gets their credit card statement, and the name of the merchant on their statement doesn't match with who they purchased from, the customer can refuse the charge and 9 out of 10 times, the money is refunded to the customer. This protects the customer from fraudulent charges. Where would that leave you – out the product and then getting a "charge-back" from companies like ccnow. If ccnow gets too many chargebacks, the credit card companies will cancel their accounts. If you get caught in a factoring scheme, you get blacklisted and won't be able to get a merchant account in the future. I would check out the financial and legal backgrounds of any company willing to accept credit cards on your behalf. Scams usually have a life of 3 to 7 years before they get busted. Ccnow may very well have a stellar reputation and have a 100% legal right to do what they say they'll do. But I am still wary of factoring. My companies are going to be around for a lot longer than 7 years, and I wouldn't take a chance on losing my privileges.

Message 6: Subject: Re: BWC: Merchant accounts for the UK?

From: Ann Zustak

Yes, it is illegal. But if the company that is providing the service acts as the reseller, that is perfectly legal.

Message 7: Subject: BWC: can't find

From: Kaci Dunham

I'm looking for a really old post. It was a non-biz type of thing. I think it was called a letter from God. It told how God was preparing you for the man/woman you were meant to be with and it went on into detail if any of you have that saved I would really appreciate it if you would resend that to me. Thanks in advance. :)

To leave, e-mail we-are-bwconnected-digest-request @thewebdepot.com with the word "leave" in the body.

To subscribe, e-mail we-are-bwconnected-digest-request @thewebdepot.com with the word "join" in the body.

Notice how the different messages are loosely organized. Sometimes responses to old posts will come up, as readers get to old mail. Sometimes messages will get ignored, or a large amount of e-mail will be sent regarding a certain thread.

If the list is unmoderated, as with the list in the example here, then the e-mails are redistributed as members contribute them. If the list is moderated, someone first approves an e-mail before it goes out. If you are the moderator, you are like the host of the party. A moderated discussion list is like an elegant cocktail party, where only polite conversation takes place. You, as the moderator, filter e-mails submitted by members in order to only allow appropriate messages to be delivered to the group. Unmoderated lists are more like a casual picnic, where e-mails are posted as they're sent. Perhaps the host will reprimand a member after an inappropriate post. Maybe not.

Figure 2.2 illustrates the differences between moderated and unmoderated lists.

Hosting vs. Participating

Discussion lists offer e-mail marketers two different ways to communicate with a widespread audience. A discussion list works by distributing one subscriber's e-mail to the whole large group (hundreds to thousands) of subscribers. Because of this system you simply have to participate to become part of the existing community. If you conduct yourself in a professional manner, by offering polite, informative, well-crafted posts, you will be able to meet your marketing communication

Party members talking randomly

"What does everyone think?"

Moderator

Party members take turns to speak,
on the topic

Figure 2.2. An unmoderated discussion list (top) vs. a moderated discussion list (bottom).

goals. "Post" is the term used to describe an e-mail that a discussion list member sends into the list to be redistributed to the other list members. There are two ways to do this: participate in existing lists or host your own list. We'll discuss the pros and cons of each.

A good way to get started with discussion lists is as a participant. To do so, you simply subscribe to lists with audiences similar to your desired audience (search in the resources listed at the end of this chapter) and, once you've followed a couple existing conversations, jump in yourself by sending an e-mail to the posting address. When you participate in a moderated list, you gain additional credibility, because a list host, generally respected by members, has accepted your post as valuable. More details about becoming involved as a participant in discussion lists are in Chapter 3, which covers online networking, and Chapter 8, which covers online public relations.

Once you dip your toes in the pool of discussion list participation, you should consider taking the plunge and hosting your own discussion list. When you take on the role of discussion list host, you are the one who owns the list. This comes with a great responsibility. You are responsible for the cost of hosting, the security and privacy of your subscriber database, and the quality of the discussion that goes on in your list.

The benefits of hosting your own list are substantial from a marketer's point of view. You can define the exact subject matter that will be covered. You can determine how frequently the list is published. If you'd like, you can make it a revenue-generating vehicle through which you can advertise your own business or sell advertising sponsorships. Over time, your readers will come to feel as though they have a personal one-to-one relationship with you; these potential clients will see you as a trustworthy and legitimate business. Best of all, as the moderator, you are instantly afforded credibility and industry expertise.

This chapter will show you how you can start and sustain your own discussion list. The example moderator we're using throughout this chapter is Eva Rosenberg who hosts the I-Sales HelpDesk— WebReview discussion list and AskTaxMama e-mail newsletter.

How Will You Host? Free vs. Fee Hosting

Depending on your budget and brand image, you might want to use a free mailing list service to host your list. These companies (such as Topica, ONElist, and eGroups) offer customers free hosting and distribution of your list in return for ad space in the e-mails that go out. An example, shown in Figure 2.3, is a text advertisement, attached to every message distributed to a free e-mail discussion list hosted by ONElist. Customers use a Web-based interface to start up and monitor their mailing lists. List owners can set up the specifications of their list (such as moderated, unmoderated, archived, headers, footers,

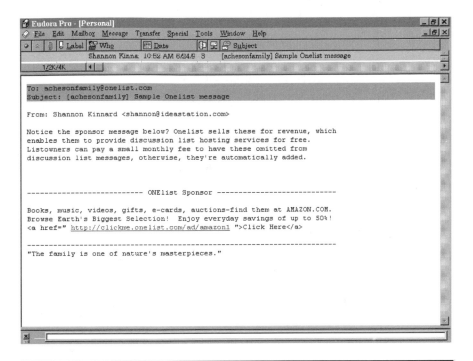

Figure 2.3. Sample message from ONElist.

labels) and can make adjustments to their member database easily, including importing existing mailing lists. Topica lets users search the archives of all Topica-hosted sites, as well as subscribing and unsubscribing themselves. ONElist lets users share files. eGroups lets users have calendars and instant messaging.

Before choosing your list host, remember that while these free services sound like a great deal, do you really want to let them have control over the ads run in your list? What if they sell space on your list to your competitor? eGroups has a $4.95-a-month option to leave out ads. Also, consider if it will clash with your brand image to send your customers an e-mail from a service known for its freebie service? Can you demand top customer service and quality from a free service? More information about the technical aspects of hosting is in Chapter 11, "Technical Know-How."

Define Your Purpose

The first task is to define your editorial purpose. Are you offering a forum on a particular industry in general, a specific product (perhaps yours), or something else? Rosenberg's two lists are very different. I-Sales HelpDesk is an e-commerce discussion list, AskTaxMama is up Rosenberg's own alley, providing tax information, alerts and communication for her tax clients. For non-clients, she seeks to offer honest, useful information about how the tax system works. Her overarching purpose is simply to be really helpful.

Discussion Lists as a Profit Center

Will you be footing the bill for your discussion list or will you sell ads? The I-Sales HelpDesk—WebReview discussion list is an advertising vehicle. Rosenberg says that the number one goal of the list is to generate an income through either paid advertising or ads to affiliate programs. While only one third of the days are sold, the other days have generated income through affiliate programs. Still other days have earned her some credit at sites she would otherwise have to pay for.

Rosenberg has considerably increased the subscriber base for her other list, AskTaxMama. In addition, TaxMama generates income through affiliate programs, paid advertisements, and sales of recommended products. Her subscriber base for TaxMama is very important. The more readers she has, the more income she can generate, because the higher your subscriber numbers, the higher the rate that can be charged for advertising or sponsorship. But if you don't sell out your ad space, all is not lost. Rosenberg uses unsold space in each of the discussion lists to publicize the other discussion list and increase traffic to her site. Similarly, consider placing straightforward ads for your services in your e-mail newsletters. You could also join one of the many affiliate programs available online and create an advertisement for them in which you receive compensation based on your affiliate sales.

Your Reputation

You are naturally positioned as an expert when you are the host or publisher of an e-mail publication. The credibility you procure and respect you gain is based on your moderating style. Make a commitment to run your list honestly, fairly, and with a dedication to quality information.

Rosenberg says that one of her goals as moderator of I-Sales HelpDesk—WebReview is to increase her credibility and visibility on the Internet. It increases the bottom line, she says. And she takes the responsibility of guarding her reputation very seriously.

By increasing your credibility through offering top quality moderation, you can increase income to all your business ventures. For example, Rosenberg limits advertising to products or services that she can honestly recommend. She refuses advertising for anything that even smells like unsolicited commercial bulk e-mail (also called "spam"), such as Multilevel Marketing (MLM) or other things without valid products or services. People who have left her with a bad impression from their posts or behavior aren't accepted as advertisers. Her method is working: The list has generated enough credibility for the moderator that she receives constant publicity and invitations to speak at and write for various seminars and publications.

Likewise, AskTaxMama has gained her such a reputation for expertise that she is increasing her paid speaking engagements and getting major sponsors for upcoming seminars. Rosenberg, as TaxMama, was interviewed for a feature in the May issue of Pacific Bell's Small Business/Home Office publication. On the first Monday of 1999, she was a guest on Jim Blasingame's "The Small Business Advocate" radio show *(http://www.smallbusinessadvocate.com)*. She was interviewed nationally on Rick Barber's radio show on KOA and is invited back for a repeat visit and she is lined up to write daily "Tax Tips" for the site CyberTip4theDay *(http://www.CyberTip4theDay.com)*. Bob Sullivan is planning to post excerpts from AskTaxMama as a weekly tax tip feature on his Small Business Adviser site, and Rosenberg has picked up new tax clients from around the country.

Simplify Signups

Make it easy for your users to sign up to your list. By automating the process, you simplify signup for both your subscribers and for yourself. An excellent example of an easy-to-use signup page is shown in the case study of ISS Group, shown at the end of this chapter.

Prelaunch Advice

Before you actually "launch" your list (i.e., make the first post and send it off to your subscribers), you must do three important things to get prepared.

1. First, set up a welcome/confirmation message. This text will be given to your list host as a way to automatically tell subscribers the rules for your list. In it, you should thank them for joining, tell them the instructions for subscribing, unsubscribing, and posting, and outline the rules for the types of posts that are appropriate.

2. Get subscribers! You need someone to welcome and to make the discussion happen. To do this, you need to set up your list hosting service (see Chapter 11, "Technical Know-How"), which will give the subscription instructions for your list. Most subscription instructions look something like Rosenberg's:

   To subscribe to "Ask TaxMama" send an e-mail to taxwriter@taxmama.com with "Subscribe" in the subject line and your full name in the body of the e-mail message.

   If you would like to subscribe and participate in this I-helpdesk—WebReview, send an e-mail to i-helpdesk_ webreview@list.mmgco.com. Put the word "subscribe" in the subject line of your message.

3. List your list! You must publicize your discussion list across the Internet. There are some resources at the end of this chapter as well as throughout the book for getting your list's name out there. Then you must wait for some people to join! This prep work will pay off when your list gets off to a running start. However, if you start with too few people, you'll spend all your time trying to get a discussion started. Instead, you should spend your time getting your list's name out there.

Formatting Your Discussion List

Before sending that first post, you should write a header and footer to frame each e-mail that is distributed to your list members. The header is the introduction to your list and usually includes the list name, volume and issue information, and the date. The footer usually contains instructions for subscribing and unsubscribing, instructions for posting, and your disclaimer.

Decide if the digest version of your list will just be a compilation of posts, in chronological order, or if you will organize them to help readers better follow ongoing discussions. Some discussion lists, such as the LinkExchange Daily Digest, shown in Figure 2.4, are set up so that first, new topics are introduced, and then, ongoing topics are presented grouped together. Ads are always placed at the top. This helps readers find their way around quickly and easily.

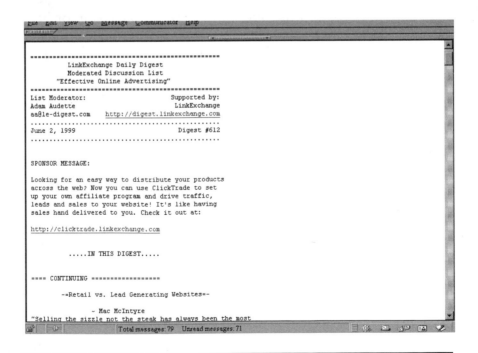

Figure 2.4. Sample copy of the LinkExchange Daily Digest.

Taking the Plunge!

This is it, the welcoming first post! Send an e-mail to your list's posting address that welcomes your charter members, introduces yourself, restates your editorial and content goals for the list (from the welcome/confirm message), and throws a couple questions out for answer or comment. Once you find a few active members, nurture them...they'll help you sustain your list through slow subject times!

Keeping the Troops Under Control

You are in control of your list. If at any time you lose control of your list, it will cease to be useful to you or your participants. If someone goes out of control (this happens more on unmoderated lists), first warn the offending party, then cut him or her off. For example, if someone starts posting unsubscribe requests to the list instead of to the correct unsubscribe address, it goes out to the whole list, many times. One suggestion is to unsubscribe the sender manually and publicly, restating the unsubscribe directions for the whole list as a gentle reminder. (Another option is to simply block posts from that address.)

Legal Responsibilities

Discussion lists are a less refined communications tool than, say, a promotional direct mail or a one-way e-mail newsletter. The atmosphere is more of an over-a-cup-of-coffee conversation, which means grammar, value, and even sometimes manners frequently fall by the wayside. This spontaneity, although sometimes unrefined, is good because it adds a level of relationship building to the community. However, because of this, it is your responsibility to use a disclaimer that states that posters (members who contribute to the discussion) are responsible for their own posts (e-mails that they send in).

Self-Promotion Within

The only way to ensure your list's success is to get new members signed up and keep all members involved. New members, eager to establish themselves, will give your list a breath of fresh air and will keep it interesting and valuable to all users. Ray Gabriel from the Association for International Business *(http://www.earthone.com)* advises that e-mail publishers ask their own subscribers to help them promote their e-mail discussion list. Encourage them by explaining that more subscribers mean greater discussion and publicity. The more minds in this meeting of the minds, the more resources will come out. Don't be shy about tooting your own horn within your own list.

Case Study: ISS Group

Internet Security Systems (Figure 2.5) was founded by a college student. The now $1 billion company has a significant dedication of resources to discussion lists. However, in the beginning, founder Chris Klaus started humbly, making a newsgroup posting about his security software program, which he had developed while doing a summer internship the summer before his freshman year at Georgia Tech.

The software tool is designed to probe networks using hundreds of vulnerability tests. It detects weaknesses in a system and provides detailed corrective action for eliminating security holes. Today, ISS products are used by thousands of companies around the world, in over thirty government networks, and by nine out of the top ten U.S. banks.

When Klaus sent the shareware version (software available for free download) of his software product to the newsgroup, the response was positive, to say the least. The following day, he was hit with more than 200 e-mail responses asking to buy the commercial version. The first product, ISS's Internet Scanner, was born. He sold the first copy for $1,000 to an Italian research site. He sold another to Novell for several times that amount.

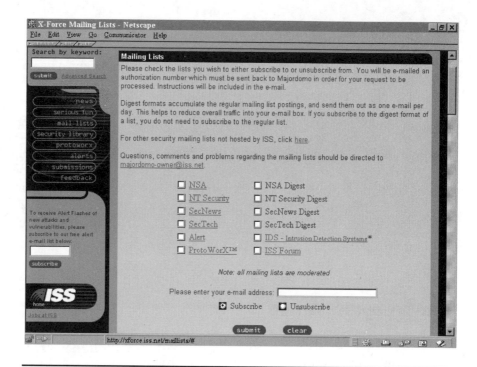

Figure 2.5. ISS signup page.

The company's e-mail discussion list program, of which Klaus is still a contributing member, has grown to about 80 mailing lists, including open discussions, partner lists, customer lists, and product announcement lists reaching over 100,000 people.

Resources

- The List of Publicly Accessible Mailing Lists (PAML) is a directory of mailing lists and discussion lists. Available in both a Web-based and a Usenet version, PAML is located at *http://www.NeoSoft.com/internet/paml/*.

- Liszt *(http://www.liszt.com)* is an enormous directory of Internet discussion groups: mailing lists, newsgroups, and

Internet Relay Chat (IRC) channels, best known for their mailing list directory. Search or browse their database to find lists about almost any subject, from A to Z.

- List-Moderators is an unmoderated e-mail discussion list for hosts/moderators of discussion lists. To join, send an e-mail to *join-list-moderators@list-moderators.com*. There is also a digest version that you can join by sending an e-mail to *join-list-moderators-digest@list-moderators.com*.

- ONElist, at *http://www.onelist.com*, is a mailing list system that allows members to create e-mail lists or subscribe to a variety of lists. Subscribing to and maintaining lists are free.

- Net-Happenings, at *http://www.scout.cs.wisc.edu/scout/net-hap/index.html*, distributes daily announcements about Internet resources to network users and providers. To subscribe, send an e-mail to *listserv@cs.wisc.edu*. In the body of the message, type *subscribe net-happenings YourFirstName YourLastName*.

- Listhost.net, at *http://www.listhost.net*, offers consulting and list management as part of their services. Listhost.net News presents strategies for list publishing, autoresponder usage, and e-mail marketing.

- TechMailings by Andover.net, at *http://www.techmailings.com*, is a thorough collection of discussion lists available on the Internet.

- Everything E-Mail, *http://everythingemail.net/email_discussion.html*, lists resources for publishing a discussion list, finding other discussion lists about discussion lists, and tools and products for list owners.

Many of the resources listed in Chapter 1 could also be used for discussion lists. The difference between a discussion list and an e-mail newsletter, technically, is just the information flow. With a discussion list, it's two-way; with a newsletter, it's one-way.

Cheat Sheet: Planning, Launching, and Sustaining a Discussion Group

1. Join some discussion lists in areas (fun and business) that interest you. Participate and follow along to familiarize yourself with the process.

2. Choose a hosting company or service and learn how to use their software. Every program has its own directions for use, but they all work by redistributing one message to a group of e-mail addresses.

3. Define your purpose and subject matter. What central topic is both of interest to a large group of people *and* would help you in your business if you were recognized as a leading expert? Then decide if you will moderate or let the list be unmoderated.

4. Define a schedule for distribution. If your list is to be moderated, consider the time you'll have to spend approving posts every time one comes in, because you'll want to be attentive to keep readers' attention.

5. Set aside a budget. Will you be footing the bill for hosting, or will the publication be advertiser or sponsor supported? If you will have sponsors, create a kit that defines rates and policies (see Chapter 9 for details).

6. Write a welcome message that will automatically be sent when new subscribers sign up. In it, include instructions for subscribing, unsubscribing, and posting. Include rules for appropriate and inappropriate content. Introduce yourself, your goals for the list, and your company. Finally, welcome the new arrivals and thank them for joining.

7. Publicize your list by going to indices and directories of discussion lists. Join other discussion lists and tell them, through your signature file (see Chapter 4), that you have a new list for them to join. Encourage early subscribers to tell their associates about you. Buy advertising space in other e-mail pub-

lications. Because subscribers to one newsletter are likely to subscribe to several, this is an efffective way to drive traffic to your discussion list.

8. Decide how each post will be formatted. Write a template for your header, your footer, and your disclaimer. Set up a recognizable format so that users can become familiar with each issue and learn how to scan posts for topics that are important and relevant to them.

9. Send your first post! Be enthusiastic, inviting, and a little controversial to get discussion hopping from the first post.

10. Maintain your list by using the following tactics: Enforce the rules that you set up in the welcome message (if you let one person get away with a commercial advertisement, you'll have to let others do the same, and your list will lose subscribers and quality). Be very appreciative of active members who post frequently (consider sending follow-up thank-you notes after they post). Solicit discussion with your own public and private posts encouraging members to talk about their areas of expertise.

3

Online Networking

The only difference between online networking and offline networking is the interface. Just as you may attend an industry event in your hometown to meet future partners and shake hands with potential customers, you can attend industry events (such as newsgroups, discussion lists, and chat rooms) online.

The difference is that you get to go to these online events at your convenience (and conveniently, in your bathrobe on your home office computer, if you are so inclined!). The online community is a cozy, friendly, and helpful world of people who join these e-mail-based discussion lists, participate in newsgroups, and socialize in Web-based forums. They're there to do more than business, although doing business is the bottom line. They're there for networking, support, and friendship with like-minded peers.

Where in the world is the online community? It's on e-mail, the Web, and other networked systems, and you have to join and participate to become a part of it. First you have to *find* online networking opportunities by seeking out and joining different communities that reach a good audience for you. Next you have to participate, using the following techniques for becoming a part of the community, not an annoying street vendor. Remember that your focus is on building relationships.

Use the Web for Networking

Networking opportunities on the Internet include discussion lists, chat rooms, and newsgroups, in which participants can "lurk," meaning they just read ongoing discussion, or can get involved and meet others to build relationships. Before jumping into any discussion, learn the rules of Netiquette, the Internet version of etiquette, a set of strict instructions for marketing communications in these groups (more details about the rules of online marketing are in Chapter 10). To make sure you adhere to the specifications set forth by a group you join, read the FAQs (Frequently Asked Questions), rules (like the example in Figure 3.1, which they have named *Rules of Play*), or guidelines for posting before you make your first post. "Posting" is the term used to describe a message that you send to continue an existing discussion or to start a new one.

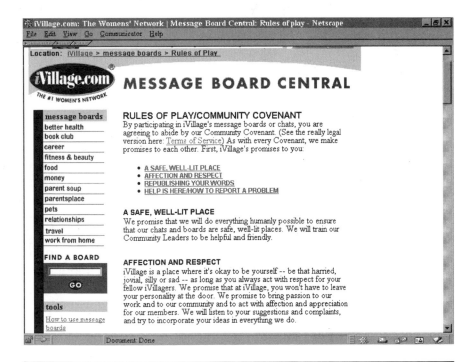

Figure 3.1. iVillage message board.

Finding online discussions to participate in for networking is not difficult, if you know where to look. Some of the possibilities include forums, discussion lists, chat rooms, newsgroups, and e-mail newsletters.

- *Forums.* Forums are available through proprietary services such as America Online and CompuServe, as well as different Web supersites such as iVillage and The Mining Company. Not only do these places present opportunities for you to participate in conversations, they are on constant lookout for experts who can lead forums on a niche topic. The added credibility of leading a forum will contribute greatly to your online presence. The Motley Fool, an online business that encourages and teaches do-it-yourself investing, launched their business by going to America Online and creating (for free) a forum about their services. They built up a huge fan club through forums and now host a Web-based business at *MotleyFool.com*, shown in Figure 3.2.

- *Discussion Lists.* In Chapter 2, you learned how moderating a discussion list can promote your business. In this section, we look at how participating in discussion lists hosted by other business owners (yes, even competitors) can promote your business. There is an added legitimacy afforded to your comments when they are published in a moderated discussion list owned by another business because this means that someone else (presumably someone who is a respected expert in your industry) finds your comments useful and intelligent enough to pass on to subscribers.

  Respect the rules by matching the tone of the publication and staying within boundaries that are established. Building a relationship with the moderator by sincerely and thoughtfully commenting on the things you like about the list will help you build relationships with the users. Aside from the business it brings you, positive feedback is the major highlight of being a list moderator.

- *Chat Rooms.* Chat rooms can be found on various Web sites and using different chat software, such as IRC (Internet Re-

Figure 3.2. The Motley Fool Web site.

lay Chat) or ICQ (which stands for "I Seek You"). Both allow
one-to-one or many-to-many real-time conversations. To connect to one of these programs, you must download and configure the software. An excellent resource for more information
about IRC is available at *http://www.user-com.undernet.org/
documents/howto.html;* more information about ICQ is available at the company's Web site *http://www.icq.com.*

- *Usenet Groups.* Usenet is a collection of online discussions
grouped into communities. The interface for Usenet is shown
in Figure 3.3. To access Usenet with Netscape Communicator, click on the Discussion Groups button in the bottom corner of your screen. Other browsers also have ways to access
these groups. Usenet resides in a different place on the Internet
from the Web and is accessed through your Internet Service

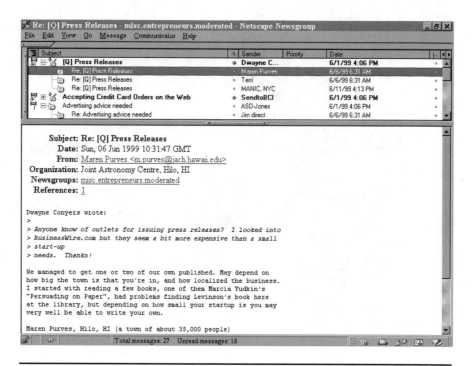

Figure 3.3. The Usenet group misc.entrepreneurs.moderated.

Provider (ISP), similar to the way your e-mail is read using a different interface than a Web site. Usenet discussion groups are generally referred to as newsgroups.

Newsgroups used to be an effective way to meet other professionals and business contacts. However, as a largely unmoderated forum, it has been abused by people hungry for the commercial exploitation of the Internet:

- Newsgroups are filled with mass-distributed commercial messages that are sent by the thousands to newsgroups. Unfortunately, instead of focusing on helping members of these groups and building relationships with each member, some marketers blanket newsgroups with their commercial messages. Just as an in-box gets filled with unwanted commercial messages (also known as getting "spammed"), so does Usenet.

– The way it works is this: automated software scans newsgroups for e-mail addresses and then strips the address, compiles a list, and sends spam to all those addresses, making it unappealing for people to try to participate, knowing that a flood of spam will result. As a result, it's less likely that using Usenet to network will be productive.

Please do this (in fact, do all your e-mail marketing) with sincerity. There's no use sending an announcement about your latest product to every industry-related group on the Internet. However, to send a follow-up post that responds to a question about a previous product you offered by saying there's an update is perfectly acceptable (because it's sincerely helpful).

If you decide to use newsgroups, create a secondary e-mail address, either through a free service or using an alias or extra account through your Internet service provider. This allows you to deal with the massive amounts of spam you'll undoubtedly receive in a more effective manner.

Ira M. Pasternack, publisher of Marketing Tip of the Day, recently did a series of e-mail newsletters on how online networkers can take advantage of Usenet without being bombarded with spam. Pasternack recommends using the customizable program My Deja News, which is available for free at *http://www.dejanews.com* (shown in Figure 3.4). The program allows you to set up newsgroups that will put you in touch with many of the people with whom you should be doing your online networking. As you find posts to which you'd like to make a comment or answer, decide if you should respond privately to the original sender or if you should write to the entire group. If you aren't sure how to start, play it safe and send your message privately first.

- *E-Mail Newsletters.* E-mail newsletters are one-way, so you can't participate in them in the same way that you can with discussion lists. However, newsletter publishers (as we mentioned in Chapter 1) are often grateful for free, well-written, informative articles. Consider finding some e-mail newsletters that reach the audience you'd like to reach. You can write one article and recycle it among different publishers that show

Figure 3.4. My Deja News is a great beginner's guide to Usenet.

an interest, or you can write original copy for certain e-mail newsletters that have a very desirable audience for you.

Find Mutually Beneficial Opportunities

As you consider which forums to target, try to think beyond the obvious: the places that talk about issues in your industry. The goal with online networking isn't so much to find clients (although that's nice, too), it's to find people who, once they know about you and your business, will send a steady stream of clients to you. But we can still start with the obvious...

- *Network Using Clients*. Find places where your clients and customers are doing their online networking and research.

You'll not only reinforce their purchase decision, you might make a post that will be corroborated by a client, who can assure others on the list that you offer a good product or service (see Figure 3.5). In this way, clients are important to your online networking activities. Giving them service above and beyond what they're expecting lets them, in good conscience, recommend you to others. Be sure to keep them apprised of new products, services, developments, and opportunities with your company, so that they can keep people informed about you, even when you're not there.

- *Unofficial Salespeople.* Offering commissions, reseller agreements, or other incentives to complementary businesses is a great way to turn other people who are in or associated with your industry into unofficial salespeople for you. Sharon Tucci of Slingshot Media, which runs the subsidiary Listhost.net, a mailing list hosting service, gives a percentage of each sale back to the person who brings her new business. In addition, she sends thoughtful presents during the holidays and refers business back to her unofficial salespeople. Not only does this build a relationship, it encourages further referrals and leads.

- *Influencers.* Getting a well-known online professional to know your product is like getting a celebrity endorsement. The best influencers tend to be discussion list hosts and moderators. Subscribers turn to these people when they are considering a purchase, so it is wise to contribute your expertise and comments regularly to lists, supplemented with private, personal e-mail to the moderator when appropriate.

  Keep in mind that online influencers are very busy and field hundreds of e-mails per day, so make certain that any e-mail you send to them is valuable to them: Forward a mention of them or their company, send your testimonial or anecdote of how their list helped you, or apprise them of a development in your company that is relevant to them.

- *Referrals.* Ask others for referrals to expand your network of reputable professionals. Nancy Roebke, a recognized online networking expert, says that if you are interested in targeting

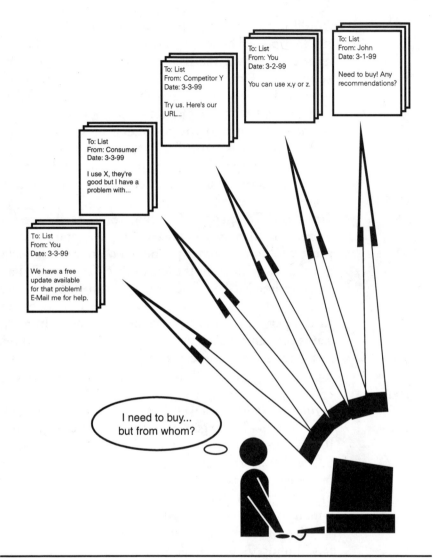

Figure 3.5. Who do you think the user will buy from: company X, Y, Z or you?

a specific market, you can ask others for leads. For example, she recommends that if you regularly work with a certain group and find that, across the board, they make good clients, then you should request referrals in that industry. Similarly, if you're interested in breaking into a certain industry as your client base, you should get online and request referrals for people in that industry. She outlines the following approach: Post online with a message that says, "I am currently looking to speak with CPAs about the new tax laws. A good lead for me would be a CPA you currently know, like, and trust. Feel free to have them contact me via e-mail."

Set Networking Goals

Decide that you're going to set up a schedule and a goal for the number of contacts you will make. Keep in mind that you're going to have a lot of reading to do in order to keep track of all the conversations going on in all of your different lists. The first schedule should be how many lists you will have at any one time. Schedule how many new ones you will join per month and how many you will ditch (if they do not bring you any results). Keep that schedule going.

The next schedule is how many posts you will make per month. Keep in mind that you will end up with some feedback, so schedule time to respond to these private posts and build relationships. Likewise, you should keep an eye out for posts of people whom you might want to contact privately to strike up a personal relationship.

Getting To Know All About You

Once you join a few lists, you'll start to familiarize yourself with regulars and you'll become comfortable with posting for yourself. If you found and joined discussion lists after reading Chapter 2, then you're already started with e-mail discussion lists. In addition, the Web-based communities (such as chat rooms) and forums on proprietary networks like America Online are places to find people with whom you should network. While some of these aren't e-mail based, they fit into this book because they integrate with your e-mail-based marketing endeavors. For example, if you make a post to a marketing forum on AOL that mentions how you gained a new client who subscribed to your e-mail newsletter, others will perhaps subscribe to your e-mail publication. Or you might make a post on Usenet (that includes your signature file) inviting others to join your members-only e-mail announcement list that announces weekly specials at bargain basement prices.

What you don't want to do is join a forum that is for a specific discussion and blatantly promote your e-mail newsletter, even if it is on the same topic as the forum. For example, let's say that you are a photographer specializing in wedding photography. You might join a list that discusses wedding planning. There are two ways you could announce your services on this list. Consider the following sample posts:

1. Subject: Trying to save money on wedding photos?

    Hi brides-to-be! I'm offering a special deal on a wedding photo package for the month of September. Buy a 62-shot album and save 15% over normal rates. Contact me for details!

2. Subject: Consider planning the big day in September.

    I've noticed that bookings for my photography services always drop in September. Do any brides-to-be know this is an unpopular month and so brides can get better rates from wedding-services vendors? I'm offering special rates for September to increase business.

If there are brides on the list that are planning a September wedding, post 1 might get their attention, but it might just seem tacky. And there's nothing to respond to, so the thread will die.

However, the second post will get conversation going about why September is a bad month. It might even make some brides realize that they might change their date to take advantage of special rates. If members of the list are already planning a September wedding, the post will probably make them ask about the special rates. Either way, the photographer can continue to post in this thread, giving him additional opportunities to get his name in front of his target audience.

Another good way to jump into a new group is to ask members to share their favorite online communities with you. The people who participate in these groups are your peers, and chances are they will know of other places where you will be able to network successfully. Ask them what online communities are important for them.

Chatter Up!

Once you find forums you'd like to participate in, you'll want to observe the discussion of others as it progresses. Ira M. Pasternack of Marketing Tip of the Day advises keeping an eye out for messages that are the beginning of a thread, meaning that there is a string of responses to a specific message. Notice the tone of the responses: Are they positive or negative? If they're positive, this indicates that that type of message is a good model for you when you craft your posts to the list.

As you post responses to other people's messages, be considerate of bandwidth and other's time. Only include the appropriate portion of the message with your response. (A previous message often has the ">" character preceding text.) An example might be as follows:

> *To: Business Owners Discussion List*
>
> *Subject: RE: Need help in collecting an overdue payment*
>
> *> ...the result was that I was stuck without payment and the client doesn't seem to have any intention of paying. Should I chalk it up to experience, or try to go after the client?*
>
> *I suggest that you take the client to small claims court if it's a large amount and if you have the time. First, though, draft a lawyerly letter that threatens this course of action. Maybe that will be enough to get them to pay up. Otherwise, small claims court is only about $40. If you win, they'll have to reimburse you.*

With e-mail, you're not shaking hands face-to-face with one person at a time. You're virtually connecting with hundreds to thousands of potential prospects. Consider the potential reach of your e-mail when you answer inquiries that come through your site, participate in discussion lists, or simply contact a potential vendor. There are a number of different reasons why someone else might receive an e-mail from you (and possibly forward it on to someone else).

A great way to build your subscriber base is to get in front of other publications' subscribers. Write an article (or even hire a freelance writer) that is useful to a particular e-mail publication's audience. List your publication, yourself and your company at the end of the article, making sure readers understand that they can come to you for more information. Barb Nelson (barb@si-partners) is a savvy e-mail marketer who builds her database of content by simply promising to run free advertising in addition to a summary tag line for any authors (who meet her criteria for publication) who will allow her to publish their articles.

Online you've got quite a good-sized potential audience—if you contact others with mutually beneficial opportunities. Not everyone will be a good candidate for online networking, which is fine because there are way too many people out there for you to try to reach anyway. Worldwide estimates project 160 million Internet users in the year 2000, according to IDC/LINK 1996. As you surf the Web, remember to connect and to play by the rules. As with every tool in this book, take the methodical, polite, sincere approach to online networking.

Making Strangers into Friends

Good old-fashioned schmoozing (finding out about the person with whom you are talking) is a technique that is natural for very few people, face-to-face. It's a little easier to schmooze through e-mail. There's more time to figure out the perfectly witty, complimentary, or winning comment to win over the guy on the other end of the modem. The goal is to agree enthusiastically, disagree politely, ask questions respectfully and describe your own success graciously.

Remember to mind your manners! In one discussion list, a member that complains about the actions of another member of the discussion list can reflect poorly on the discussion list publisher. There are several benefits to participating in online conversations, and making an effort to be likable and helpful:

- It will keep you and your company in the spotlight.

- It can make others recognize the business that you're in (and that you're an active and knowledgeable participant in your business).

- It helps to build your reputation. Now you are recognized for your expertise, and, more importantly, for your accessibility.

- It helps you to build a personal fan club of people who send business your way.

The most important person to get to know is the big kahuna: The host of whatever list, forum, or discussion in which you are participating. One suggestion is to send the host a note after you've been involved for a little while. Just introduce yourself and compliment the person on a job well done. People love to feel appreciated.

If, down the road, your company does something that is of interest to the whole community, but is also a blatant self-promotion, you can e-mail or phone the host personally. Explain that you'd love to share with the group the information about your new development, but you didn't want to abuse the host's free service with a commercial message. Chances are, the host will post the information for you and appreciate the gesture. The endorsement of the host is much stronger publicity than any post you could make yourself.

Get Personal—Contact Others

The strategy behind the tactic of online networking is to build personal business relationships with a wide range of people online in order to get your name out there. The more people there are who know what you do and respect your company's reliability (to deliver quality service, on time, at a fair price), the more opportunities you create to field incoming leads.

Nancy Roebke is the editor of Network Ink, an e-mail newsletter about networking, and the executive director of ProfNet, a professional networking organization that sets up chapters all over the country. She advises targeting those people who are in constant contact with the types of people who can become clients. In other words, focus on people who can bring you a steady stream of leads. Figure out what category of people are good for your business. So don't focus on particular people, focus on what those people do. Consider the following categories of professionals:

- Bankers

- Lawyers

- Accountants

- Printers

- Realtors

Think about the fields that currently bring you a lot of business, but also think of the ones from which you don't have any clients. Roebke suggests making a list of fields of businesses that would best help you, then finding them online and making an introduction.

To penetrate the online community, you'll have to log some serious time online. This involves subscribing to discussion lists and interacting with other subscribers, subscribing to newsletters and interfacing with the hosts, surfing the Web and writing to people you read about online...basically, getting involved. One nice thing about online networking is that it doesn't actually feel like work. It's fun! It's like going to a dinner party without having to deal with the anxiety of not knowing anyone else, because you can lurk first, participate second.

Online networking, the subject of this chapter, is the crux of marketing with e-mail. Everything you do as part of your e-mail marketing plan—from publishing an e-mail newsletter to making a sale to providing customer service—comes back to online networking. Doing it wrong can seriously damage your reputation and get you labeled a spammer (see Chapter 10 for an in-depth look at spam on the Internet). If you take the time to learn the accepted protocol for online networking, it will make your activities down the road much easier. The online community can smell a sales pitch from a mile away, and repairing damage is much harder than preventing mistakes from the beginning.

The Internet is not a broadcast medium, like television, print, and radio. It's not about one person sending out a message to a large group of people with a slow and cumbersome means of response. Instead the Internet is a real-time, interactive, one-to-one marketing tool. Personal e-mails make networking personal. Why would you send someone a follow-up private post to their public post? There are several reasons: to ask for more information, to offer a contrasting point of view, to answer their questions, to thank them for their help, or to tell them how their post influenced a decision you made. It's the start of a friendship, so be sincere!

Play by the Rules

The rules of online networking are the same as those for offline networking. According to Roebke, you should first ask other people about their businesses. Find out how you can help them. What is their product or service? How much does it cost? What kind of leads would they like? How can you be of service to them?

When they reciprocate and it's your turn to tell them about you, avoid sales talk. Instead, give them concise teasers of valuable information, indicating that more resources are available on your site or through your autoresponder (see Chapter 5). This way, you let your Web site do the sales after proving your expertise in your field. Be genuine and build friendships with people in a position to bring you referrals.

Resources

- Network Ink (subscribe by sending an e-mail to *subscribe@just-business.com*) just started its second year of publication as the leading online networking e-mail newsletter on the Internet.

- Just Business, at *http://www.just-business.com*, offers a wealth of information about online networking to find referrals online, including a library of articles, autoresponders, discussion boards, an ask-the-experts tool, and weekly newsletters.

- About.com's chat site, at *http://chatting.miningco.com*, is a resource about and listing of all the places to go on the Web to chat. This site is frequently updated by host Julie Martin and includes the latest news and tools for getting involved in online chat, and Chatter, an e-mail newsletter about chatting on the Internet.

- Forum One, at *http://www.forumone.com*, is a search engine and directory-style database of all the Web forums available on the Internet. Search through categories from business and finance to health to education to arts.

- Marcom Exchange, at *http://www.marcomexchange.com*, is an interactive forum for marketing communications professionals. Visitors can access news, resources, marketplace, Marcom links, "Idea Exchange," and the "Creative Café." Free membership lets users into a media room that publishes member news.

- Deja.com, at *http://www.dejanews.com*, started as a searchable database of all the discussions that take place on Usenet, but has grown to a multi-service company that also offers ratings on Internet products, a tracking service, Deja Tracker, that monitors follow-up to posted messages and instant messaging. Other community-building services include a What's Happening e-mail that announces new members to the Deja.com community, a member photo gallery, and a Founders 101 that helps you found your own community.

- Usenet 2, at *http://www.usenet2.org*, is an attempt to create a structure in which the traditional Usenet model of cooperation and trust is reinstated. Using a minimal set of restrictions on abusive behavior, Usenet 2 will create an environment like the pre-commercial Usenet. This means that people still disagree, people still send nasty messages known as "flames," but people don't use it as a place for advertising space.

Cheat Sheet: Engage Your Online Networking Plan of Attack

1. Do an Internet search to find forums that have desirable target audiences. Consider setting up America Online and CompuServe accounts as a way to take advantage of their proprietary forums, especially if your product targets an audience that is newer to computers and the Internet.

2. Make a target list of discussions that you will subscribe to and join. Active lists are very time-consuming, so prune your list down to a manageable amount of traffic. Consider setting up a goal of a certain number of new lists per week to review, deciding after a few weeks of participation if you are going to be an active member, an inactive member, or an unsubscriber.

3. Make a short list of which forums you will focus on. These should change over time as you determine which pull valuable leads and which just pull busywork.

4. Set aside a certain number of hours per week for online networking. This includes the time you spend reading and responding to discussion in the forums you've joined.

5. Set a goal for how many new posts you will make per week.

6. Keep in mind that your goal is to become part of these communities, not just to hawk your wares.

7. Send posts publicly to the list and privately to certain members with whom you'd like to set up a more intimate relationship.

8. Measure your response and refine your actions constantly.

9. Write articles based on the hot topics that you see on the lists and send them to e-mail newsletter owners as a way to get published on these lists as well, reaching a whole new audience.

10. Integrate your online networking with signatures (Chapter 4) and rules (Chapter 10).

4

Signature Files

In the offline world, it's easy to mark your signature. Just a simple squiggle or a beautiful cursive mark was enough (everyone knows about ol' John Hancock and his overboard autograph). Then came e-mail, and at first, you could get away with a simple signoff: Sincerely, Shannon. No more! Now your signature has to comprise information about who you are, what you do, which company you work for, the address for your URL, and, of course, how to subscribe to your e-mail publication. A great signature file is the best way to add subscribers to your subscriber list.

It is this signature, with your e-mail call-to-action, that is going to do the most work for getting subscribers to your publication and then building a relationship with them. Now that e-mail is a tool of electronic commerce, signatures have a whole new meaning. They're the tag line at the end of each and every e-mail that you send out (who knows where that e-mail may end up...the forward key is mighty popular). Your signature can be a powerful marketing tool, but making one is much more complex than simply putting pen to paper!

What Is a Signature File?

Your signature (the Net slang term is "sig") file is the tag line that attaches automatically to every e-mail message that you send out. It includes the pertinent stuff—name, e-mail address and URL—and should include a compelling message or a directive (Subscribe to our newsletter! Request our autoresponder!). Consider your sig file as if it's your electronic business card. Just as you hand over your card when you network in real life, so you do when online.

As you create your signature file, include the following three important components:

1. General information: name, company name, and contact information.

2. The benefit to subscribers: Show how you're going to make others smarter, richer, better, or happier (with a free subscription to your e-mail newsletter, perchance?).

3. A call to action: List how they can respond or take you up on an offer. If you're paying attention to the other chapters in this book and creating your own e-mail publication, here's the place to promote it!

Imagine that your favorite magazine is going to write an article about your company. What would the headline say? In one or two sentences, you should be able to convey a meaningful summary that presents the cool thing about you that would draw people in and make them do what you want them to do. The best call to action starts with a verb and then follows with what is in it for the respondent.

If you can't do this, you're trying to convey too much information. It is not necessary to describe all your services in one signature. Instead, create multiple signatures based on the audience that will read your message. The example at the end of chapter comes from Shel Horowitz, who has a complicated, extensive system of targeting a group of e-mail signatures to a group of e-mail newsletters in which he participates. While it's not necessary to go to this length, it certainly doesn't hurt Horowitz's marketing efforts.

How to Decide What to Put In Your Signature File

This section itemizes what you need to create an electronic signature that serves a marketing purpose and gets results!

- *Keep it short and simple.* Brevity is essential. Keep your entire signoff message under six lines. If you go over, many of the list moderators will chop off the end. Plus, a quick read is easier for most readers to digest. Be concise with your signature or it won't get read. Think of your signature as a mini–business bio or an electronic business card.

- *Make it memorable.* Use your signature file as a way to show personality. Doing this in conjunction with all the other marketing functions might be a tall order, but it helps people remember you. When recipients of your e-mails and subscribers to discussion lists to which you post read your memorable signature, it works as a branding tool.

  Lisa Bryan, a witty copywriter who used to manage a copywriting service called Word Works (shown in Figure 4.1), emphasized her clever copywriting abilities with zingers and funny sayings at the end of each e-mail. To gage their effectiveness, she recently ran a contest polling recipients, asking them to vote for their favorites. She says that her "Lisa-isms" are her brand and have attracted a lot of attention to her business. She says people have told her that they read her posts to public discussion lists just because they know there will be something funny at the end. The most important thing is that people remember her. In addition, her creative tag lines serve to reinforce her brand image as a creative copywriter.

- *Get creative!* In her recent article, "Using Signature Files as a Networking Tool," Nancy Roebke, Executive Director of ProfNet, a networking organization, gives a creative suggestion for using signature files to elicit responses from all who see it: "Use your sig file to do a little market research. Ask one question, and tell respondents how to forward you their response. Once you have reached your desired number of respondents, change the question." What creative tactics can you think up?

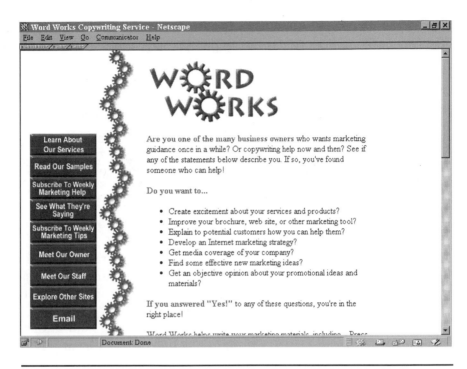

Figure 4.1. Word Works copywriting service's home page.

- *Offer free stuff.* You can do this by promising exclusive information, personalized consultation, free products, or anything that you can sum up in a brief sentence. Offer free sample products, limited services, and subscriptions via snail mail or e-mail. Some things that are easy to offer for free are autoresponders (see Chapter 5) filled with valuable information, a free subscription to an e-mail newsletter, or a special offer, event, or sale.

George Matyjewicz, an online marketing consultant, recommends taking a straightforward approach. His advice is to simply present your offerings to prospects. Say who you are, what company you are with, what you do, where you can be found, and what services you are highlighting. His signature reads

George Matyjewicz, C.M.O.
mailto:georgem@gapent.com

GAP Enterprises, Ltd.
http://www.gapent.com/Marketing Your Web
http://www.gapent.com/myweb/Automated Press Releases
http://www.gapent.com/pr/CyberSolutioning (tm)
http://www.gapent.com/cybersol/"How-to" Guides
http://www.gapent.com/howto/Affiliates Program http://
www.gapent.com/gapptr/

- *Use a call to action.* If you're using any of the tools from the other chapters of this book, namely, an e-mail newsletter, a discussion list, or autoresponders, you already have your non-threatening call to action. It's nonthreatening because it offers your target audience a way to respond to an automated system versus the more time-consuming, sometimes (and for some people) less appealing personal communications. At this point, you're just offering people a way to learn more about you and your business.

- If you want the recipients of your marketing e-mails to respond, ask them to respond! It's also perfectly acceptable to ask for them to respond to you personally. Include a line that asks readers to contact you or visit your site. To do this, you must use action verbs in your tag line, playing on the needs of your intended reader. For example, "E-mail us mentioning this special code and receive a free consultation on designing your professional Web presence."

- *Skip the sales pitch.* Roebke warns against any type of hardcore sales approach, "Please don't tell us that we can make a million dollars a minute (or anything that remotely sounds like that) by contacting you about your product or service that slices, dices, and does our laundry. We won't take you seriously, and it is a terrible waste of the most valuable real estate you have online—your signature file."

  The following signature file, one of Roebke's own, simply states what she's available for, making a sales offer without making a sales pitch:

Learn to Network!

Increase income, cut costs, and put an end to cold calling.

Get our FREE series of articles that teach you the secrets of successful networking. mailto:files@ProfNet.org Today!

ProfNet – Helping Business Professionals Find More Business

Variety—The Spice of Sigs

Who says you can only have one signature file? Roebke says, "I see a lot of people try to accomplish everything in their sig file, when having multiple signatures is a far better option." Mix and match a variety of renditions of your signature to the different places it will appear. The e-mail program Pegasus (available at *http:// www.pegasus.usa.com*) allows users to prerecord a number of different written signatures and choose one each time they send an e-mail. Customize your signature for each place that it will be sent. Shel Horowitz says that he has over 25 different signature files and uses them all! (Read them all, plus their separate objectives, in this chapter's case study.)

Information

At a minimum (and besides all the pieces listed earlier), include all the following details in your signature: your name, your company name, and your company's URL. Then, if there's room, include other pertinent details: your phone number, your e-mail address, and your mailing address. In his most commonly used file, Horowitz has the following pieces of information (a good example of each of our directives):

Shel Horowitz, mailto:shel@frugalfun.com, 800-683-WORD/413-586-2388

News releases, brochures, newsletters, ad copy, re-sumes, etc.

Books to save you money on business (Marketing Without Megabucks) and pleasure (The Penny-Pinching Hedonist) – preview them, get free marketing advice, arts travel zines & more: http://www.frugalfun.com

Test for Clarity

Run your message past a few people to make sure that you've made your point. Choose your words carefully to sum up your marketing message. Susan Klein, a marketing professional with Forty Software (shown in Figure 4.2), says that her signature file is written to speak directly to her target audience. She uses the following entertaining and informative signature file message when she posts to discussion lists filled with her target audience of business professionals:

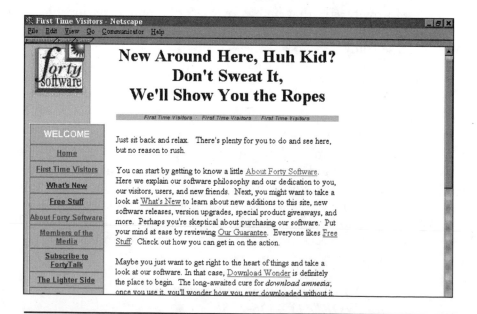

Figure 4.2. Forty Software's home page.

"It's 10:00 a.m. Can't find that file you downloaded for your 11:00 meeting? Visit <u>http://www.forty.com</u> and get the cure for your Download Amnesia."

Use signature files as an introduction to pique a potential client's interest, but don't give out too much or too little information. Remember to be short, precise, and relevant. Offer people a way to get back to you or to respond to your call to action.

In order to have a truly effective directive in your e-mail message, you should check for clarity by testing the message out on several different people in your target audience (not your boss, and definitely not a subordinate). Have a user group of consumers in your target audience who have volunteered to give you feedback (use a simple questionnaire that quizzes them on comprehension of your marketing message).

Speak Directly to Your Audience

Direct your signature file to a very specific audience...those who are interested in exactly and precisely what you have to offer. Don't try to reach everyone. This attracts the right people and doesn't waste your time filtering through inquiries from people who don't want or can't afford your services. Barbara Bix, a health care marketing professional who publishes the e-mail newsletter Health Care Marketing Plus, says her signature file, which offers a sample or subscription to her e-mail newsletter, is effective in weeding out the riffraff, keeping her list lean with highly targeted prospects. The vast majority of her subscribers are a homogenous group of health care professionals with marketing responsibilities. She averages less than two unsubscribes for every issue she sends. The net result is a highly targeted list of exactly the people she needs to reach.

Her signature reads:

Health Care Marketing Plus, mail to:hcmkgplus@world.std.com

If you would like to get the next issue of Health Care Marketing Matters, please send me your e-mail address.

This free online publication discusses ways to uncover untapped marketing opportunities.

A Note about ASCII

ASCII is a character set that excludes special characters, formatting, and fonts. ASCII art is when a bunch of ASCII characters are put together to create something else. For a simple example, consider this: You can't type an arrow pointing left with the ASCII character set, but you can use the less-than symbol and a dash to create "<-". Be cautious about putting too much in your signature file or you risk really annoying the recipient. However, should you choose to use ASCII art in your e-mail, use it for a specific purpose: to entertain, to set your information apart from the rest of the message, or to brand your image.

Test and Measure

Through different sample signatures, different calls to action, and different vehicles for responding, you can measure the creative execution of your signature file. For example, Jose Camilo measures the results of his signature file through leads it generates in visits to his Web site. His signature reads

Jose Camilo Daccach T. mailto:jocada@norma.net

Calle 12 No. 8-13 Cali, Colombia. South America

Tel: +57 2 886 2388 Cel: 93 551 5917

The DELTA report http://delta.hypermart.net/ ERD.html?fir

He says that about twenty responses per day are from the last line of his signature file, "Note that I can change the part after the question mark to anything I want, hence I can change it every month or with different messages to measure its impact." You can use this same technique to measure the effect that your free posts to different newsgroups have on the consumers who see it.

Setting Up Your Signature File

Most e-mail programs offer a way to set up a signature file. Some of the more popular programs are described in the following sections.

Using Pegasus

1. Go to the Tools pull-down menu and choose "Options."

2. Click on "Signatures." You will be presented with a list of nine signature spaces to edit.

3. To create a signature, click on the Edit button next to the one you want to use (start with one, then two, etc.)

4. Fill out the box for the Sent via the Internet option.

5. Enter a name to identify that signature (for example, if it is for a specific forum) and press "Save."

6. To choose a signature, create a new message and double-click the signature check box to open the signature dialog box.

7. Select a message signature using the pull-down menu.

Using Outlook

1. Using the Tools pull-down menu, choose "Autosignature."

2. In the space provided, fill out your preferred signature and check the box that says "Add this signature to the end of new messages."

3. To add the signature to new messages, do nothing; it will be automatically added.

4. To add the signature to existing messages (such as forwards and replies), choose the Insert pull-down menu and click on "Autosignature."

Using Eudora

1. Eudora comes with a default signature called standard, which you can change to create your primary signature.

2. From the Tools menu, choose "Signatures." The Signature window is displayed.

3. Right-click anywhere inside the Signature window and choose "New" from the context menu. Eudora displays the Create New Signature dialog, asking you for a name.

4. In the dialog, enter a signature name and click "OK." A Signature window is displayed.

5. Enter your signature text in the Signature window.

6. Save the signature file using the File menu Save command.

7. Close the Signature window.

Using Netscape Communicator

1. From the Edit menu, choose "Preferences."

2. Select "Identity" from the Mail Groups category.

3. In the Identity panel, type your name, e-mail address, reply-to address, and organization.

4. Create a separate file in WordPad or another plain text editor. Save it on your hard drive.

5. To attach this file to your messages, which will create the signature, type the absolute path at the Signature File box or click "Browse" to locate the file you just created.

6. Click "OK."

7. The signature will be added to all your outgoing messages.

Case Study: Shel Horowitz of Frugal Fun

Shel Horowitz has more than 25 signatures that are used on outgoing messages. Each is designed with a different audience in mind. Similarly, you can use different signatures depending on the audience you're reaching.

Standard

First is Shel's standard signature, set as the default, used most often. The goal is to promote copywriting, books, and the Web site:

Shel Horowitz, mailto:shel@frugalfun.com, 800-683-WORD/413-586-2388

News releases, brochures, newsletters, ad copy, resumes, etc.

Books to save you money on business (Marketing Without Megabucks) and pleasure (The Penny-Pinching Hedonist) – preview them, get free marketing advice, arts/travel zines & more: http:// www.frugalfun.com

Marketing

Because his standard focuses on his main line of business, these variations address other services, namely emphasizing consulting and strategy more than copywriting:

Shel Horowitz, Director—Accurate Writing & More (Northampton MA)

High-return, low-cost marketing materials and strategy development

Author, Marketing Without Megabucks: How to Sell Anything on a Shoestring

FREE monthly marketing tips, how-to articles, more:
http://www.frugalfun.com

mailto:shel@frugalfun.com, 413-586-2388 (voice), 617-249-0153 (fax)

Marketing and Article Writing

The following signature is useful when discussing advertorials or areas where someone wants a writer with both a public relations/marketing and journalism background:

Shel Horowitz, Director—Accurate Writing & More

High-return, low-cost marketing materials and strategy development

Author, *Marketing Without Megabucks: How to Sell Anything on a Shoestring* and *The Penny-Pinching Hedonist: How to Live Like Royalty with a Peasant's Pocketbook*

Editor, *Down To Business* / *Global Arts Review* / *Global Travel Review*

Over 800 published articles

mailto:shel@frugalfun.com http://www.frugalfun.com
413.586.2388

Accurate Writing and More—General/Marketing

Shel's standard signature with his company name attached is useful when he corresponds with people who find him first through his company. But his marketing strategy is to brand his own name, not his company name, because he has good name recognition in his local area.

> *Shel Horowitz, mailto:shel@frugalfun.com, 800-683-WORD/413-586-2388*
>
> *Director, Accurate Writing & More*
>
> *News releases, brochures, newsletters, direct mail, ad copy, resumes, etc.*
>
> *Books to save you money on business (Marketing Without Megabucks: How to Sell Anything on a Shoestring) and pleasure (The Penny-Pinching Hedonist: How to Live Like Royalty with a Peasant's Pocketbook) – preview them, get free marketing advice, arts/travel zines & more: http://www.frugalfun.com Fax: 617-249-0153*

Accurate Writing and More—Editing/Book Doctoring

This variation emphasizes a specific, different set of services:

> *Shel Horowitz, mailto:shel@frugalfun.com, 800-683-WORD/413-586-2388*
>
> *Director, Accurate Writing & More*
>
> *Editing * Book Proposals * Ghostwriting * Publishing Consulting * Marketing*
>
> *Serving writers and publishers since 1981 Fax: 617-249-0153*

Posting to Discussion Lists

The next four are custom versions used when Shel posts messages in the I-Sales and I-Advertising discussion lists, with three- and four-line limits, respectively. He has a primary and alternate for each, depending on what he wants to emphasize.

I-Sales

> *Shel Horowitz <mailto:shel@frugalfun.com> 800-683-WORD/413-586-2388*
>
> *LOW-COST, HIGH-RETURN MARKETING: strategy, materials from book author.*
>
> *http://www.frugalfun.com – 200 pages of free money-saving advice*

I-Sales Alternate

> *Shel Horowitz <mailto:shel@frugalfun.com> 800-683-WORD/413-586-2388*
>
> *MARKETING WITHOUT MEGABUCKS: strategy, materials, 384-page book.*
>
> *http://www.frugalfun.com – 200 pages of free money-saving advice*

I-Advertising

> *Shel Horowitz, mailto:shel@frugalfun.com, 800-683-WORD/413-586-2388*
>
> *News releases, brochures, newsletters, ad copy, resumes, etc.*
>
> *$ave on business and pleasure—visit http://www.frugalfun.com for free*

marketing advice, book previews, arts/travel/business zines & more.

I-Advertising Alternate

Shel Horowitz <mailto:shel@frugalfun.com> 800-683-WORD/413-586-2388

Affordable, effective marketing materials/strategies from the author of Marketing Without Megabucks: How to Sell Anything on a Shoestring

http://www.frugalfun.com for free marketing tips, cheapskate advice, 'zines...

Accurate Writing and More—Resumes/Careers

Frugal Fun offers a diverse range of services, so they need a diverse range of signatures. Local clients hire them for resume work, but the company also has occasional clients who use them for resume writing. This signature is used when someone comes to them for these services through the Web:

Shel Horowitz, mailto:shel@frugalfun.com, http://www.frugalfun.com

Director, Accurate Writing & More

ph. 800.683.WORD/413.586.2388 (since 1981)

Affordable Professional Resumes – in person (MA) or by fax/e-mail/phone

Resumes published in five national resume books

Assistance in starting, operating, and marketing a business

Author, Marketing Without Megabucks: How to Sell Anything on a Shoestring

Public Speaking: Long and Short Versions

Shel also works as a paid public speaker. He uses the following two signatures to market himself for these projects:

Shel Horowitz, mailto:shel@frugalfun.com,

800-683-WORD/413-586-2388

Featured Speaker, American Marketing Association— CT Chapter Conference; National Writers Union regional conferences; others. Instructor, University of Massachusetts. Heard live on radio stations from Taiwan to Tennessee.

Author of books to save you money on business (Marketing Without Megabucks: How to Sell Anything on a Shoestring) and pleasure (The Penny-Pinching Hedonist: How to Live Like Royalty with a Peasant's Pocketbook) – preview them, get free marketing advice, arts/travel zines & more: http://www.frugalfun.com Fax: 617-249-0153

or

Shel Horowitz – Featured Speaker, American Marketing Association—CT Chapter Conference; National Writers Union regional conferences; others.

Instructor, University of Massachusetts. Heard live on radio stations from Taiwan to Tennessee.

mailto:shel@frugalfun.com

800-683-WORD/413-586-2388

http://www.frugalfun.com Fax: 617-249-0153

Global Arts/Travel

Frugal Fun publishes Web magazines, so when Shel works with writers and advertisers about this line of business, these are his signatures for corresponding with them:

Shel Horowitz, *mailto:shel@frugalfun.com*,

413-586-2388 (v) 617-249-0153 (f)

Editor/Publisher

Global ARTS Review <http://www.frugalfun.com/ review.html>

Global TRAVEL Review <http://www.frugalfun.com/ travel.html>

For information about our book on low-cost FUN, send any message to pph@frugalfun.com, or visit our Web site, <http://www.frugalfun.com>

or

Shel Horowitz, *mailto:shel@frugalfun.com*,

413-586-2388 (v) 617-249-0153 (f)

Editor/Publisher

Global ARTS Review <http://www.frugalfun.com/ review.html>

Global TRAVEL Review <http://www.frugalfun.com/ travel.html>

Down to Business <http://www.frugalfun.com/ dtb.html>

For information about our books on low-cost FUN and low cost marketing, send any message to <mailto:pph@frugalfun.com> <mailto:mwm@frugalfun.com> (marketing), or visit our Web site, <http://www.frugalfun.com>

Articles/Webzines

The goal of the following two signatures is to emphasize Shel's article writing and union affiliation, with and without the webzines:

Shel Horowitz, Northampton, MA, USA,
mailto:shel@frugalfun.com. NWU member.

Author, *Marketing Without Megabucks: How to Sell
Anything on a Shoestring* and *The Penny-Pinching
Hedonist: How to Live Like Royalty with a Peasant's
Pocketbook* Editor, *Down To Business* / *Global
Arts Review* / *Global Travel Review*

Over 800 published articles http://www.frugalfun.com
413.586.2388

Shel Horowitz, Northampton, MA, USA,
mailto:shel@frugalfun.com

Author, *Marketing Without Megabucks: How to Sell
Anything on a Shoestring* and *The Penny-Pinching
Hedonist: How to Live Like Royalty with a Peasant's
Pocketbook* Over 800 published articles in magazines,
newspapers, and newsletters http://www.frugalfun.com
413.586.2388.

Online Publications

The following signatures encourage recipients to become interested
in Shel's three webzines and the two tipsheets:

Shel Horowitz, mailto:shel@frugalfun.com, http://
www.frugalfun.com

Publisher, Monthly Frugal Fun Tips & Monthly Frugal
Marketing Tips e-mail newsletters, Global Arts Review,
Global Travel Review, and Down to Business webzines.
Also books to save you money on business and pleasure

800-683-9673/413-586-2388 Fax: 617-249-0153

Shel Horowitz, mailto:shel@frugalfun.com, http://
www.frugalfun.com

Publisher, Monthly Frugal Fun Tips & Monthly Frugal
Marketing Tips e-mail newsletters, Global Arts Review,

*Global Travel Review, and Down to Business webzines.
Also books to save you money on business (Marketing
Without Megabucks: How to Sell Anything on a Shoe-
string) and pleasure (The Penny-Pinching Hedonist:
How to Live Like Royalty with a Peasant's Pocketbook)*

*800-683-9673/413-586-2388
Fax: 617-249-0153*

AWM Books

The focus of this signature is to highlight the company's publishing
services:

Shel Horowitz, <u>mailto:shel@frugalfun.com</u>,

877-FRUGALFUN/413-586-2388

*Publisher, AWM Books: Books that save you money on
business and pleasure:*

*Marketing Without Megabucks: How to Sell Anything
on a Shoestring*

*The Penny-Pinching Hedonist: How to Live Like
Royalty with a Peasant's Pocketbook*

*Also affordable marketing services for publishers and
other small businesses*

*Preview our books, get free marketing advice, arts/
travel/business zines & more: <u>http://www.frugalfun.com</u>
Fax: 617-249-0153*

AWM Books—Holiday Special

The holiday version of their signature is used in November and December, to encourage seasonal gift buying:

Shel Horowitz, <u>mailto:shel@frugalfun.com</u>,

877-FRUGALFUN/413-586-2388

*Through December 15 – FREE SHIPPING (US/
Canada) on our money-saving books: Marketing With-
out Megabucks: How to Sell Anything on a Shoestring
The Penny-Pinching Hedonist: How to Live Like
Royalty with a Peasant's Pocketbook*

*Also affordable marketing services for publishers and
other small businesses*

*Preview our books, get free marketing advice, arts/
travel/business zines & more: http://www.frugalfun.com
Fax: 617-249-0153*

Web Site
Sometimes the goal is just to draw visitors to the Web site:

Shel Horowitz, mailto:shel@frugalfun.com,

877-FRUGALFUN

Webmaster, FrugalFun.com http://www.frugalfun.com

Over 200 articles to save you money and improve your life

*Home of: Global Arts Review, Global Travel Review,
Down to Business mags*

Monthly Frugal Fun and Frugal Marketing tipsheets

*Excerpts from Marketing Without Megabucks, The
Penny-Pinching Hedonist*

Radio Contact
The goal of this signature is to be booked as a guest by a radio person. Anytime Shel receives or initiates an e-mail conversation with a
radio producer or talkshow host, he uses this signature:

*Shel Horowitz, "The King of Frugal Fun" Author, 4
books. mailto:shel@frugalfun.com*

413-586-2388 (Northampton, MA) http://www.frugalfun.com

Featured on over 150 radio shows from New England to California to Taiwan.

Talking Points (Low-Cost Fun): Anyone can afford vacations, entertainment, food, shopping, romance, etc.—specific ways to slash costs.

Talking Points (Low-Cost Marketing): Flame-proof Internet marketing, zero-cost Websites, free media exposure, slash your ad costs while building results.

Frugality
Shel calls this his cheapskate signature, used to position his authority as a frugal expert. This is used in situations that have nothing to do with marketing work.

Shel Horowitz, "The King of Frugal Fun," mailto:shel@frugalfun.com

800-683-WORD/413-586-2388 (Northampton, MA) Fax: 617-249-0153

Author, The Penny-Pinching Hedonist: How to Live Like Royalty with a Peasant's Pocketbook and three other books. Featured on radio stations from New England to Taiwan...praised in Living Cheap News, Boston Globe, Frugal Bugle, others.

Book excerpts, monthly tip sheet, arts/travel zines: http://www.frugalfun.com

Resources

- ASCII Art Resources, at *http://www.geocities.com/SouthBeach/Marina/4942/ascii.htm*, is a gigantic ASCII art resource, including the free program Sigzag, which lets you create an ASCII signature.

- Flumps ASCII Art Collection, at *http://www.xs4all.nl/~klr*, is a database of pictures made out of ASCII characters. They're offered free of charge, as long as the artist's initials are kept with the picture.

- SIG ASCII Interest Group List, at *http://www.egroups.com/ group/sig-list/info.html*, is a show-and-tell ASCII/signature interest group list, primarily for all those who use a signature with their e-mail or doodle in ASCII. Conversation covers ASCII art, quotes, poetry, Netiquette, sig files, software, and how to do it in ASCII. To subscribe, send an empty message to *sig-list-subscribe@makelist.com*.

- Coolsig, at *http://www.coolsig.com*, is billed as the biggest signature collection on the Internet. This collection of phrases and quotes that you can use to spice up your signature files is collected from visitors to the site who submit suggestions to the database.

- Signature Museum, at *http://huizen.dds.nl/~mwpieter/sigs/*, showcases art and slogans that can be used in signature files. The categories include samples and comments, together with a link to the home page of the contributors.

Cheat Sheet: Make Your Signature Files

1. Open a plain ASCII document editor, such as WordPad.

2. Type your basic identifying information: name, company name.

3. Decide how you want people to respond to you, and include this information as the contact information: phone, e-mail, snail mail. Keep it brief.

4. Make a list of all the possible audiences you will reach as you undertake your online networking endeavors.

5. For each audience, write your "headline" that describes your unique selling point.

6. For each audience, sum up your call to action and response mechanism.

7. Set your collection of signatures up in your e-mail program, using the directions listed in the help section.

8. Begin your online networking endeavors!

5

Autoresponders

Imagine hot prospects considering doing business with your company. They visit your site and have questions about why your services can help them with their needs. If an article explaining this is simply listed on your site, then the prospects look it up and you are none the wiser (except your site counter might register a visitor). They may or may not contact you to use your services. Now, imagine instead that they have to request this informative article via autoresponder. The benefit is that, while they still get the information right away, you get a quick note that tells you exactly who has requested more information from your company (at a minimum, you have an e-mail address; ideally they have a preset signature file that shows their name, title, company and more). Voila, you can follow up with these hot prospects and close the deal.

Autoresponders (also known as "information on demand") are a wonderful time-saving marketing tool. Developing an effective and well-used autoresponder plan requires systematic attention to and recording of e-mails that come into your organization, through the Web site, through your other e-mail marketing efforts, and through other ways that people reach your organization. As you get further into your e-mail marketing activities, managing the flow of e-mail will take more and more time. At first, this is going to be really satisfying, but it will soon get tiresome. Don't get caught unprepared when this point hits. Instead, keep track of the nature of the first wave of e-mails that come into your organization, recording what questions recur most often and what information you have to share most often to close a sale.

The fact is that when you're new to e-mail marketing, the first twenty times someone asks you to send them a description of your top-selling product or service you'll be thrilled—interested prospects! E-mail marketing works! All these people are going to become customers. Then it might turn into a tiresome time bandit to explain the same thing over and over again, because the fact is that a lot of these people aren't going to become customers, they're just picking your brain for information and expertise. This is fine—you want to be helpful to build a good reputation online. However, when it starts to take time and interfere with the money-making part of your business, it's time to bring in the autoresponders. With these, you can answer all these questions quickly and thoroughly.

The early way to answer all these incoming questions was with a Frequently Asked Questions (FAQ) page on your company's Web site. While it still might be feasible to offer a FAQ page to answer these questions, you might end up wasting a lot of time directing people to it. In addition, it might not be the preferred way for your audience to receive information from you. Having the autoresponder option is a time- and cost-saving approach.

The Definition of an Autoresponder

Autoresponders are text files that are returned via e-mail, automatically, when requested. They are requested by sending an e-mail to a designated address, which is set up for the purpose of automatically responding with another e-mail. These e-mails are sent automatically, as shown in the diagram in Figure 5.1. Hence the name "autoresponder." Other names include "infobots" and "e-mail on demand."

One example of autoresponders is the one shown in Figure 5.2. As a marketing tool, Idea Station used to offer a list of mass opt-in e-mail distribution vendors for free via autoresponder. Because this is a printed document that you're holding in your hands, you don't have the benefit of the most current information. Therefore, as a service to you, the reader, Idea Station used to interact with readers by

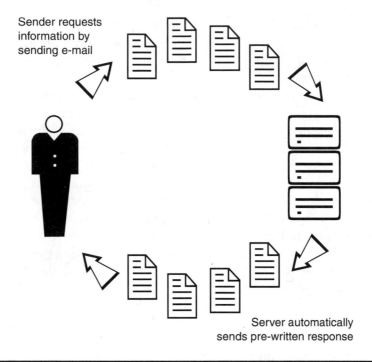

Sender requests information by sending e-mail

Server automatically sends pre-written response

Figure 5.1. How an autoresponder works.

offering an autoresponder listing all vendors in this industry. The great thing about this autoresponder technology is that e-mail can be sent to the inquirer immediately, without the need for me to do anything. When you use an autoresponder to market your expertise in your field, you often achieve sales without having to do anything (except cash the check!).

Autoresponders can be used for a multitude of purposes, from simply relaying standard information, as shown in the preceding example, to customer service, marketing, and promotions. The goal is to respond to prospects, clients, and other important inquiries quickly, without making them wait or, worse, sending them to your competition.

To encourage prospects, clients, and others to contact you, devise your autoresponder program with their needs in mind. What does someone who wants to work with your company need to know? Contact information? Pricing? Policies? Here's a hint: Set up your autoresponders so that each e-mail that is sent into the autoresponder

E-mail Marketing Vendor List

Created 10/23/99 5:24 PM
Last Updated 07/31/00 11:34 AM E.S.T.

This autoresponder does not automatically add your name to a database. In fact, we update frequently, and the only way for you to receive updates is to send a new message to vendors@ideastation.com.

Bonus Mail
Product: Bonus Mail
Price: $.19 per message

CLICK ACTION
Product: E-mail Relationship Management
Price: $5,000-$10,000; $.015-$.05 per e-mail

e-ads™
Product: e-ads™
Price: $349 / yr. subscription + $.01 per mailing

Echomail
Product: Echomail
Price: $5,000-$10,000; $.04-$.08 per e-mail

Exactis.com
Product: E-mail Marketing Solutions^{SM}
Price: Cost per message: $0.005 - $0.10
Monthly Minimum: $1,000 - $5,000
Set up fees: $250 - $2,500

L-Soft International, Inc
Product: LISTSERV (R), LSMTP (R), ListPlex (R), EASE
Price range: $500-$24,000

Message Media
Product: UnityMail
Price: Depends on Package ($7,000 - $30,000)

MyPoints.com
Product: MyPoints.com's Cost Per Click (CPC) Web Marketing Program
Price: $.50 per click, up to 100,000 clicks, then price break

SparkLIST.com
Product: Business E-mail List Hosting Service
Price: Cost per message: $1/1,000 e-mails
Monthly Minimum: $50
Set up fees: $50 - $5000

Figure 5.2.   Idea Station's partial list of vendors.

is copied to you. People don't necessarily understand autoresponder technology, so they will sometimes write notes to you in the body of their message. If you copy these messages to your personal address, you can follow up on them. It's also a good idea to get these messages so that you can do a personal follow-up with people who request information about your company.

The ideas in this chapter should be adapted and expanded to fit your business. Any piece of information that prospects need or want in order to do business with you (from forms to contact information to promotional material) can be prewritten and sent to them. As you read this chapter, jot down your ideas for autoresponders that can be constructed and offered to your target audience.

Make Money While You Sleep!

I realize that this claim sounds too good to be true. But good autoresponders can save you time by answering questions while you are off doing other things (like sleeping). And, hey, time *is* money!

Autoresponders are a valuable part of your e-mail marketing program because they position you as an expert, help to automate customer relations and sales processes, and create a free offer that you can use to publicize your name and company.

As with most e-mail marketing endeavors, autoresponders save you money. It is less costly to have a prospect request an automatically returned response than to spend time returning phone calls, sending faxes on demand, or sending mail, with the associated paper, printing, and postage fees.

In addition, it's satisfying for your prospects to receive immediate feedback on their sales inquiries. You have the benefit of knowing who is requesting information and the benefit of knowing what response was sent. No one has to wait on hold or wonder if their question will be answered. This keeps your business competitive.

You can set up an infinite number of responses that answer an infinite number of possible inquiries. Because they're automated, an autoresponder can process a large volume of requests easily and quickly. In addition, it doesn't matter what length you're sending as your autoresponse text: a 20-page document takes the same resources as a paragraph. In an information-glut era when spam is making it difficult to get an effective message responded to on a one-to-one basis, autoresponders can do an army of work. Autoresponders are one of the best tools at your disposal.

Here's one caveat: Make it clear that when people request an autoresponder, you will respect their privacy by not using their e-mail address for other purposes. Follow-up is acceptable (Such as an e-mail that asks, "Thanks for requesting our autoresponder. Did you receive it? Are there any questions I can answer?), but hitting them with a sales pitch is a no-no.

How to Create an Autoresponder

The setup will vary somewhat depending on what service you use to host your autoresponders. The basics remain the same, however. Just ask your autoresponder service vendor for specifics on how to set yours up.

- Create a text file that contains the exact text that you want to send back to anyone who sends an e-mail to your autoresponder address.

- Format it with hard returns at the end of each line. Depending on the e-mail program that your recipients use, you might end up sending them an e-mail in which each paragraph appears as one very long line. To avoid this, use manual returns.

- Create an e-mail address that you will use to name the file.

- Upload the file to the service. For some services, this may be through a Web site. For others, you might have to use a program (such as FTP or Fetch) that transfers your files to their service.

- Be sure that the contents of your file are in ASCII (plain text rather than HTML) and that if you use a file transfer program, you transfer in ASCII as well.

- If you want a copy of each request for an automated response to be copied to a real e-mail address, be sure to forward one copy of all the e-mails coming into the autoresponder address to a second address. Sometimes people don't understand that they're sending to a machine and they will include a personal message. It might be a sales order, so you don't want to miss it!

- Test the autoresponder by sending a message to your autoresponder address.

The Next Generation: Personalized Autoresponders and Sequenced Messaging

As the technology advances and autoresponders become more popular, the customization and personalization so popular with e-mail newsletters and promotions are now becoming popular for autoresponders. Automation gets information to prospects quickly and results in faster turnaround on sales.

The next generation of autoresponders will collect demographic information and preferences from prospects and return to them (addressed specifically for them) the exact information they want. In addition, more robust autoresponder programs include automatic follow-up, in which the first response is appended with later automatic e-mails sending additional information, offers, or reminders. The e-mail marketer determines what specific information is sent in the follow-up message. If you consider that it often takes several repetitions of your message to have an effect on a prospect, an automated autoresponder follow-up program is a great marketing tactic.

Sequenced messaging lets you predefine personalized content and send according to a sequenced delivery. One company that is currently seeking a patent on their Adaptive Sequenced Messaging (ASM) technology is e2 Communications. "This provides marketers with a process-based approach to customer and lead management," touts the company's literature.

Another such program is available at *http://www.aweber.com/ ?9696*. With this program a prospect first requests information from your company. The information is instantly sent, with a notice that follow-up information will be forwarded at a later date. The address is added to your database. After a predetermined interval, the follow-up message is sent.

What to Put in Your Autoresponder

You can include just about any question that comes to you more than once in your autoresponder. Because the text is prewritten and automatically sent, you want documents that are standard, relatively timeless, and used repeatedly. Think in terms of who will be requesting these autoresponders. Design content for prospects, clients, and members of the media.

I had a creative writing instructor at the University of Florida that gave me an excellent piece of advice on how to be a productive writer. "Just find someone who is a good talker and write down what they say." I share this advice with you because it might help you find that great mind (and great talker) in your company. That lets you easily find excellent information to compile in your autoresponders. Simply interview the company expert on a given topic, make this essay available via autoresponder, and you're all set to build and strengthen relationships with your target audience.

The following are some examples of what you might include in your autoresponder program.

Instructions for Working with Your Company

When a new client comes to you, there are things that have to be hashed out at the beginning of the relationship. Automate the information that they need to know about you and a list of questions for information that you need to know about them. For example,

- A form that requests all their contact information and the names and details about all the people you'll have to be in contact with: accounting, management, public relations, sales, marketing and administrative personnel.

- A form that gives them all the contact information they'll have to have for you.

- A "getting-to-know-you" form that asks them questions. Their answers help you build your customer database (good for the long-term relationship that you're building with each customer).

- A "getting-to-know-us" form that outlines how you work with clients.

- A list of prices, including instructions for how they can modify their current arrangement with you (for example, if they want to grow or shrink their budget with you).

- Forms that they can easily fill out to place orders with your company.

- A description of the benefits of working with your company.

- Directions to your offices for in-town and out-of-town visitors.

- A list of references and other clients with whom they may discuss your strengths and weaknesses in order to make a purchase decision (make sure that you have permission from these other clients...including their e-mail address if this is their preferred method of communications).

- A referral page that they can give to others to recommend your services for you and generate leads.

Articles

The articles that you offer in your autoresponder must be written to speak directly to your target market. To do this, make a list of the common problems that your target market might face. For example, if you would like to reach entrepreneurs, you might make a list that includes the following:

- Cashflow Shortages: Tips for Stretching a Dollar

- No Time for Marketing: How to Automate With E-mail

- Can't Find New Customers? Try These 5 Easy Tips

- Whether or Not to Incorporate: How to Decide

Solutions to their problems are the only thing that your target audience will request. Now try to write a headline that matches each of those problems. Examples might be:

- Cashflow Shortages: "How to Find Great Business Deals on the Internet"; "How to Barter With Other Businesses."

- No Time for Marketing: "The Five-Minute-a-Day Plan for New Leads"; "Using Autoresponders To Market While You Sleep." (Hey, that last one sounds familiar!)

- Can't Find New Customers: "Secrets for Getting Customers to Come to You!"; "Ten Places to Find Customers."

- Whether or Not to Incorporate: "Certified Public Accountants vs. Attorneys-at-Law: The Incorporation Showdown."

Writing the articles isn't as difficult as you might think. (Gene Fowler is quoted as saying: "Writing is easy. All you do is stare at a blank sheet of paper until drops of blood form on your forehead.") The trick is to follow this no-fail, satisfaction guaranteed, step-by-step guide to writing a respectably useful article for your autoresponder (you can quote me on that).

- *Step 1.* Define your topic. You've already done this by writing the headline. (See how easy it is already?)

- *Step 2.* Create a blank outline with the following details:

  - Introduction

  - Thesis

  - Point 1

  - Point 2

  - Point 3

  - Conclusion

- *Step 3.* Fill in the worksheet you just created with one sentence per section. At this point, the introduction can start with a simple sentence that outlines your article's purpose. (Step 5 will remedy the problem that this is a rather boring way to present an article). The *thesis* outlines your three (or more, or less) points about your topic. Then list a complete sentence for each of your points. Finally, your conclusion should give your readers a glimpse at what they can accomplish now that you've enlightened them with your informative article. When you're done, your paper might look something like this:

  - *Introduction:* This article will explain how entrepreneurs can use the Internet to find great business deals.

  - *Thesis:* Great deals on products can be found through Web sites, banner ads and e-mail newsletters.

  - *Point 1:* Web sites of major retailers, such as Office Depot.com, and small retailers, such as iPrint.com, offer great prices compared to retail stores.

  - *Point 2:* As you search the Web, keep an eye out for banner ads that offer discounts if you click on them.

  - *Point 3:* Sign up for e-mail newsletters and e-mail announcements whenever you come across them, because this is the only place that many business-to-business online retailers post specials.

  - *Conclusion:* When you are in the market for new products and services for your business, turn first to the Internet to get the best deals.

- *Step 4.* Strengthen your article by using quotes from sources (perhaps a customer or employee) and list examples or further resources. For each of the points you make, try to find someone who has, in fact, used the advice you've given and has results to share. The best lessons are taught by those who have tried your tips.

- *Step 5*. This is where you actually start writing (or rewriting) your article. The hard work is now beginning, but at least you'll start with something on paper. Now it's time to go back and rewrite your article. Eliminate the words "introduction," "thesis," "point 1," "point 2," "point 3," and "conclusion," and put your copy into five-paragraph format. You should have something resembling an article, but needing some smoothing out.

Popular (Easy) Formats for Articles

Still stuck? Consider copycatting some tried and true article formats. The following could work for you:

- *List Articles*. "top ten reasons to"; "top five ways to"; "top fifteen places to"; "top twenty strategies for".

- *News*. In this case, you might want to try offering a press release about your company's newest product, service or client.

- *Lessons*. Step-by-step tutorials that apply to your industry are useful. If you write one that shows how to do the service that you offer to clients and it shows the level of complexity and expertise involved in the service you provide, it may end up convincing them that it's better to hire you than to do it themselves.

Ira Pasternack of Clearly Internet writes in his e-mail newsletter Marketing Tip of the Day, "If you effectively teach them something in the free article, they will be likely to have confidence in your ability to continue to help them if they pay for your services."

Get Feedback

Encourage recipients to give you feedback on your autoresponders. Not only will this help you keep tabs on the effectiveness of your articles, but they'll help you improve your autoresponders by telling you what else you could offer them or how you could make your autoresponders more useable.

Another result of encouraging feedback is that is helps you build relationships with your audience. It is this relationship that puts value into your e-mail marketing program because this relationship is based on trust.

Layout
Because your autoresponder is plain text, there are a few formatting tools that will make them easier for your prospects to read. Keep line lengths under 65 characters to ensure that your paragraphs wrap as you want them to (not as different e-mail readers force them to). Use short paragraphs, with one idea expressed per paragraph and an extra blank line inserted between paragraphs. Use spaces instead of tabs, and leave out all special characters. Even curly quotes ("") and em dashes (—) send incorrectly with some programs. Attachments can't be sent as autoresponders.

Case Study: Severina Publications

Severina Publications offers a full autoresponder program from their site at *http://www.severina.co.uk/marketserv/auto/whatout.htm*. Their Web site is shown in Figure 5.3. This full-service Internet publishing and Internet marketing company which practices what they preach: They offer autoresponders to clients as a service to build clients' businesses, but they also offer a full library of autoresponders as part of their own Internet marketing strategy. Autoresponders include both articles and information about working with the company. The following autoresponders are in the company's Autoresponder Central list. Request them by sending a blank e-mail to the addresses given.

- *12steps@severina.co.uk* retrieves a list of 12 ways to promote your Web site offline.

- *10@severina.co.uk* retrieves a list of 10 questions that you should ask prospective Web designers before placing your business with them.

- *Link@severina.co.uk* retrieves a list of link sites on the Internet.

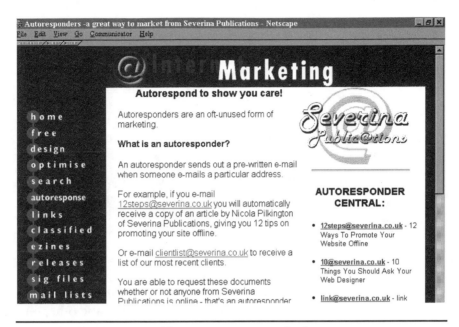

Figure 5.3. Severina Publications' autoresponder home page.

- *Classified@severina.co.uk* retrieves a list of classified ad sites on the Web.

- *ezines@severina.co.uk* retrieves a list of e-zines on the Internet.

- *Clientlist@severina.co.uk* retrieves a list of Severina Publications' most recent clients.

Resources

- Autoresponders.com, at *http://www.autoresponders.com*, by Voron Communications offers autoresponders and information about buying and using this tool.

- Autoresponders.net, at *http://www.autoresponders.net*, is another site that sells autoresponder services and has free information about them.

List Your Autoresponder on Your Site

Ira Pasternack with Clearly Internet offers the following code for use on your site to let people request your autoresponder. Place this code in the HTML on your Web site:

```
<FORM METHOD="POST"
ACTION="mailto:email@host.com?subject=clicker">
INPUT TYPE="SUBMIT" NAME="Button" VALUE="Click Here" <FORM>
```

Replace *e-mail@host.com* with the correct address of your autoresponder. If your autoresponder requires a specific subject, replace *clicker* with that subject. If your autoresponder can have any subject, replace *clicker* with any unique phrase that will allow you to identify that a particular request to your autoresponder came from your Web site (as opposed to from someone simply e-mailing the address on their own).

- DataBack Systems, at *http://www.databack.com*, offers information about autoresponders, mail lists, and other e-mail technologies, and is available by autoresponder, of course. To retrieve, send a blank e-mail to *services@mailback.com*.

- Autoresponder Central, at *http://www.web-source.net/links*, is a collection of articles and free resources available via autoresponder.

- Sendfree, at *http://www.sendfree.com*, offers free autoresponders and autoresponder advertising. The program works like this: You place another Sendfree member's advertisement in your autoresponder, and for every two requested, one of your ads is run in another member's autoresponder. The company then sells the extra reserve of ads as a way to fund the program.

Cheat Sheet: Planning an Autoresponder Program

1. Make a list of all the standard pieces of information that visitors to your Web site often ask you for. List answers that you find yourself sending repeatedly to people who inquire about your business.

2. Make a list of all the standard information you have to send to a new client teaching them how to work with you, including forms, agreements, information lists, and other instructions and policies.

3. Make a list of all the industry-related topics in which you have expertise. What topics can you write (or have you already written) about?

4. Make a plan to systematically create each of the documents on your list and, using the outline in this chapter, to start writing some articles. Execute the plan.

5. Check with your current ISP, hosting company, or Web designer to see if they offer autoresponders. If not, sign up with an autoresponder hosting company. Choose one based on ease of use, dependability, and price.

6. Create all your autoresponders by sending each of the documents you've created to the autoresponder hosting company's servers, either through a file transfer program or the hosting company's Web-based interface.

7. Promote! List your autoresponders on your Web site, in your signature file, and in all your other e-mail and offline marketing materials.

8. Set up your autoresponders with a call to action and unique instructions on how recipients can act to become clients. Set up alias addresses or other measurement tools to pay attention to which autoresponders are requested. Measure results and pay attention to opportunities to create more autoresponders.

9. Create a schedule to update and refine your autoresponder offerings on a regular basis.

6

Customer Relationship Management

Are your e-mail systems designed to build relationships with prospects and customers who come to your Web site, subscribe to your e-mail newsletter, and buy your products or your services online? Will you be able to set up a 24-hour-a-day, 7-day-a-week support system? Or will you drop the ball and simply set up a policy that says you'll get to these online consumers at your convenience?

It costs more to acquire a new customer than it does to retain an existing one, a fact that makes it imperative for you to define how you will manage relationships with your customers using e-mail. E-mail isn't just being used to develop new customer relationships but also to create better post-customer relationships. Kenneth Johnsen, president and COO of How2.com, a provider of online customer care services, says that his company's site automates post-purchase customer care activities like rebate processing, extended warranty sales, and product manual access. The goal is to allow the businesses who work with them to enhance customer retention, increase revenue opportunities, and improve operating efficiencies. "Our Internet-based software solution transforms rebates, warranties, and product manuals from customer service liabilities to retention and extension opportunities," says Johnsen.

Supporting customers through e-mail is a vital part of your e-mail marketing plan. Service is one of the most effective ways for vendors to differentiate themselves from competitors. Competing on price isn't easy when, with the click of a button, your prospect can price check with your competitors. Make it a point not only to use excellent customer service via e-mail as a way to bring people in, but to retain them for life with e-mail-based customer communications practices. Virtual Vineyards, an online wine retailer whose home page is shown in Figure 6.1, uses e-mail as one of their key customer retention tools. Working with the firm Digital Impact (*http://www.digitalimpact.com*), they target their messages using database marketing. Their software detects whether a recipient can receive HTML and if the message has been opened. Messages are tagged to track how many bottles are sold and who bought them. They use this data to find which customers are more inclined to buy expensive vintages. They also send an online newsletter to 75,000 opt-in subscribers touting specials, links, and commentary from the company's founder.

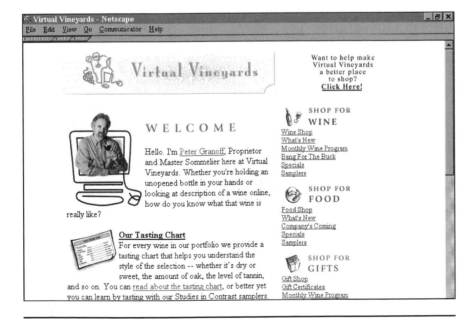

Figure 6.1. Virtual Vineyards' Web site.

Customers are growing increasingly comfortable with working via e-mail, and companies are recognizing the widespread cost savings and faster sales cycles that result when they employ e-mail-based customer service systems that are integrated with the rest of their e-mail marketing plan. According to Forrester Research, during the next two years, the tools, processes, and plans to manage the flow of customer e-mails will mature as e-mail rises to an acceptance level equivalent to toll-free calling.

Each piece of data about every customer is what drives customer relationship management. This means centralizing customer information: transactions and interactions. Then the promotional offers and upsell offers are tailored to the customer's actions. One way to do this is to combine front-end customer relationship management applications with back-end fulfillment operations, such as when Smith-Gardner launched a customer-focused e-business platform called Ecometry. The company focuses on customer loyalty by focusing on the interactions in the sales and service processes.

Combine consumers' preference for e-mail-based communication with the fact that it's a less expensive route to communicate with them. Add in the advanced database technologies that enable customer tracking, and you've got a surefire solution for exceeding customer expectations and retaining them for life.

Treat E-Mail Like a Sales Counter

As the online shopping frenzy continues to grow out of control, stores that address customer service online are pulling themselves out of the confusion and presenting their customers with responsive, satisfying sales support. Consumers are beginning to make comparisons between online and traditional shopping experiences. Winning the online vote demands a dedication to real-time customer service as part of the online shopping experience.

Your online customers should be able to turn first to e-mail for questions, the medium less time-consuming than driving to your store, more convenient than mailing a letter, and less expensive than making a long distance call. You have a responsibility to prioritize their needs by ensuring the resources for a quick, friendly, and personal response. As an online marketing strategy, e-mail-based customer service can save money, build relationships, and increase sales, but if incoming e-mails are ignored or poorly handled, the effects can be detrimental. Your image is on the line!

Setting Up Your E-Mail Customer Service Plan

The first word in "customer service" is "customer," right? So customers' needs take priority. If they have to sit and wait for your response, your customer service is about you, not them. E-mail marketing must be planned with a system that ensures timely response.

Seventy-four percent of Internet shoppers in 1998 believed that companies responded poorly to inquiries by e-mail, according to a study by Jupiter Communications. Turnaround time is a major factor from a consumer point of view. Because the Internet has a sense of immediacy attached to it, people want to have support, especially in technology-related fields, right away. This can make e-mail customer service rather tricky. Even if you are a two-person firm, the following action plan will help you set up your customer service policy.

- *Step 1*. Automate.

- *Step 2*. Delegate.

Sound easy? It actually is if you start at the beginning by setting up a system and making sure it is clear to both prospects and employees.

As your company and your client base grow, so will the number of incoming e-mails. But the biggest impact on your incoming e-mail volume is going to be the effectiveness of your e-mail marketing campaign. So while you want your e-mail marketing to be successful, you want to beware the problems of too much success: Don't get caught unprepared. Be ready to ramp things up quickly. People like to communicate by e-mail, and you'll have to adapt to follow their lead or risk losing to those competitors who have a great system in place.

Considering that, by shopping online, consumers are the ones making business on the Internet possible, so it's up to businesses to keep them there. If they're not comfortable with the customer service they receive while shopping online, they're not going to continue to do so! So make it a priority to put the resources in place to support your online shoppers.

Automate!

Automation should be set up from the start. Consider all the ways that your Web site can be set up to let customers self-serve. Just as a voice mail system will walk you through different options, a good automated customer service system can do the same. For example, you might have a media relations page that automates and delegates so that information is automatically sent to the right person. As shown in Figure 6.2, you could create different autoresponders and e-mail addresses set up for all the following options:

- To request our most recent press release as well as a list of all available press releases, which can be requested individually...

- For a list of experts at our company who are willing and available to talk with the media...

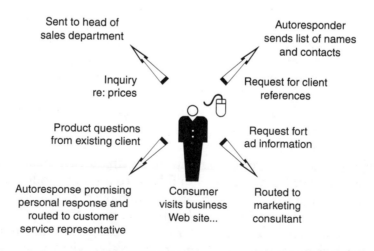

Figure 6.2.   How a system of automation and delegation might work.

- To retrieve a list of client testimonials and contact names of clients who have agreed to be contacts for the media about our products...

- For sample quotes from our management team on a variety of topics...

- For a list of story ideas that use our company, as well as a list of recent publications that have featured our company's products, services, or experts...

The goal is to use automatic responses anytime the information is standard, such as a price list, a contact list, or directions to corporate headquarters.

Another reason to automate is if you can't send immediate personal responses. This allows inquirers to know that their e-mail was received and assures them that it will be answered. It can also tell them *when* to expect an answer. For example, Intuit, which sells accounting software and related products, sends an immediate note to inquiries that come in from their Web site. In the note, Intuit indicates at what time they will send the personal response. Their message reads: "Your message is very important to us and we are committed to responding as quickly as possible. We will respond to your message within 48 hours." True to their promise, they deliver a response with the information requested.

Routing Systems

Would you ever leave a prospect who phoned you on hold while you headed off to lunch? Of course not! If you turn off your computer at night and leave incoming messages to your "sales" address going unanswered, it's the equivalent of shutting the door in a customer's face or leaving the phone ringing (or worse, leaving that prospect on hold while you go out to lunch!).

An automated routing system to process incoming e-mail might be the best solution for your growing organization. A good system will take the place of having a group of aliases, filters, and autoresponders. Instead, all e-mail comes into one address. The e-mail is immediately acknowledged and labeled with a tracking number that can be used for future reference. These codes can also be used for quality control and market research.

Messages are appropriately distributed to one central place per department, rather than individuals. Then the people in that department can access the incoming e-mails and respond to them as they are received. A typical process goes like this: A customer sends a message to your organization. The server routes it based on the subject and predefined filters, and simultaneously slaps a tracking number on it and sends a confirmation receipt to the customer. One of the delegates responsible for answering the messages receives the incoming message, composes a reply, solves the problem, and sends the message back to the server, which makes a copy and sends a copy on to the client.

Mass Customization

Your outbound e-mail messages will make the best impression on customers when they are customized. Now don't be fooled into thinking that a simple "Dear John" mail merge is enough to trick today's savvy consumers into thinking that you're sending them a personal or individually written note. Rather, let them tell you that they'd like to customize their message to receive, for example, the first two content modules you're offering, but not the last two. The message that will make the best impression is the one that is meaningful to the customer...and that customer will tell you what is meaningful if you give them a chance.

Personalization can be included as a nice touch, but it isn't the thing that builds the relationship. The relationship is built by sending meaningful information based on feedback given and preferences stated by your audience—whether you have 400 or 400,000 members in your database.

An example of an excellent use of mass customization are the programs that use technology like that offered by Digital Impact *(http://www.digitalimpact.com)*. In a recent campaign for the online retailer Wine.com, Digital Impact looked at which products were often purchased together. After analyzing this customer behavior, they determined what offers would be most appealing in the future and based recommendations on this data. They also use a "Subscription Management and Profile (SMP)" page to allow customers to select their own preferences, further optimizing personalization. William Park, the company's chief executive officer and chairman, stresses the importance of combining behavior-based datamining and analysis, explaining that "this heightened level of personalization truly narrows the gap between guessing and knowing." Similarly, your own program should take individual customers into account: finding the happy medium between individual e-mails and blanket mass marketing.

Another example (and one that takes CRM to the next level) is a product offered by Salesmation *(http://www.salesmation.com)*. Their eCampaign Plus! product lets marketers automate and individualize the delivery of e-mail. Their technology combines online click stream behavior, offline demographics, and legacy data as a way to build campaigns for marketers.

Define Your Policy

Whether you choose a manual or automated routing system, make sure that you get input from everyone responsible for being involved and then make sure that everyone knows the policy and adheres to it. Even if you are a one-person business, a customer service philosophy, guiding mission statement, or list of core values will help you prioritize and make decisions. Know what things contribute to the bottom line at your company, and then nurture those things. At most companies, it boils down to two things: quality and service.

American Express *(http://americanexpress.com)* once offered this simple but effective definition of its corporate values on its Web site. It simply read:

- About Our Company

- Corporate Information

    - We have built our business around the single, simple premise of helping people achieve their financial objectives.

- Company History

      – A century ago, John Tappan started a small business in Minneapolis to help ordinary people plan for a better financial future. As we enter our second century, we are well positioned to continue our history of success.

- Corporate Giving

      – Doing what's best for our communities. It's one of our corporate values. We believe we must be good citizens in the communities in which we live and work, not only because it's the right thing to do, but because a healthy community provides a good environment for our employees, financial advisors and business, and the people who live in these communities.

And their reputation is everything to them. They live by the above motto, just as your company should post and adhere to a corporate policy, especially a corporate *e-mail* motto that respects and informs your audience. Never forget that the key to a successful e-mail marketing program is to build relationships with your audience.

Go Above and Beyond Their Expectations

When was the last time you made a purchase and were totally wowed by the way the business went overboard to be helpful? If you remember, you're like most people. And if you're like most people, you probably continue to do business with that company because you expect and respect their excellent customer service.

On the other hand, when was the last time you went to a restaurant and the waiter was rude to you? If you're like most people, you not only remember, but you probably aren't eager to return to that restaurant, even if the food is good. No one wants to be treated poorly when they are spending their hard-earned money. However, if the food is good, you probably *do* end up going back. Why is that? We've grown accustomed to subpar customer service. Now if a competitor restaurant offered the same food *and* great service, you'd probably give them your business.

What does this mean for you, the business owner or marketing executive? It means that if you can offer great customer service—not just good, but better than the competition—you can rope in a competitor's customers and make them yours. The reason most businesses don't offer great customer service isn't because they don't want to, it's because they don't have time and systems that allow them to. But you can automate much of the process, and your customers never have to know. All they know is that they feel special.

Dave Sundin is a Marketing Manager and Customer Service Manager for Crowline, one of the largest independent boat builders in this country. He has been stepping out ahead of his industry by marketing Crowline's products on the Internet for years. He has committed the company resources so that their online offering far exceeds an electronic sales brochure, which is the extent of online marketing that he sees most of his competitors doing. The process that Crowline is implementing includes a fully moderated forum that lets customers get immediate feedback, even if it comes from other customers (which saves Crowline time and money). They also use a complete database-driven system to promptly handle lead follow-up. They've also defined their e-mail management policy, referred to as their "e-mail ethic." It simply states that they will offer both fast and customized responses to incoming e-mails. He says that these systems have their customers buzzing.

Tracking Post-purchase Satisfaction

Tracking customers' activity and following up appropriately throughout the life of your relationship with them lets you offer customer service to them before they come to you with problems or dissatisfaction. Think of the implications of keeping tabs on every customer's actions through sophisticated database tools:

- A customer buys the same major item, such as a microwave oven, two months apart. You follow up with an e-mail just to make sure that there wasn't a defect with the first one.

- A bank is set up to notify a customer relations manager every time a client's savings account goes over $5,000 and stays there for more than two months. At that point, the bank sends an e-mail to the customer and advises her about their money market accounts, which can earn the customer higher interest on that account.

- A used automobile dealer notices that a client has only used one oil change discount coupon in eight months. The dealer sends a friendly e-mail reminding the customer of the importance of oil changes and announcing their new pickup service, in which they pick a car up, service it, and return it to the customer.

Database technology has progressed to a level of functionality that goes beyond simply pinpointing and targeting a desirable demographic. Now, the focus is on actually building and maintaining relationships with customers. Take "e-care" of your customers. Amazon.com offers an excellent example of this. They service their customers from the moment of purchase through delivery. Their transaction-based program supports new customers by sending an e-mail to confirm the purchase (complete with a tracking number to ensure timely and accurate follow-up, should the customer have questions) and a second e-mail to announce when the book is shipped and when it should arrive. This supports and builds their brand.

As the Internet pushes even one-man shops into global markets, this relationship grows in importance. Customer relationship management software has been around for a while, but only the most forward-thinking of these companies incorporate e-mail into the customer care mix. Consider using these products to retain and grow your customer relationships:

- Siebel, at *http://www.siebel.com*, offers customer management applications that use a database to collect information about each customer's unique situation and route and manage communications via a variety of methods, including e-mail.

- Vantive, at *http://www.vantive.com*, offers e-Customer Relationship Management tools that manage and integrate communications through the Web, e-mail, phone, and in person to provide customer service.

- Clarify, at *http://www.clarify.com*, offers eFrontOffice, a software product that integrates and personalizes all "customer touch points," which means customer interaction via the Web, e-mail, and telephony, in a single environment.

- MarketFirst, at *http://www.marketfirst.com*, offers an electronic marketing automation system that fully integrates your marketing platform, from planning to execution, including media management and reporting. Their eMarketing Blueprints product tailors solutions to a particular market.

- @once, at *http://www.@once.com,* provides outbound e-mail management combined with strategic, marketing, and creative services. Their focus is on full-service, full-circle campaign management, running from the creative and strategic side back to data collection and tailoring messages based on user feedback.

Ensure Perfect Grammar and Spelling

If e-mail is going to be your way to communicate with your customer, be vigilant about grammar, spelling, and form. An e-mail that makes you look uninformed, uneducated, or unbusinesslike will do more harm than good, by positioning you in your customer's mind as having questionable abilities. Resist the urge to go along with the abbreviations, shortcuts, no-caps, and emoticons—such as a smile, represented by :)—that are so common in personal, non-business-related e-mail these days. Use complete sentences, capitalization, and polite greetings/closings in your e-mail relations with customers.

Second-rate communication skills have a negative impact on your credibility. Grab a grammar book and improve your vocabulary and grammar skills. I keep three books—the *St. Martin's Handbook*, *Webster's Dictionary*, and *Roget's Thesaurus*—on my desk at all times.

Tell Customers Where to Go for More Information

Include in your response the personal names, e-mail addresses, and toll-free numbers for further questions or comments. There's some marketing flexibility here, too. With e-mail customer service, there's not the extra cost of paper mailings or lengthy long distance phone call bills. And because the nature of the Internet allows hyperlinks, it's easy to direct someone to more resources with a URL or autoresponder, keeping the original e-mail concise.

Respond Personally

It's important to let customers know that there's a person behind their customer service e-mails. E-mail-based customer service is "high-touch," meaning it requires an individual approach. Brinker International, the parent company of Chili's restaurants, answers e-mails within an hour with a personal answer from the guest relations representative. They fully research answers and send a personal e-mail, not a prewritten answer. The quick response is especially good marketing because of this personal touch. More detail about Brinker's policies are in this chapter's case study.

Save Money

Resources should include automated systems, full-time customer service representatives, or a system for distributing incoming e-mails to the proper department. Atlanta-based AirTran Airways, whose home page is shown in Figure 6.3, uses an e-mail services bureau that is set up on a database that automatically "reads" messages, filtering them to different departments based on certain keywords that it looks for within each message. This saves the company money, because it is a less costly medium. The objective for AirTran is to move as much customer service as possible away from more expensive traditional methods like telephone call centers. It also assures fast and accurate customer care.

Follow Through

The main reason why you should stay in touch with customers after the initial purchase is to find repeat business. After that, their loyalty should be rewarded with excellent customer service. Why? Customers are likely to keep purchasing from companies that provide them with

Figure 6.3.   AirTran Airways' home page.

excellent customer service. So if you can take that one step further, by providing follow-up and follow-through, you'll really impress them. For example, is your product something that is normally used up after a certain period of time? Try sending an e-mail two weeks before the product is due to run out and remind your customers to reorder.

GoldMine Software has a built-in tool that automates this follow-up process. By combining e-mail with a calendar follow-up program, the software automatically sends out e-mail follow-ups. Their Web import tool grabs contact data from people visiting a Web site (after the visitor fills out a form). The data is e-mailed back to GoldMine for an automatic response, and then the recipient is put on a sales track for further follow-up.

Find Hidden Opportunities

Now that you see how customer e-care works in most organizations, how will you customize it for your company? Consider the needs of your customers that bring them to your business in the first place.

What types of follow-ups are nonthreatening (meaning nonsalesy) fits for your business? Consider the following possibilities (or think of your own):

- *Gift Reminders.* As you make a sale, collect demographics from visitors to your site as well as existing customers. Is your product a good fit for a certain holiday? Consider implementing a gift reminder service, in which customers tell you what upcoming gift purchases they have and you send them reminders and ideas for fulfilling their needs with you.

- *Billing via E-mail.* Do you recognize the customer service opportunity of something as mundane as your monthly billing? As consumers turn to the Internet and their computers for a growing number of daily activities, including bill paying, they seek out further opportunities for this type of convenience. Additionally, as security measures on the Internet continue to improve, electronic billing is gaining in popularity. So combining e-mail-based billing with customer service might just be the opportunity you're looking for to find opportunities to sell more to your existing clients.

  Consider the fact that sometimes, bills are the only communication between you and your customers. So don't just request payment from them, turn the activity into a relationship builder. You know how your credit card statement often comes with special offers and announcements? Why not include an electronic insert, such as an advertising banner, in with your HTML e-mail billing statement?

- *Demographic Fits.* Do you reach a certain demographic? Think about the niche you serve or the subcategories of customers in your entire customer base. If they have special needs or interests, focus on serving them with a follow-up reminder or special offer.

- *Maintenance.* Is your product going to need maintenance or is it a maintenance tool for your customer? According to their usage and purchase habits, consider sending a reminder when it's time to purchase. For example, if customer A buys a bag of dog food every six weeks, begin sending reminders at five weeks (to remind A to buy from you). If customer B buys an air conditioner, consider sending a reminder to buy filters every six months.

Case Study: Brinker International

Brinker International is the parent company of Chili's restaurants. One of their sites, *http://www.chilis.com*, is a resource for all things Chili's: who they are, how to join them, what's new on the menu, buying gift certificates, finding their restaurants, starting a franchise, and how to communicate with them on and offline. More important, the site offers answers to guest questions 24 hours a day, 7 days a week.

Julee White, Brinker's manager of guest relations, says that most correspondence comes into the office during evening hours, during dinner time: "Since the majority of our business transactions are conducted during evening hours, e-mail has provided our corporation a very efficient and effective manner of offering guest relations and customer service during our peak hours of operation. It also provides an available format for our guests to immediately respond and comment on an evening visit at one of our restaurants, thereby offering Brinker International invaluable feedback on levels of service and quality of product."

Brinker International's Guest Relations policies, procedures, and standard of service rate their guests as number 1 in their creed, The 8 Flames of Brinker. The other flames are Food, Team, Concepts, Culture, Partners, Community, and Stakeholders. The guest relations department is responsible for all incoming inquiries, guest comments, guest corporate gift certificate sales, and monthly statistical reports for in-house executives. White believes that the guest relations department "is second to none in the industry."

How do they achieve this level of success? They run with a department of five full-time employees with experience in both restaurant operations and corporate management. The Brinker International company has nine restaurant "concepts," totaling over 900 restaurants in 20 countries. Their focus is exceeding guests' expectations, which means that they take every single comment, question, or complaint to heart. Every single one is very important to them and always receives personal care and concern. Brinker

International receives an average of 75 e-mails every day. "The number is growing by leaps and bounds," says White. "It's an indication that electronic mail is the preferred method of communicating with service-oriented businesses."

Their process is this: An area director responds to a guest's verbal comment within 24 to 48 hours, followed up by written correspondence. A guest relations specialist responds to their guest's written comments within the same business day (8:00 A.M. to 5:30 P.M. CST). If a comment is received on a weekend day or holiday, the guest will be contacted the next business day. If research is required to satisfy a guest inquiry, the guest is notified that his or her inquiry has been received and is appreciated, and that a response is forthcoming.

Resources

- Aditi Corporation, at *http://www.aditi.com*, offers a customer e-mail management software product called Talisma. The software, for customer support staff, organizes inquiry mail, responses to Web forms, and e-mail aliases (such as *help@company.com* or *sales@company.com*), and offers outsourced support and customer development services.

- Brightware, at *http://www.brightware.com*, offers, along with a host of other products, the Brightware E-mail Relationship Management System (ERMS) consisting of the Brightware Answer Agent for e-mail automation and the Brightware Contact Center for e-mail management.

- Online Satisfaction, at *http://www.onlinesatisfaction.com*, is an online customer service company that offers strategy consulting, evaluation and education. In addition, they offer staffing for companies that want to temporarily outsource customer management services.

- GoldMine Software, at *http://www.goldmine.com*, automates the customer service process. GoldMine will automatically send out e-mails, faxes, and schedule calls. But e-mail is the essential method of communicating with the customer. The Web import feature of their software grabs contact data from people visiting a Web site (after they've filled out a form), the data gets e-mailed back to the company for an automatic response and then the people are put on a sales track for further follow-up.

- BeNow, at *http://www.be-now.com*, is a business-to-business database marketing company that believes the future of direct marketing for businesses lies in highly sophisticated one-to-one focused technology. They believe in integrating online and offline techniques, meaning direct mail and e-mail, to best serve customers.

- Mustang Software, at *http://www.mustang.com*, has a product called Internet Message Center that routes incoming e-mail messages to the people best able to answer them. The product works with existing Internet mail servers and clients like Microsoft Exchange, Outlook, Outlook Express, Netscape, Lotus Notes, cc:Mail, Eudora, and others.

- Digital Impact, at *http://www.digital-impact.com*, has tools to personalize e-mail marketing. E-mails are tailored by content and format based on individual preferences and profiles.

- EchoMail, at *http://www.EchoMail.com*, automatically receives, manages, routes, responds to, and tracks inbound e-mail originating from a Web site or an Internet address. EchoMail/CC is being used by major brands' customer service departments and call centers to increase the quality and speed of service to their most valuable asset—their customers.

Cheat Sheet: Steps for E-Mail Customer Service

1. Decide what resources you have to allocate to your customer service plan in order to implement a system that responds efficiently to e-mails that are sent to your company.

2. Make a comprehensive list of the process that will be used to answer incoming e-mail. Automate what can be automated, delegate what can be delegated, and handle the rest quickly.

3. Don't consider the sale the end; it's just the beginning. Implement a database program that takes care of customers from the moment they begin to research your company through their purchase and along the course of the lifetime of your relationship with them. This can be as simple as a follow-up thank-you note via e-mail, or as complex as a customer relationship management software solution.

4. Consider if you need to purchase software that automatically routes incoming e-mails and sends them to the appropriate customer service representatives or specific departments in order to save time otherwise spent redirecting messages and to speed up the time it takes to respond to customers.

5. Automation means setting up as many automatic response mechanisms as possible to shorten the time between when a question or comment comes into your organization and when a response is sent out. Use automated tools to handle and track e-mail to make sure that every piece of e-mail is answered.

6. Delegate e-mail to the appropriate people and let them be in charge of responding for their own area of responsibility.

7. Set up a customer service policy and share it with your entire organization. Enlist not only the support of these people, but also their input. To have their buy-in, it is essential that they feel a part of the planning.

8. Brainstorm about reminders or special touches that suit your market. Implement a program wherein you send these e-care reminders to retain customers while strengthening your relationship with them.

7

Promotions and Direct E-Mail

Special promotions and direct e-mail campaigns are technically like e-mail newsletters, because they're mass distributed from the publisher to the subscriber base. However, they don't have a schedule, and rather than containing news, they usually contain special promotions. What's the difference between direct e-mail and spam? Only that the recipients have asked to receive the direct e-mail: they've subscribed for special offers in particular, predefined categories.

Direct e-mail is more robust than direct mail because measurability is improved. No longer is the destination of your targeted offer just a mailbox; now you are sending your message to an actual person—but with this greater reachability comes greater accountability (because you'll want greater effectiveness). For you, the e-mail marketer, direct e-mail promotions mean that you have more precise information about your target audience, because the members of this audience provide the information themselves. You have better information about what they want to hear about because they've listed their preferences voluntarily. You can reach them using the vehicle that they prefer, which just happens to be less expensive for you. Finally, you have more accurate and more detailed methods for measuring response. The process is shown in Figure 7.1.

With direct e-mail, there are three ways to measure response rates. First, you have an accurate picture of the number of people who re-

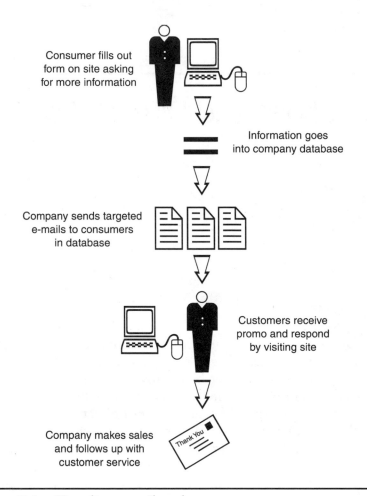

Figure 7.1. How direct e-mail works.

ceive your message. An e-mail that cannot reach its destination box comes back as a bounced message, so those are not counted. Many e-mail programs actually send receipts to the sender indicating that a message was received and indicating that it was opened. Using code embedded in an HTML message, the marketer can track when the e-mail is received, viewed, and acted upon. So by using measures of the recipients' activity (called click-through rates, which count how many recipients click on a link in an e-mail message) you can measure response. Links can either open a Web page or send an e-mail.

Third, you can measure conversion rates. Conversion refers to how many people try out a free demo, order a sample, subscribe to your newsletter, or buy your product and become customers.

There are many similarities between an e-mail newsletter and a direct e-mail piece. Each is requested by recipients. Each has mechanisms for feedback. Each should be measured and refined. However, whereas e-mail newsletters are news, direct e-mail, in its purest form, is a promotion vehicle. This includes special offers sent as announcements. Using a database for targeting and measurement, outgoing messages are personalized and tagged. These one-shot, targeted, tracked, and (most important) requested promotional e-mails are an important component in an e-mail marketing campaign.

The process is this: Collect information about your target market through your site. Use tactics such as contests and membership clubs to encourage participation. Define goals for each campaign, which include personalized and compelling messages. Do a test run before you send the actual message to the full audience. Track recipients to see how they respond, and use this information to continually refine your direct e-mail campaigns.

Collect User Information for Targeted Campaigns

The first step is to collect all those juicy pieces of data about the members of your target audience. Although it's perfectly acceptable to simply have a signup form on your site with the promise to send valuable offers in return for signup, it's much more effective to come up with a creative tactic that offers more: prizes, membership, bonus, free stuff! As you build your database of e-mail addresses, try to elicit more than just that one piece of information. Ask for zip codes and offer custom content to a particular region. Ask for users' hobbies and create special announcements based on niche interests. Find out demographics and tailor your offer or message to that particular recipient.

The more robust your user profiles are, the more tailored and valuable the information that you send to them will be. It also offers an ongoing focus group that lets you tailor your business offerings to the aggregate needs of your target market. The ClickZ Network (shown in Figure 7.2) provides free information on every aspect of the online marketing business world. Andrew Bourland, CEO and publisher, says that their profile-based mailing service lets them target specific information to specific users, according to what the user has requested. A user can set up a profile and request information on, for example, direct marketing, e-mail marketing, or setting up an e-commerce site. Then, as ClickZ creates articles on these particular topics, they are e-mailed to the user. ClickZ not only guides the content they create, it gets the right content to the right users.

Contests and Sweepstakes

Contests and sweepstakes can be very effective ways to encourage people to become a part of your database. You can run your own, cosponsor one, or offer the prize for another company's endeavors. Online consumers have taken to this marketing tactic with gusto. Be warned, though, that consumers who flock to these free offers might

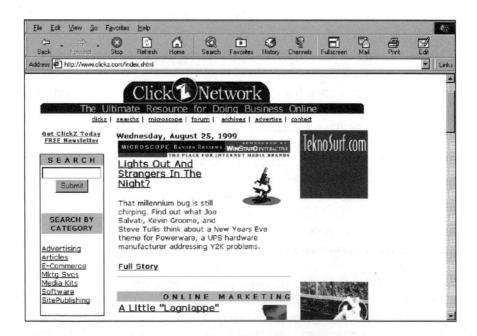

Figure 7.2. The ClickZ Network at *http://www.clickz.com*.

be more interested in a free deal than becoming long-term clients, so consider if this is the way to build your database. Julie McCormack of the Internet travel company Worldwide Escapes offered an online contest, but she came across problems when a sweepstakes site got wind of her contest and entries started coming in from a nontargeted audience. She collected more than 2,300 entries.

Unfortunately, Julie planned the promotion as a way to build the company's database of good target customers (in this case, frequent business travelers to Asia who wanted adventure travel packages). What she got was a lot of people who must sign up for every single contest on the Internet. It meant that she had to clean their database and toss about 75% of the entries out of the pile. Still, she gained 900 new subscribers to her online newsletter.

The biggest logistic risk, then, of an online contest is that you might not end up with a valuable database. Since quality, not quantity, is what matters here, target your contest so that it is announced in places where your target audience will hear or read about it. Tailor your message and offer so that your contest is of interest to your audience. Once you've done this, the only other risk to watch for is the legal one.

The legal aspects of a contest or sweepstakes on the Internet are related to the fact that the Internet has a widely dispersed audience. If you're making a contest available online, make sure that it is legal in every state where it's offered. Evelyn Ashley, founding partner of Red Hot Law Group of Ashley LLC, a law boutique for emerging growth technology companies, advises that companies run contests in accordance with the Fair Business Practices Act (the FBPA) of each individual state. She outlines the following guidelines:

- Post rules on the site, including the promoter's name and address, the verifiable retail value of each prize that the contestant has a chance of receiving, and the odds of winning the contest.

- Include a disclaimer that denies responsibility for lost entries and for failure due to computer viruses or Internet lapses.

Penalties for breaking the FBPA include breach of statute, with various penalties and fines in different states. More important, Ashley says that because contests are public, if any given state takes actions against promoters or sponsors, this tends to be public as well. Unless you believe there's no such thing as bad press, a bungled contest could be destructive to your company's image.

Frequent Visitor or Frequent Buyer Plans

Consider a promotional e-mail marketing program that speaks to your existing customers. Not only does this build your database with valuable entries, it also reinforces their purchase decision, encouraging repurchase and turning them into unofficial salespeople for you. Try an offer that only your frequent visitors or frequent buyers can act on. Amazon.com and CDNOW keep track of users' interests, preferences, and past purchases. This enables them to keep prospects and customers informed of any specials or any new CDs that are released by the customers' favorite musicians or books that have come out by the customers' favorite authors.

Another option might be a frequent flier-style club for consumers. For example, an online retailer of upscale kitchen supplies might offer a Frequent Cookers club, where customers are awarded three levels of membership: Chef, Gourmet, and Cordon Bleu. Each level relates to a certain amount of dollars spent with the company; each affords its own perks: free products, free cooking lessons or an invitation to a cooking seminar, recognition in the company e-mail newsletter, or something similar.

Define Your Direct E-Mail Goals

After you build your database of prospects, consider your goals in sending e-mail communications to them. Most often, promotional direct e-mail campaigns are effectively used to drive a peak in online sales, trials, or traffic to a Web site. Because the e-mails reach consumers who are used to shopping online while they're online, an analogy is that direct e-mail is like an in-store impulse item sold at the counter next to the cash register. While they're online, consumers might as well swing over to your site and act on your well-defined offer. Direct e-mail is an excellent way to break through the clutter.

Unfortunately, as marketers embrace e-mail as an advertising (rather than relationship building) medium, consumers are hit with a barrage of incoming information assaults. Consumers received an estimated average of 1,166 e-mails each in 1998. Jupiter Communications estimates that the number of messages sent to users will increase by 50% to 1,606 per user per year by 2002. For consumers who are also in the technology business (and therefore more likely to be online shoppers) those numbers are probably low. Forrester reports that under one third of consumers already ignore e-mail messages from unfamiliar parties. Your goal as an e-mail marketer isn't just for your recipients to receive your messages, but for them to read, process, and act on them. As a marketing channel, e-mail is cost-effective to implement and offers better response rates than any other message vehicle.

Direct e-mail lets consumers control the campaign. Because they not only choose to receive your message but choose *how* to receive your message, it's more likely that your message will have an effect on the recipients. They control how many messages they receive from you, and they control what type of content they receive from you. In return, they know that they are going to reap the rewards of being honest with you about their desires.

To Whom It May Concern

For your e-mail marketing promotions to be effective, remember to take into account *why* consumers have given you their e-mail addresses and asked for information. Remember, the robustness and accuracy of your database is important, not the size. Having 6,000 apathetic recipients in your database isn't worth much, but having 600 truly interested people in your database turns it into a gold mine for you. To design your direct e-mail campaign around your database, design your database around your target audience. One suggestion about how you label your audience might be by status (i.e., does the entry represent a current customer, prospect, media, business associate, or personal contact?).

Let's imagine, for example, that you are the proprietor of a company that sells toasters. On your site, you might offer a signup form for your different promotional lists. As you collect these names, you're building what is called a house list. Let's say you collect the name and zip code of everyone who signs up. In addition, you ask them their specific interests, which might be as follows:

- Maintenance and Care of My Toaster (category A)

- Recipes for Cooking With My Toaster (category B)

- Specials and Discounts for Buying a Toaster (category C)

- Toaster-Related Trivia (category D)

- Toaster Company Corporate News (category E)

Now, people can self-select themselves for the appropriate category, giving you excellent, accurate, and free market research about your audience. Consumers who are in the market for a new toaster will sign up to be included in category C. Current customers will sign up for categories A and B. Random visitors to your site might sign up for category D. Members of the media or financial analysts will sign up for category E. Once your database is built and filled with e-mail addresses and zip codes, you can build special marketing promotions based on the hobbies, interests, and lifestyles of your audience...your self-selected, very interested audience. Then, when members of your whole audience consider purchase or repurchase (for example, if someone moves from category D to category C), they'll stick with you, because you've built a relationship with them. This relationship is reinforced every time you send them a customized, personalized (albeit automated) e-mail newsletter.

The one-to-one marketing process can be automated with e-mail personalization software that targets recipients and tailors content to them. Cliff Allen of GuestTrack (see Figure 7.3), which offers this type of software product, co-authored the book, *Internet World Guide to One-to-One Web Marketing*. Practicing what he preaches, Cliff recently ran a campaign that used information that recipients entered in a questionnaire on his site to send a series of e-mails. Each e-mail was not only personalized, it was customized with different pieces of data that he collected through the questionnaire. In a follow-up phone call with a prospect, Cliff recalls the prospect asking him if he actually wrote each e-mail manually. It took Cliff a while to convince the prospect that the messages are actually personalized and customized by the server.

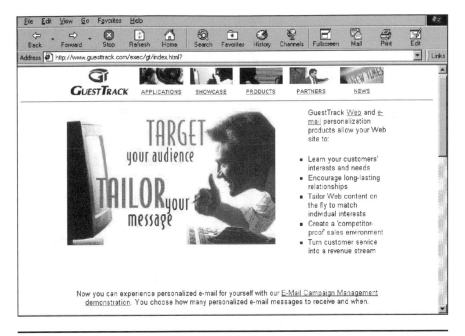

Figure 7.3. GuestTrack's Web site remembers visitors when they return to the site.

Create a Call to Action (and Make It Snappy!)

E-mail is an immediate medium. Users are conditioned to receive a message, read the contents, then act on it. Action means they'll reply or delete it once it's read. If it's too difficult to reply, chances are the e-mail will get deleted. If you can grab your recipients with a compelling "act now" message that only requires a click to respond, they're more likely to respond to your urgent or time-sensitive marketing message. iPrint.com is an Internet-based printing shop that lets users design their own stationary, business cards, and other printable products using a Web interface. Aaron Rudger, direct marketing and metrics manager at iPrint.com says that their e-mail marketing program has been very successful. They use database marketing to send out mailings of lists that they've compiled in-house. E-mail marketing is at the core of their strategy for encouraging repeat purchases from customers. He says that e-mail is effective from the standpoint of cost per sale, but the response is low, from 1% to 10%. Still, with such an inexpensive delivery mechanism, it's worth trying, measuring, refining, and trying again. One of their most popular promotions is the 5-Second Special, in which recipients are given a special URL through which they can take advantage of a limited-time discount offer.

The Direct Marketing Association has published a list of self-regulatory guidelines for use in direct mail. These ethical rules for communicating are as important online as they are offline. As you form your direct e-mail campaign, be sure you follow these rules:

1. *Honesty and Clarity of Offer*. All offers should be clear, honest, and complete so that the consumer may know the exact nature of what is being offered, the price, the terms of payment (including all extra charges), and the commitment involved in the placing of an order.

2. *Accuracy and Consistency*. Simple and consistent statements or representations of all the essential points of the offer should appear in the promotional material.

3. *Actual Conditions Article*. All descriptions, promises, and claims of limitation should be in accordance with actual conditions, situations, and circumstances existing at the time of the promotion.

4. *Disparagement*. Disparagement of any person or group on grounds addressed by federal or state laws that prohibit discrimination is unacceptable.

5. *Decency*. Solicitations should not be sent to consumers who have indicated to the marketer that they consider those solicitations to be vulgar, immoral, profane, pornographic, or offensive in any way and who do not want to receive them.

6. *Disclosure of Sponsor and Intent*. All marketing contacts should disclose the name of the sponsor and each purpose of the contact.

7. *Accessibility*. Every offer and shipment should clearly identify the marketer's name and postal address or telephone

number, or both, at which the consumer may obtain service. If an offer is made online, an e-mail address should also be identified.

8. *Marketing to Children.* Offers and the manner in which they are presented that are suitable for adults only should not be made to children.

9. *Use of the Word "Free" and Other Similar Representations.* A product or service that is offered without cost or obligation to the recipient may be unqualifiedly described as "free."

10. *Price Comparisons.* Price comparisons, including those between a marketer's current price and a former, future, or suggested price, or between a marketer's price and the price of a competitor's comparable product, should be fair and accurate.

11. *Use of Test or Survey Data.* All test or survey data referred to in advertising should be valid and reliable as to source and methodology, and it should support the specific claim for which it is cited.

12. *Testimonials and Endorsements.* Testimonials and endorsements should be used only if they are (a) authorized by the person quoted, (b) genuine and related to the experience of the person giving them both at the time made and at the time of the promotion, and (c) not taken out of context so as to distort the endorser's opinion or experience with the product.

13. *Use of the Term "Sweepstakes."* Sweepstakes are promotional devices by which items of value (prizes) are awarded to participants by chance without the promoter requiring the participants to render something of value (consideration) to be eligible to participate. The coexistence of all three elements—prize, chance, and consideration—in the same promotion constitutes a lottery. It is illegal for any private enterprise to run a lottery without specific government authorization. When skill replaces chance, the promotion becomes a skill contest.

14. *Personal Data*. Marketers should be sensitive to the issue of consumer privacy and should collect, combine, rent, sell, exchange, or use marketing data only for marketing purposes.

Pretest Different Creative Executions

Consider your database to be your own little marketing research focus group. The people in it don't even have to know they're being used for this purpose! Before you send a message to your database, grab a few different random samples of names and test different versions of your message out on them. Which one pulls better results? Use that one to go out to your entire database.

Send, Track, Tailor

The marketer's dream come true is e-mail's flexibility and low cost. It's no big deal to send a message and, based on response, make a change and re-send to another segment of your database. This process can go on for the life of your campaign, as in the diagram shown in Figure 7.4. In fact, your campaign should be run this way. As you develop and implement your campaign, remember that the flexibility of the medium allows you to improve with every message. Practice using a variety of different creative approaches in your messages and see which one is most effective for encouraging a response.

You'll learn that the most effective approach consists of messages that are brief, are easy to read, and quickly communicate your offer and call to action. The beauty of databases is that they allow direct e-mail to fulfill the promise made by direct mail (regular postal mail). That promise is that you, the marketer, will know if the precise user you target receives and reads your message. With a piece of paper mail, you've got no guarantee that it wasn't put on the counter unread, covered by a bookbag, knocked behind the fridge, or tossed in the garbage on the way from the mailbox to the house. With e-mail, you can track when it was delivered, opened, and acted on. John Audette, president and CEO of Multimedia Marketing Group, recently ran a successful opt-in e-mail campaign for one of MMG's

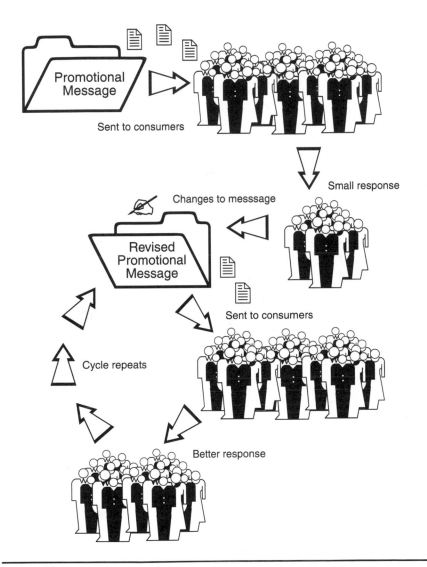

Figure 7.4. Test, track, and constantly improve your e-mail marketing efforts.

clients. In this campaign, they targeted a specific audience (by job title) with unique e-mails (with trackable URLs). The campaign showed a 25% click-through rate on messages sent. Of those people, 30% were conversions (meaning they tried the product for free).

Case Study: E-Tailer's Digest CyberCelebration

As the e-commerce discussion list E-Tailer's Digest neared issue number 100, they decided to turn it into a special event to boost membership and make their newsletter more appealing to advertisers. They threw a cybercelebration to celebrate. The home of the party was a Web site that included a place for readers to make toasts, for readers to upload pictures of themselves, a sing-along and member-sponsored door prizes.

On- and offline party-planning expert and author Patty Sachs planned the event, which was held on October 21, 1998. To promote the event, 3,600 press releases were sent out to targeted media contacts and the site created for the event was listed in 400 search engines. List members were encouraged to promote the event to friends.

When the results were tallied, the party was deemed a success:

- 2,714 people attended during the eight-day celebration (2,002 visitors on the first day).

- 450 visitors came to the sing-along.

- 412 new members joined E-Tailer's Digest at the party.

- 127 members sent an invitation to friends and colleagues.

- List members donated a total of 31 prizes.

A side result was that two different companies asked E-Tailor's parent company, Webbers Communications, which designs Web sites and Internet marketing campaigns, to offer the cyberparty as a template or an added service.

Resources

- Annuncio Software, at *http://www.annuncio.com*, provides Internet marketing automation solutions.

- Acxiom Direct Media, at *http://www.directmedia.com*, offers full-service e-mail delivery, tracking, and campaign management, as well as a host of other direct marketing services. Their e-mail solution uses real-time tracking and performance reporting.

- The Direct Marketing Association, at *http://www.the-dma.org*, is an association for marketing professionals interested in direct marketing. Their site is a resource for industry news and resources, conferences, seminars, and special interest councils.

- GuestTrack, at *http://www.guesttrack.com*, is a software program that lets you tailor e-mail and your site to match your customers' interests and needs.

- MessageMedia, at *http://www.messagemedia.com*, offers e-mail campaign management services that enable ongoing, meaningful dialogue with customers in real-time, event-driven, and scheduled marketing campaigns.

Cheat Sheet: Plan Your Direct E-Mail Promotional Campaign

1. Set up a mechanism on your site to collect names from visitors who are interested in receiving more information from your company.

2. Collect their names, demographic information, and other pertinent details to help you customize future campaigns.

3. Use contests, membership clubs, and other creative techniques to convince your audience to give you detailed information.

4. Define your goals for the entire campaign (if you're sending a series) or per e-mail.

5. Personalize outgoing messages, and send these to a subset of your database who are matched for a particular offer.

6. Create a compelling call to action. Write copy that is short, clear, and direct.

7. Test different creative executions on a small segment of your market.

8. Send the first message and collect the results.

9. Set up a tracking mechanism or use software to keep tabs on the following for each company:

   • How many people received the e-mail?

   • How many recipients clicked on the response mechanism?

   • How many respondents became customers or tried the product?

10. Tailor subsequent messages according to the aggregate results of each send-out.

A Final Word of Warning About Opt-In Lists

I once attended a conference where a speaker made an analogy comparing opt-in lists and dating: "You can't rent love," he said, making the point that an e-mail marketer selling, for example, office supplies is going to have better luck building a house list of people interested in a weekly newsletter on office management than a one- (or two-) shot promotional e-mail offering deep discounts on office equipment.

A Sample of How Press Can Generate More Press

A good press release about what's happening with your list or your company can generate publicity. If you happen to land a mention in a high-profile publication, that's another excuse to send out a press release and tell more people about your company. This example shows how one company took advantage of a Forbes article by sending out a press release about their hit (subsequently landing them this very sidebar that you're reading right now)

Lyris Technologies Profiled by Forbes Magazine:
Article Highlights Lyris Product Benefits
And Successful Client Results

BERKELEY, CA — (INTERNET WIRE) — 04/05/00 — Lyris Technologies, the leader in permission email marketing software, announced today that the April 17, 2000 issue of Forbes Magazine will include a detailed profile of Lyris in an article about electronic mailing list campaigns.

The Forbes article ("Get Listed" by Jennifer Godwin, page 428) highlights several key ways in which Lyris Technologies software and outsourcing benefit both list administrators and members. These strengths include automatic handling of bad email addresses; extreme reliability for sending to million-member lists; and intelligent processing of auto-responses that would otherwise disable a list or alienate its subscribers.

"Opt-in email marketing is clearly a hot topic these days, and an increasing number of businesses are realizing how persuasively they can communicate through their customers' in-boxes," said John Buckman, CEO and founder of Lyris Technologies. "As we prepare for a public offering next year, we're thrilled that Forbes has recognized our success and the significant return our software brings the companies that use it." Current Lyris Technologies customers noted in the Forbes article include Novell, Random House and Southwest Airlines.

About Lyris Technologies

Lyris Technologies, Inc. is the leading developer of list server software for permission email marketing, and anti-spam software for server-based protection against unsolicited commercial email. Nearly 2,000 Lyris List Manager and MailShield licenses are in use today, with customers ranging from Fortune 500 corporations to fast-growing Internet startups. Based in Berkeley, California, Lyris Technologies is a privately held company and can be reached at *http://www.lyristech.com.*

8

Online Public Relations

Many members of the media use e-mail as an integral part of their work. They use it to find sources, to interview sources, and to work with editors. At a basic level, online public relations consists of contacting members of the press and freelance writers, and convincing them to write about you. It's not as simple as it may sound, though, because the press is bombarded with incoming information and their agenda is often different from your agenda. As part of your e-mail marketing plan, you should incorporate online public relations: sending news, announcements, and alerts that can be reprinted, or acting as an expert whose comments can be incorporated into various hot topics and issues of the day.

Working with members of the media is the same as working with your prospects and customers. At the heart of the tactic is the relationship. It's all about building relationships. Focus on being helpful, streamlined, and genuine in your communications with the media. Just as selling your products or services starts by building a relationship with your prospects, selling yourself as an expert to members of the press starts with building this relationship with writers. Just as you don't abuse your relationship with a customer or prospect through e-mail, don't abuse your relationship with a writer or reporter.

Use ongoing e-mail communications with the media to support your other e-mail marketing endeavors to attract media attention and create a buzz about your site and your product or service. There is a two-step process for building relationships with this important target audience: Get your message out there so that they can contact you, then deliver the goods when they ask you for information.

As a matter of fact, many of the sources in this book were culled from press releases sent directly to me, from contacting public relations professionals to talk with them or their clients (thanks, folks!), or indirectly through lists I read regularly.

Make the Press Come to *You!*

For starters, quite a few sites online will allow you to submit your press releases to be redistributed to the press or searched through by the press. Through services such as BusinessWire(at *http://www.businesswire.com*) and InternetWire *(http://www.internet wire.com)*, your company name and information are available to members of the press when they're looking for specific sources. Some of these sites even offer publicity for you through their own outgoing e-mail marketing efforts.

PR Newswire offers an e-mail service called ProfNet Briefs (see Figure 8.1) for three beats: Business, Healthcare, and Technology. Weekly blurbs of story ideas and expert sources are sent to subscribing journalists, who can follow up with ideas and issues that match stories they're working on. As a way for writers to find you, join ProfNet's Experts Database to be listed as an expert in your particular field. ProfNet has become so successful that they are moving their service into a new platform, Organik 3.0 from Orbital Software. The company connects reporters and experts through ProfNet Leads e-mail newsletters. If you're trying to get news of your publication out to the world, this is an excellent place to start. It is also a good case study about how e-mail can create a business.

Dan Forbush of PR Newswire says that the key to a well-received brief is focus: "In one way or another, virtually every good lead is a trend story or 'sign-of-the-times' item. The trick," he says, "is to figure out the larger story you belong in, and to pitch both simultaneously." He says that the way to get publicity using this service is to make short, clear statements with vivid use of metaphors and telling personal anecdotes. He emphasizes sending short messages (one or two paragraphs), without any attachments, and respecting reporters

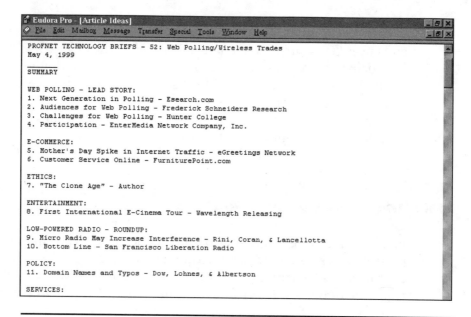

Figure 8.1. ProfNet Technology Brief no. 52.

by never sending the same note to more than one reporter at a time. "Write tightly and colorfully with vivid use of metaphors." His advice for potential sources is quite simple: Be polite to reporters. Cooperate with reporters.

In addition, your press releases can be sent to different e-mail publications (discussion lists and newsletters) that will rewrite or republish them for you. Many of these are read by writers, who lurk online to find good sources (including the author of the book you're holding right now). As members of the media contact you for follow-up, express your interest in building a relationship (by offering to add them to your database or subscriber list), then keep them posted. But only keep them posted if they ask for regular communications from you. Otherwise, simply leave them alone!

Contacting the Media Online

Contacting the media online, as with other forms of e-mail marketing, begins with permission. It's really more effective to send a release to someone who wants to receive it. The media, probably more than any other industry, get bombarded with incoming information. It's much nicer for them if you allow them to make a choice about what they receive from you and in what form they receive it.

A growing number of professional writers and journalists are addicted to e-mail because they can easily cut, paste, file, and delete information, rather than cluttering up their desks with huge press kits. This is good for you, too, because if you want to create a sense of urgency and immediacy about your outgoing news release, it's nice to send it immediately via e-mail. In fact, many professional online e-mail public relations professionals won't even try to go after media people who list their communication preferences as snail mail, because by the time snail mail arrives, it's too late for a quickly breaking story.

Finding the e-mail addresses of the media really isn't the goal. While it might seem acceptable to find an address and forward a press release, don't do it! Instead, take a methodical approach to building your database, one relationship at a time. Only add reporters who show interest in you and your product after a polite introduction, or better yet, after they contact you.

There are also lists of writer and reporter e-mail addresses that you can buy. Chances are that these are going to be out of date or untargeted (such as the information address for a publication, not the contact information for a specific reporter). A more important problem for purchasers is that these e-mail addresses are going to have been abused by others who bought the same list before you. Simply put, any time you can buy an actual list, you'll be buying a list of e-mail addresses that have been passed around and hammered by spammers. These lists will never be as effective as one you build yourself. Effective online publicity requires that you contact specific journalists with personalized, targeted, custom information.

Going With a Pro

There's a reason public relations firms exist. They've already done the hard part of building relationships with the media. Not only do they have the contacts that matter, they also know how, when, and with what information to contact these influential people. In some cases, you will find that publicity pros are very chummy with the journalists with whom they work. Plus, it's their job to maintain these lists. Wouldn't it be easier to let those people, who already have the ear of the media, talk about you and your great news?

If you decide to outsource, be very particular and methodical in your search for the firm that fits your company. First, do a search on the Internet to find a list of online publicity or online public relations agencies. Contact writers with whom you have relationships or who cover your industry (trade magazines are a good place to look) and ask them who they would recommend. Make a list of agencies. Next, log on and start surfing. Visit the Web sites of all the agencies on the list. Narrow down your possibilities to agencies that have appealing sites. Contact each agency on your short list and tell them you might be interested in hiring them. They should send you an idea of prices, how they work and, especially, references. Follow up on their references to see how pleased their clients are with their work. Then, taking your budget and research into consideration, make your choice!

Building Your Own Media Contact List

If you decide to do your own public relations work, rather than hiring an agency, then you'll have to build your own list. From here on out, every time you read an article (on or offline), you'll have to search out bylines and bios for e-mail addresses and an invitation to write to them with ideas. Most newspaper writers, many magazine writers, and a good portion of online writers include this information with their articles.

Create a database in Excel or, if you're an experienced database pro, Access, or use a contact manager. Start collecting (at a minimum) the following information about the people attached to the e-mail addresses attached to articles:

- Name

- Publication

- Beat or area of interest

- E-mail address

- Lead time (how much time do they need to finish a story before it's published...important for seasonal ideas)

The caliber of your database is more important than its size. It's better to have 100 interested parties receiving your message than 500 people who are going to toss it in the trash. In fact, it's best of all to simply have one person at a time receive a short note from you stating the availability of a press release and asking permission to send it. Be conscientious about who you contact and how current their information is. This is another reason to first get permission and then build a database: It will be as important to the media that your information is current as it is to you.

Where To Find Addresses

Offline, you can find addresses in most print publications. Pick both publications that are in your industry and ones in vertical industries that you would like to reach. For example, if you're an accountant, you might want to look in finance and accounting journals for writers who cover topics related to your industry. However, you should also contact journalists who write for a specific industry, such as pharmacies, and pitch an idea that relates your topic to this market, such as Accounting Tips for Drug Store Owners.

At the beginning of most magazines is a masthead that lists things like the editor-in-chief, managing editor on down to beat reporters and research assistants. A sample magazine masthead is the one in Figure 8.2, for *digitalsouth* magazine. This is a good place to start collecting addresses. Some magazines, such as Internet trade publications, list one address for every name listed. Some might only list generic addresses for the publication. Use what you can find until you build a relationship with a specific person at the organization.

Television is an important medium to target as well. With WebTV putting television audiences online and, more important, with personal computers showing up in living rooms on an increasingly frequent basis, television is proving its capability in driving traffic to the

digitalsouth

2 | 2 JANUARY/FEBRUARY 99

www.digitalsouth.com | www.dbusiness.com

PUBLISHED BY AMERICAN DIGITAL MEDIA

EDITOR-IN-CHIEF
Jason Kelly, jkelly@digitalsouth.com

CONTRIBUTING WRITERS
Michael Bernos, Mark Bridgwater,
M.M. Cloutier, Cheryl Crockett,
Shannon Kinnard, Timothy Mullaney

ART DIRECTOR
Michelle Glennon, Glennon Design
glennon@mindspring.com

CONTRIBUTING PHOTOGRAPHERS
Daemon Baizan, Kent DuFault, Michael
Northrup, Steve Rucker

MARKETING/CIRCULATION DIRECTOR
Brian Todd, btodd@digitalsouth.com

Figure 8.2. *digitalsouth* magazine's masthead.

Web. As you watch the news and news-style shows, keep a close eye out for e-mail addresses in the credits section. Consider taping these shows (especially lunchtime news and cable news segment shows) and replaying the credits section at half-speed to get the names of producers for sections related to your business. Keep in mind that the producer of a segment is more likely to include you in an upcoming segment than a specific reporter or journalist.

Last, turn on the radio and tune into both music-format stations and news stations. Get in touch with deejays and build a relationship with them. Take special notice of syndicated radio show hosts, like Kim Kommando and Rush Limbaugh, who have the potential to reach a nationwide audience at different time slots throughout the week. They often have their own Web sites and announce their e-mail addresses on the air.

Be creative and broadminded in your endeavors. Don't just target the magazines that are obvious or the ones that have a large circulation. If you don't have subscriptions to all the magazines out there (hey, who does?), visit the public library and go through the magazines that they stock. Let friends and associates know that you'd like their old issues of magazines and ferret through these as well.

Don't just focus on staff writers though! Freelancers are a great source for coverage, since they often cover different topics for different magazines. Once they find reliable sources they like, they'll latch on and use them more than once if possible. Freelancers are also likely to resell their articles down the road, and one article can have ongoing and wide circulation beyond its first printing. Consider hanging out online at some of the places where writers hang out (search *freelance writer* on any search engine and you'll be presented with a ton of resources, the leading one being *http://www.inkspot.com*) and contacting them privately if they advertise their need for a particular source.

It's fine to contact editors, who will normally push your information on to the writer who covers topics suited to your information. But writers have the final say on whom they include in an article, so it's better to directly build the relationship with them.

Be Persistent (But Not Annoying!)

Because e-mail is a sensitive medium and because the media get so much e-mail, it's important to make a helpful and thoughtful introduction of yourself before sending press releases. Start with compliments on articles, tell them that you might make a good future source, and ask if you may contact them in the future (and how they prefer to be contacted). Always respect their preferences and deliver information in the format that they prefer, whether that is phone, e-mail, fax, or regular mail.

Because e-mail is a personal medium, think about wording your statement so that it is concise and friendly, versus an impersonal press release. In an information-overloaded society, the folks writing professionally are positively bombarded! It's easier for them if you can make your main points stand out with bullets and break up the paragraphs with subtitles. Most readers don't scroll down past the first page for most e-mails they receive, so make the first page count.

Consider offering media alerts as an opt-in e-mail newsletter from your Web site. Then as members of the media sign up, you can ask them for details. What kind of information do they want updates on? New products? Your celebrity CEO? Special events? Story ideas that you'd be a source for? Let them tell you, then respect their wishes. The key is sincerity in building this valuable relationship with different writers—one at a time.

The Rule: An Hour a Day of Online Marketing

The best part of your marketing plan is the social routine of sending and answering e-mails, so enjoy it. Whether you're answering a reporter's query, posting to a discussion list, thanking a client for referring you to a prospect, or sending some other e-mail that connects you with the online world, it's this hour every morning (or noon, or night) that keeps your presence pervasive.

Initial Contact

The first opportunity to seek with your hour a day is to make introductions. When you find writers who cover your beat, send them a note that says you're interested in what they cover and you might have information of interest to them. Ask for their permission to send them ongoing information.

There is a slight difference between contacting a writer first and contacting a prospect first. Because writers are public figures of sorts, you can contact them out of the blue. Prospects for your business aren't. No matter how polite you are, your e-mail is still unsolicited.

So, What Do You Want?

Figure out what you want to happen, then summarize it and talk to the writer, through e-mail, as a person just doing their job. Don't play games about what your real purpose might be; writers just want to know the point. Don't insist that they care. There is nothing more frustrating for a writer than replying to an e-mail press release and saying that it doesn't fit the topic, only to get a reply that argues that it *is* a perfect fit.

Actually, there is something more frustrating: having someone *call* to insist that information should be included in your article. Don't ever do this. It leaves a really bad taste in the writer's mouth and will adversely flavor future attempts that you make to contact the writer.

Then, What Do You Send?

Anne Marie Baugh, a publicist and the owner of Write-Promotion *(http://www.write-promotion.com)*, describes a press kit as "an exaggerated press release turned into a package." She lists the components as follows:

A. An Introduction Letter

B. One or Two Press Releases

C. A Fact Sheet (This contains the facts about you or your business.)

D. Bio Sheet (Which is a biography of you and your accomplishments.)

E. Copies of Published Articles

F. Company Literature

G. A Business Card

Follow Through

As you build your database of media contacts, send them consistent pieces of information (but don't overdo). Periodic updates with valuable tips and ideas remind them of who you are, what you do, and how much you know and can contribute. A bombardment of press releases annoys them and gets your e-mail filtered to the trash box.

Follow Up

Create a standard letter that you can send to writers when you see articles that could (or should) have mentioned your company. The content should indicate that the next time they write a similar type of article, you'd like to be considered as a source. Don't overwhelm them with information, and do be polite! Give them enough to let them file you away in their database of sources to use you as a future reference.

Keeping Your Company's Name in the Spotlight

It's difficult sometimes to keep perspective about what really is newsworthy about your company. Rather than waiting for an event that is hot and pushing for a big media push, keep your media feed on simmer. For example, if you sell women's clothing, you'll want to gather a database of fashion editors. Keep them posted on how your product fits into their upcoming story ideas, remembering their lead times. You might want to send them holiday fashion trends for December, dressing on a budget in April, keeping cool while looking hot in July. Find an angle and create a close circle of journalists who are interested in your finely tuned niche.

Remember to be brief. Don't send a long-winded press release or it might not get read. In fact, the part of your e-mail most likely to be read is going to be the subject line, so it's very important that you think hard about what to put in here. Include, at a minimum, your company name. If you're writing about a particular subject, include this. If you're writing to a freelancer for a particular publication, include the name of the publication as well. Another way to make things easy on the writer is to send your message as the plain (unformatted) text of an e-mail. HTML is hard to cut and paste; attachments are an annoyance.

What are some possible media buzzes for your company? Some possibilities might be in the answers to the following questions:

- What's special about your people?

- What's unique about the way your product is presented?

- What's cool about the founding of your company?

- What's great about your office space?

- What are you doing to keep your customers or employees happy?

- What innovative e-mail marketing are you implementing?

Build Your Own Media Wire

There's no reason why you can't make your own media wire available to reporters, journalists, and writers. To do this, go back to Chapter 1 and take the same steps you would take to build an e-mail newsletter for prospects, but instead, target it to the media and create content in the form of story ideas, expert quotes and news releases. Figure 8.3 shows a sample effort aimed at reporters.

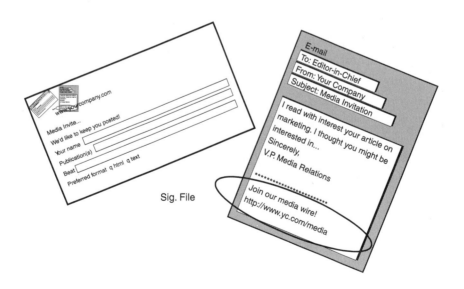

Figure 8.3. Tactics that combine to create a successful e-mail media relations program.

Create your media wire as a segmented database, if you can. Your business definitely has more than one angle that can be covered by the media. For example, an online retailer of lingerie, such as Victoria's Secret, might create a media list that targets the following areas...

- Fashion: What's Hot This Summer...In the Bedroom

- Sexuality: Victoria's Secret Launches Three-Part Women's Health Series

- Relationships: Spice Up Your Romance with Something Lacy

- Plus-size Women: Ditch the Drape with Sexy Lingerie For Womanly Women

- Internet Marketing: E-mail Newsletters That Build Relationships in More Ways Than One

- E-commerce: Victoria's Secret Hits 1,000th Online Sale!

Segmenting your database according to the recipient's preferences is a good way to make sure that your hard work in developing and pitching ideas is targeted and well received. Brainstorm constantly to meet the demands for fresh, original, and interesting ideas for content, and the media will love you.

Case Study: Bootstrapper's Success Secrets

When Kimberly Stansell, an entrepreneurial trainer and author of *Bootstrapper's Success Secrets: 151 Tactics for Building Your Business on a Shoestring Budget* (Career Press) decided to re-launch her Web site, she turned to online public relations. She first sent an invitation to visit her site to a list of 100 media contacts, approximately 90% of whom were journalists who had previously interviewed her for feature stories, expert quotes, or referrals. The other 10% were people in the media whom she contacted based on an e-mail address she had picked out of their byline. A few of them responded by thanking her for letting them know about the site. Another group of announcements went out to publishing peers. A total of 327 e-mails were sent on January 25, 1999.

The press release/invitation was worded to indicate that Kimberly and the recipient had worked together previously. The majority of the results were positive, garnering her mention or features in *Entrepreneur* magazine, *Parenting Magazine*, and *Success* magazine.

Tracking traffic revealed 100 visitors within the first 18 hours. Dozens more continue to drop by daily, she says. "The e-mail blitz has also stimulated a lot of word of mouth; as of 03/01/99, I've had 606 hits— keep in mind that my site is not registered with any search engines."

As a result of her invitation to the media, many have contacted her for projects (including this book—I received one of the invitations). Kimberly's site is located at *http://www.kimberlystansell.com*. Her release reads:

> *Dear Broadcast, Print, or Electronic Media Professional:*
>
> *Since we have worked together in the past on various media projects, I am inviting you to be among the first to check out a new offering on the World Wide Web. There's now a Web site dedicated to helping people realize their dreams with a little or no money. It's my namesake http://www.kimberlystansell.com.*
>
> *Go take a peek. There you will find the Bootstrappin' Tip of the Week, a weekly installment of business building tips delivered free to your e-mail. The site also includes a Success Library of articles, information, and resources for shoestring entrepreneurs. If by chance you haven't seen or read my book, Bootstrapper's Success Secrets: 151 Tactics for Building Your Business on a Shoestring Budget (Career Press), then you can use my site to learn more about the popular guide and my forthcoming work, Witty Workin' Woman.*
>
> *Should you need an expert's comments for one of your projects, just give me a call at 310-568-9861 or e-mail me at kimberly@kimberlystansell.com. I'd be delighted*

to share some of my entrepreneurial insights as well as put you in touch with others from my network.

Here's to much success in 2000!

Kimberly Stansell

Entrepreneurial Author & Trainer

kimberly@kimberlystansell.com

http://www.kimberlystansell.com

Phone: 310-568-9861

Resources

- Internet Publicity Resources, at *http://marketing.tenagra.com/ pubnet/*, offers an introduction to Internet publicity techniques, links to resources, instructions for the do-it-yourself publicist, and information about outsourcing to paid professionals.

- InterActive Agency, Inc., at *http://iagency.com*, is a full-service agency that uses the online realm to create a buzz and drive traffic to client sites. They also offer a wire service to reporters.

- Multimedia Marketing Group Public Relations, at *http:// www.mmgco.com/pr/*, specializes in online public relations, not just to the big media outlets, but also to the thousands of smaller publications online. They understand that collectively, the little guys are very important to your campaign. They've been working with the Internet press since 1995.

- PR Web, at *http://www.prweb.com*, is a free database (for public relations professionals too!) where you can submit your press releases to create a searchable database for writers.

- MediaMap, at *http://www.mediamap.com*, is a software program that databases information about the media and their preferences for use by the public relations industry. Their site lets you have a peek into their database and is a great way to make initial contact with the press by sending relevant information to the proper writers.

- EdCals.com, at *http://www.edcals.com*, another Media Map product, lists thousands of editorial calendars from different publications, allowing you to pitch appropriate stories that are especially relevant to the recipient.

- Internet Wire, at *http://www.internetwire.com*, sends your press release out to subscribers, mostly writers and journalists, who can request full text through the e-mail distribution.

- PR Newswire, at *http://www.profnet.com*, offers a central collection-and-distribution point for queries from reporters. They work on hundreds of media projects weekly through their query service, outgoing briefs and expert database. They also offer an informative member primer at *http://www.profnet.com/howtoleads.html*.

- Pet Peeves of the Press, at *http://www.gapent.com/pr/pet_peeve.htm*, is a checklist of the top complaints of members of the media regarding incoming information. Compiled from comments by members of the Future Media Organization, these guidelines are a valuable resource.

- The Internet News Bureau, at *http://www.newsbureau.com*, offers news gathering and distribution services for businesses and journalists. For $225, they'll distribute your release through the Internet to their database of media contacts.

- The National Writers Union, at *http://www.nwu.org*, offers a backdoor and slightly sneaky approach to getting to know freelancers. Their e-mail discussion lists are populated by a large number of freelance writers. While it's unacceptable to contact the writers on the list by blasting the list with a press release, you can certainly contact them privately if their post or signature suggests that your information might be of interest to them.

Cheat Sheet: Steps to Build an Online Public Relations Plan

1. First decide if you're going to spend money to outsource your online public relations or if you're going to spend time to build your list in-house.

2. If you decide to outsource the work, you'll want to first do an agency search. Look online for online public relations firms in your area or in your industry.

3. Make a short list of agencies and sites that you like and contact them, picking the one with the best references and most affordable prices. (But remember, you get what you pay for!)

4. Keep reading, because even if you're going to outsource, you should know what they can do for you.

5. Design a database in which you will collect all your names, contact information, and interests.

6. Fill your database. Go online and offline to snoop for the e-mail addresses of writers, editors, producers, and reporters.

7. Introduce yourself. Offer your expertise.

8. Keep an ongoing dialogue with them through regular releases, scheduled information, or your own media wire.

9. Join discussion lists and participate frequently on topics that you can speak about intelligently. Perhaps the comments you make on the lists will reach a widely distributed print publication down the road.

9

Advertising in E-Publications

As the number of consumers using e-mail increases, so too does the opportunity to reach them via e-mail. Marketers know this, and so competition for the attention of those consumers is fierce. This is why e-mail should be thought of as a relationship-building tool (rather than another online advertising vehicle). Having made that warning, know that advertising in e-mail publications that already have a loyal and attentive subscriber base can be very effective.

Advertising in e-mail publications can mean one of two things for you. You're either buying advertising space in another publisher's e-mail newsletter to reach their audience or you're selling advertising space in your own publication as a revenue stream. This practice (buying and selling advertising space in e-mail publications—both discussion lists and newsletters) more than doubled in the third quarter of 1999, according to Haim Ariav, senior vice president of business development for DVCi Technologies in New York City. "While $24 million may not sound like much in the scheme of $1.2 billion spent on online advertising," says Ariav, "these monies have been generated largely without the benefits of the sophisticated ad-serving technology now available for banners." However, as the practice becomes more popular, technology is developing to make it easier than ever to insert advertising in these e-mail publications.

Consider using press releases to sell your publication in two ways: subscribers and advertisers. There are several examples of press releases available on the Internet and in books specifically dedicated to the topic. Consider sending press releases to announce the existence of your publication, to announce a landmark subscriber number or to announce any major advertising deals you close. News about your publication will bring awareness, and you'll definitely gain subscribers and, if you have an advertising program, advertisers as well.

An ad in an e-mail publication is usually text, but this can depend on the format of the publication. Some publications (and eventually most publications) are created with graphics. But most publications today are text, because that is the preferred medium, according to a survey by Multimedia Marketing Group. Ariav says that technology companies are working on solutions that promise to relieve the tedium of inserting text and HTML ads or messages in e-mail promotions.

A text advertisement is normally a five- or six-line description of your offer and a call to action. Depending on your media strategy, your ad copy can encourage readers to visit a Web site, request an autoresponder, contact a particular person, or place an order. A sample ad looks like this:

```
=================================================

*** Free Cool-Sites Newsletter ***

You are cordially invited to subscribe to: Rob's wURLd
"Best of the Web"

This newsletter is family-oriented and features best of
the Web, and cool-site selections for ALL ages!!

Subscription instructions:

http://www.topica.com/lists/RobswURLd - OR –mailto:
RobswURLd-subscribe@topica.com
=================================================
```

These e-mail advertisements are proving to be a reliable and effective medium when they are properly targeted and precisely measured. Because many e-mail publications are both intimate and niche focused, e-mail marketers have an incredible opportunity to reach a specific audience. U.S. firms are catching on to the effectiveness of this new medium. eMarketer predicts that U.S. firms will increase their spending on e-mail advertising from $97 million in 1999 to $2 billion in 2003.

"Advertising inside newsletters delivered via e-mail is the fastest growing segment of the online advertising industry. Internet marketers are discovering that e-mail really works and the industry is expanding rapidly" said Jaffer Ali, CEO of PennMedia.com *(http:// www.pennmedia.com)*, which is an e-mail newsletter advertising network with more than 25 million opt-in subscribers.

Placing Text Ads in Other Publications

Before you buy advertising space in another publication, you should plan the offer that you are going to make. What action do you want the subscriber to take? Once you decide on an offer, you can create a media plan. Your first step is to decide your objectives. E-mail advertising objectives include the following pieces of information:

- *Determine your target audience.* Your target audience isn't necessarily the person who purchases your product; rather it's the person who makes the decision to purchase your product. Because there are so many niche publications on the Web, be specific about all the different subcategories of people who could make (or influence) the decision to purchase your product.

- *What message do you want to communicate?* An example advertisement that you might place is an offer that encourages people to come to your Web site and sign up for your e-mail newsletter. This is your offer: a free, informative e-mail newsletter. Use the list of "guaranteed response" words from Chapter 1 to create your actual advertisement.

- *Pick specific vehicles.* Make a list of all the publications that target this audience. Using the indices and services listed in the resources section, search on keywords that represent your audience, your industry, your competition, and your product or service. Do some research to find out the circulation, ad rates, schedule, contact information, and requirements for placement. A sample worksheet is located in Chapter 14. The best vehicles for your message are the ones that will maximize your margin by reducing the cost of bringing in a new member to your database.

Reach: Target Your Audience

In addition to considering the e-mail newsletters and discussion lists to which you already subscribe, research Ruth Townsend's database, The Directory of Ezines *(www.lifestylespub.com/main)* (Figure 9.1), to find other possible vehicles for your advertising. This directory is a resource for marketers interested in reaching e-mail newsletter and discussion list subscribers. It is a wise place to both list your publication and find details on advertising in existing publications.

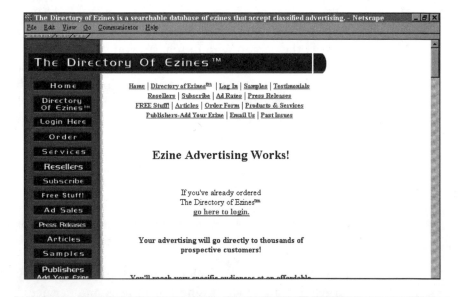

Figure 9.1. The Directory of Ezines.

Once you find possible targets for your advertising message, it's time to start doing some investigative research. Subscribe to as many as you can and read them to judge which ones are not on a par with the level of quality you want to be associated with. Toss those. In addition, research their circulation, rates, schedule, and requirements. Toss out any that are obviously out of your price range. Add this information to your media plan.

Frequency: Hit 'Em Again and Again

Decide how often and for what length of time your ads will run. One-shot advertising isn't a good idea for getting your name recognized. It takes a few ads for the name to become familiar, and possibly a few more for it to result in a response. Since this medium allows you to track response per ad, consider trying a test campaign of a long-running ad in a number of issues. Make a graph that shows response and pick the peak number as the ideal number of ads to run for your audience. Figure 9.2 shows a sample ad run of 15 ads between two similar but separate tests. The results indicate that for this particular ad, the frequency of the advertisement should be at least six times per publication.

Advertising Barters

Consider trading advertising with another publication as a way to increase your subscriber base. This is a great way to save some money (while establishing credibility for your own publication as an advertising vehicle). Trading space with other e-mail publications requires, of course, that you *have* your own publication. Assuming that you've taken the advice of previous chapters to build an e-mail publication around a niche and grow your subscriber base, you've probably got something worth trading.

Be aware, however, that even though no money is exchanged, you'll still want to have a formal, written agreement in place. Make sure this agreement outlines the expectations of the arrangement. For example, will the trade run until a given amount of impressions is reached, will it be in place for a fixed time period, or will you measure click-throughs, new subscribers, new purchases, or some other criteria?

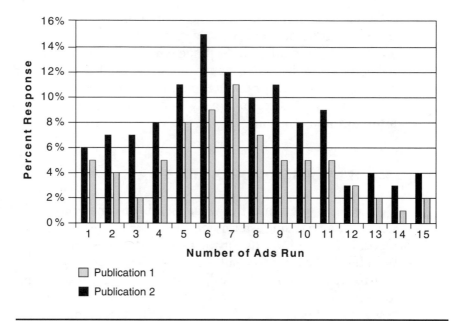

Figure 9.2. Sample run of ads in two publications.

The e-mail publication Name That Movie exchanged advertising with another publication. The owner signed up as an affiliate with another site, but the relationship became demanding. "The other publication owner was too controlling with respect to how, how often, and where his own ads should be placed," says the publisher, who advises others to make sure that the barter partners uphold their end of the deal by making sure, in writing, that you both know what's expected of the arrangement.

Using the list you've created of desirable e-mail publications for your offer, pick those that reach a target audience similar to yours. Subscribe and read a few issues. Then write to the publisher and introduce yourself. Explain that you'd like to barter ads with them. Include your reasoning: What is it about your publication (or product, or service) that might be of interest to their readers and what is it about your subscribers that might be of interest to them? Notice that this needs to be about how *you* can help *them*.

Buying Ad Space in Other E-Mail Publications

Right now, the process of buying space to run an e-mail advertising campaign is rather difficult. There's no uniform way to buy and place ads. Regarding the lack of standardization for media buyers, Andrew Bourland, publisher of the ClickZ Network, made a public plea in January 1999 on several e-mail discussion lists for e-mail publishers to adopt a standard offering for advertisers. His logic is that this would make the practice of buying ad space in e-mail publications easier and comparisons more "apples-to-apples" for media buyers, and would make creating text banners a simpler process for advertisers. His suggestion, and you may use this when designing your own ad offerings in your own publication, is for all ads to be 60 characters wide, which consistently shows up cleanly, no matter what e-mail browsers or settings are used. He also suggests putting a border above and below the ad as a way to designate the ad as such.

Tips for Getting Results

Chapter 1 has a list of words that are guaranteed attention grabbers for headlines. Keep this list handy as you create the ads that you'll place in other publications (and as you help your advertisers create yours). You don't have much space to work with, so pick a strategy. Remember that there's nothing to be gained by mysterious or cryptic ads. Don't be so creative that your audience doesn't know what you're selling or what you're asking them to do. Be consistent with your campaign, so that your audience recognizes your offer and begins to associate you with your desired brand image.

A product-focused approach to writing your ad focuses on the specifics of what you sell. Put your product or service in the best light possible and tell people where to go for more information. To ensure that your ads are successful, follow these guidelines:

- Offer something for free. Use the word *free* often in your ad. What types of things can you offer for little or no cost? How about a free subscription to your e-mail newsletter, a free ad in your e-mail newsletter, a free article sent via autoresponder, or a free gift with purchase?

- Are you hawking your wares for lower-than-the-competition rates? Then focus on this aspect of your product or service in the ad.

- Are you using your advertising to get the most bang for your buck through a special promotion? Focus on the "now" of the contest to create a sense of urgency about response.

- Tailor your message directly to the market that you're reaching. You can't get more specific than something like this: "If you're an 'Ad News' subscriber, our free article 'Ad News Bytes' is for you!"

- Run a testimonial from a satisfied customer. Better yet, run a testimonial from the list host or moderator, if you can get that person to try your product and like it.

- Tell a story that will compel people to buy. The best story makes them think of how your offer could work specifically for their situation.

What Works?

The best way for you to make efficient use of your ad dollars is to measure which ads pull the best response. The Internet allows plenty of ways to do this:

- *Autoresponders*. Create an autoresponder that addresses a tease that you might put in your ad. For example: "This summer, make sure the grass is greener on YOUR side of the fence. Send a blank e-mail to: 'greengrass@lawnproducts.com' for a ten-step program to ensure lawn success." This autoresponder will then send more information to qualified prospects, those who both have lawns and do their own yardwork. The fictional company, Lawn Products, can count each response.

- *E-mail Aliases*. Create aliases that redirect to your main account and place these e-mail addresses in each ad. Our fictional company can place the same autoresponder call to action in several different publications, renaming it each time. Tracking each individual approach will tell them where their money is best spent.

- *Trackable URLs.* Unique URLs, with counters in place, are another way to keep track of which ads pull responses. In the example PlanetRx ad in Figure 9.3, the string of characters after the URL represents a Web page unique to that ad. Instead of placing the ad in an autoresponder, Lawn Products could create different URLs for each ad with the same article on each page and place counters on each page to track visitors.

- *Discounts and Sales Codes.* By far the simplest way to measure the response you get from each ad is to ask customers to enter a special code when they place their order or if they

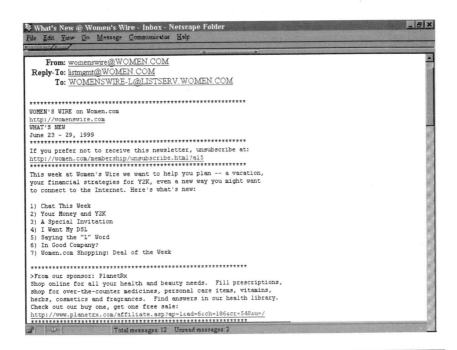

Figure 9.3. PlanetRx ad with a unique URL, from Women's Wire.

request more information. Offer a discount to encourage them to do so.

Tailor Your Future Media Buys

Make sure that the advertising space that you buy is targeted. As the number of e-mail publishers grows, so does the competition for your audience's attention. It might be preferable to advertise your product to someone else's audience (with whom they likely have built a relationship). One company that offers advertisers the opportunity to place a message in one of thousands of opt-in e-mail newsletters reaching millions of targeted individuals is XactMail (*http://www.xactmail.com*). Some of the categories that they offer: golfers, pet lovers, parents, travelers, business executives, and gardeners. Audiences subscribe to e-mail newsletters for news, information, entertainment and advice.

Advertising in opt-in newsletters increases brand awareness, drives traffic to your Web site, generates leads, and brings new customers to your company. Because these newsletters are read by their subscribers, your ad is sure to be seen. Unlike with print advertising, you can link it easily to your Web site and automatically track readers. Because the respondents to e-mail-based advertisements are seeking more information about your product, they're an easier sell once they get to your site.

E-mail allows you to track response in real time. Many vendors include detailed reporting and tracking as part of their product. XactMail is one company that does this, according to company literature: "We send you a detailed report that shows you all the details. You can test different variables to find out what produces the best response, and you can apply that knowledge to get even better results out of your next campaign." The company's services include buying and selling e-mail-based advertising for e-mail publications, including DM News, ADWEEK, Business 2.0, Industry Standard, Silicon Alley, iMarketing News, Digitrends and ChannelSeven.com.

The great thing about e-mail and the Internet is that it allows you to tailor your marketing endeavors bsased on the response. After you place campaigns, watch closely to see which tactics work and why, and tailor your campaign accordingly.

Cheat Sheet: Placing an Ad Campaign

1. Create your offer.

2. Describe your audience.

3. Make a list of publications in which you can advertise.

4. Research their circulation, rates, schedule, contact information, and requirements for placement.

5. Determine frequency.

6. Contact publications that might be feasible barter partners and try this approach.

7. For the ones with whom you can't barter, determine price and place your media buys, filling this information into your media plan.

8. Write your ads, including attention-getting headlines and a compelling call to action.

9. Measure response using any one of a variety of mechanisms.

10. Tailor your campaign to improve results.

Selling Ad Space in Your Publication

On the flip side, you can use advertising as a way to make extra revenue for your business by offering advertising in your e-mail publication. Now, not only is your publication used to position your business as a leader in your industry and to create extra sales opportunities, but you've got a bonus of monetary payoff. Aside from the monetary benefit of selling ads, it provides additional motivation for you, the publisher, to publish a great product on schedule. By reinvesting advertising revenue back into your publication you provide your customers with a better service. Another way to invest might be to up-grade your software or distribution system.

The Publisher/Editor Debate

Traditional journalism calls for a distinct division between editor and publisher. While one must be concerned with the integrity of the content in the publication, the other is concerned with selling advertising. This is the traditional print model. How is this debate affected with the advent of e-publications? It's a debate that continues.

If you are placing an advertisement in an e-mail newsletter and find that they are running it with an article that cites a competitor, what recourse do you have? And what if you're in the shoes of the publisher/editor? Which priority are you going to place on top: your duty to provide unbiased content to your readers or your duty to make money and sustain your publication and business?

Create a Media Kit

To help prospective buyers decide if they'd like to place ads with you and to help you decide where you'd like to buy e-mail advertising, you'll have to become familiar with the media kit, as shown in Figure 9.4. This section is devoted to helping you create a media kit for your publication. Your media kit can be on paper and faxed or mailed to prospective advertisers, it can be a Web site, or it can be a text document that is sent via autoresponder.

The information that you want to include in your media kit includes

- *The Name and Tagline of Your Publication.* Your tagline serves to remind your prospective buyers that you write for their intended audience.

- *Cost of Sponsorship.* Base your prices on several factors: the going rate for your industry, the size of your subscriber base, the frequency with which you publish and the number of ads

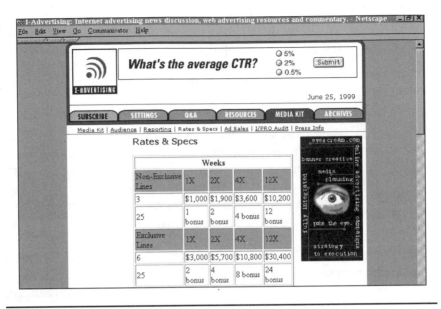

Figure 9.4. Sample media kit.

in each issue, the industry, and what the market will bear. Subscriber-based rates are usually reported in CPM (cost per thousand readers) or CPC (cost per click-through). Cost per click-through is a less accepted choice that is based on how many readers click on the advertiser's response mechanism, such as their autoresponder or unique URL.

- *Specifications of Your Publication.* Schedule, length, editorial focus, and purpose.

- *Your Subscriber Numbers and Description.* This is a quickly growing number for most e-mail publishers, so be sure to update yours frequently. Also, take a periodic poll of your subscribers and find out who they are. It's important to have an idea of your demographics in order to lure advertisers to your publication. Surveys also allow you to collect information and talk about your subscribers' aggregate qualities without violating their privacy.

- *Testimonials*. If previous advertisers have measured results from their ad campaign in your publication, include their results here. If you get positive feedback from subscribers (especially "names" in your industry) include them here.

- *Payment Guidelines*. Identify how advertisers are to pay for their campaign. Accept a variety of payment options, if possible. Publish your guidelines for agency discounts (normally, ad agency media buyers get a 15% discount, which is their commission for bringing you some business). Let them know when payment is due. If you require payment before publishing, let your advertisers know.

If you've done a good job of presenting your audience, your advertisers will be making offers appropriate to (and appreciated by) your readers. As the publisher, you provide the essential link between your readers and the products or services that they want to buy, so it's up to you to provide them with something of value. Advertising is a way to provide readers with additional information and other resources for them to get information, products, or services. If done well, your advertisements can be a major benefit to your readers.

In addition, keep up your customer relationship with past advertisers by putting them on a periodic (quarterly) announcement list that updates them on the progress of your list. Let them know that your subscriber numbers have gone up, that your prices have changed, that you're offering a special deal, and that you have some spaces available. Consider creating a special offer just for prior advertisers where you bundle together some different frequency packages.

Sharon Tucci of Slingshot Media also adds this important piece of advice: "It's not enough to tell them that so many people with the right demographic characteristics receive your e-zine in their inboxes. You must convince them that your publication's so darn good that all who receive it actually READ it!"

Case Study: E-target.com

E-target.com is a new concept in Internet marketing. Because of the impact that spam has had on the e-mail marketing industry, they're very focused on keeping things legit, finding a happy medium. E-target.com partners with e-mail newsletter owners to enable targeted e-mail marketing using opt-in lists that don't include the threat of spam. Instead of sending unsolicited bulk e-mail, E-target.com uses targeted ads within the e-zines and works with e-mail newsletter publishers that allow them to send exclusive ads that go out without the newsletter. E-target.com finds this campaign to be effective on two fronts.

First, the readership of e-mail newsletters can be targeted to the topic the e-mail newsletter covers. Second, the readership is entirely opt-in, which means the recipients have volunteered to receive the information. Brent Livingston is the founder of TSM Web Design, the parent company of the E-target.com site. He says that when e-mail newsletter publishers use a methodology to get very specific demographic information about their readers (by taking polls or asking questions when a subscriber signs up), they create a more powerful tool for selling ad space.

E-target.com is currently in the process of developing an entire automated system that will allow the publishers of e-mail publications to administer their e-mail publication via the Web. Their product caters to those publications that allow advertising within the e-zine or exclusively. The product has real-time counts and costs among many other state-of-the-art features.

Resources

- ClickZ, at *http://www.clickz.com*, is a collection of finely edited articles on the Internet marketing industry, written by in-the-trenches authors who are working in this industry. It's one of the best resources for information about Internet marketing available. Subscribe to the ClickZ Network Daily Update to get information delivered to your e-mail box.

- Severina Publications has a free autoresponder listing e-zines that you can advertise in by sending a blank e-mail to *ezines@severina.co.uk*.

- Ruth Townsend of Lifestyles Publishing offers the e-mail marketing community The Directory of Ezines at *www.lifestylespub.com/main*. For publishers, listings are free, giving exposure to potential advertisers, who buy membership to search the directory.

- "Behind the 8-Ball," an article that covers how and why to place ads in e-mail newsletters, is available through free autoresponder by sending a blank e-mail to *ezine8ball@smartbot.net*.

- PennMedia.com E-mail Newsletter Advertising Network aggregates e-mail publications that can add additional ad sales revenue for e-mail publishers while providing an easy way for advertisers to market via e-mail newsletters, without having to contact hundreds of individual e-mail publishers. Subscribers opt-in to receive content from more than 450 daily and weekly e-mail newsletters. A wide range of topics are available: daily jokes, recipes, religion, sports scores, technology tips and more. All of the publications are free and subsidized by advertising.

- MMG—The Online Agency, at *http://www.mmgco.com/adniche.html*, developed the AdNiche Tracking System, which measures real-time response from e-pub advertising. A-List software lists the top 100 e-mail publications and allows users to easily subscribe and unsubscribe.

- IDG Communications List Services, at *http://www.idglist.com*, is a full-service list management and brokerage system managing e-mail advertising placement for some of the Internet's best-read e-mail publications. Their lists boast audiences with very desirable demographics.

- BestEzines, at *http://www.BestEzines.com*, is a database that reviews the best e-mail publications on the Internet and provides advertisers with a resource to find potential vehicles for their messages.

- The World's Ultimate e-Magazine Database, located at *http://www.ezinesearch.com*, is an excellent resource for e-mail advertisers to search the Internet for e-mail publications that will reach any niche audience imaginable.

Cheat Sheet: Selling Ads

1. Create a media kit that summarizes your publication in a way that makes it, and your audience, appealing to potential advertisers.

2. Decide what an ad in your publication is worth. It would be impossible to put a generic rate here because your worth will vary depending on the frequency and reach of your publication, as well as the particular niche you serve.

3. Include all the information about your publication that a potential advertiser needs to make a purchase decision.

4. Offer your media kit on your Web site and through an autoresponder announced in your publication.

Part Two:

The Process

10

The E-Mail Marketing Rulebook

The Rules

No one "owns" the Internet. At the same time: everyone owns it! So the rules are simple: don't send e-mail unless it's requested by the recipient. Rule number one is this: don't send e-mail unsolicited. It's tough: you want to e-mail prospects to tell them about your e-mail newsletter but you can't send them e-mail unless they request it (but how do they know to request it if you can't e-mail them?)... advertising, networking and public relations. But you never reach them by sending spam!

Spam: It's a Four-Letter Word

It's fine (even recommended) to practice different approaches with your audience. It's also fine (again, recommended) to testing your message. Cleaning your database is fine. Refining your e-mail marketing program is fine. Constant correction and improvement are a natural and an encouraged part of building, executing, and evolving your e-mail marketing program. You will make mistakes, and you will learn from them. But of all the mistakes you make, please don't make the mistake of sending out unsolicited, bulk e-mail, also known as "spam."

Spam is a major and growing concern for every e-mail marketer. You do not, I repeat, *do not*, want to be labeled a spammer. Spamming means sending e-mail to someone with the motive of promoting your product without getting permission from them first. You need to have people somehow request your e-mail. If you publicize that your announcement list, e-mail newsletter, or discussion list is available (by listing it on your site, in databases, and in other places on- and offline), prospective subscribers will find you.

Spam is a problem even for non-spammers because all e-mail marketers are at risk of being perceived to be spammers. At some point, the sheer volume of e-mail could be detrimental to the practice of e-mail marketing. In fact, Tom Geller, founder and administrator of The Suespammers Project, says that this already seems to be the case with America Online. "I've maintained an AOL account since 1993, and it's simply unusable for mail now," says Geller, who cites a spam–to–real message ratio of 20:1. "Spam becomes a problem, so sysadmins put up filters; the spammers figure out ways around the filters; sysadmins improve their filters; ad nauseam. Spam forces system administrators into a weapons war that we shouldn't be forced to fight, at our own expense." This, he says, is the issue that eludes end users, even though it costs them money as their ISPs have to spend time playing this game. "Spam is a problem of social engineering, not machine engineering. For social issues, strong laws and active litigation help a lot," which is why he founded the organization SueSpammers.org.

Netiquette is a word that represents the unofficial rules of polite behavior on the Internet. It has evolved online, without formal legislation, through the majority sentiments of the Internet community. E-mail marketers should seek to adhere to the highest standards of behavior: respecting recipients by delivering on what they promise. "Only through confirmed opt-in and strict documentation are you 100 percent protected against accusations of spam," says SueSpammer.org's Geller.

Slingshot Media's listhosting division, Listhost.net, handles the distribution of e-mail newsletters and discussion lists for clients with subscriber bases that include tens of thousands of names. Sharon Tucci, the CEO, is all too familiar with the repercussions of spam for e-mail marketers. Several clients, playing totally by the rules laid forth in this chapter, have been caught off guard by subscribers who claim they never subscribed. Part of her role is to continually educate clients and prospects about spam and UCE (unsolicited commercial e-mail). The major misperception is that it's okay to contact someone and ask for permission. She tells clients that it's unacceptable even to send a preliminary "May I e-mail you again?" e-mail to anyone with whom you've not had prior contact. She says that any clients who do so will be first warned, then terminated.

Meaningful Is Good, Unsolicited Is Bad

The prevalence of mass-distributed e-mails that offer get-rich-quick schemes, miracle drugs, and sexy young things who want to talk just to you has given consumers a mistrust of all mass-distributed e-mails, legitimate (such as e-mail newsletters) or not. Your responsibility as an e-mail marketer is to never, never cross the line in zealousness to market with this medium. This means that your first few months might be slow going.

"The most important lesson that we and our customers have learned is to target e-mail messages to a list that has been created with care," says Karen Fegarty of MailWorkZ, which offers software to distribute e-mail messages and handle feedback. "The most effective and positive response rates come from creating meaningful messages sent to people who have requested this information. This 'opt-in' list can be created through a variety of ways." One example she emphasizes is to ask for e-mail addresses at your company's physical store, if you have one. One way to do this is to print up business cards for the specific purpose of promoting your free newsletter and sticking one in the shopping bag of every customer. (iPrint, at *http:// www.iPrint.com* offers affordable business cards in quantities of 500 and up, for an extremely affordable price, and with a simple-to-use design interface.)

The ongoing problem of spam has made Internet users resentful of senders, because it costs the recipients time (and resources) to receive, review, and delete each message. This means that you walk on eggshells as you build your reputation as a legitimate e-mail marketer. It's okay that your first few months are slow going, because you'll have the time it takes to build a core group of loyal subscribers who understand your mission and feel that they have a relationship with you.

Before you start to feel as if this spam problem paints a dismal picture for mass e-mailing, remember that the Web has a good percentage of unsavory content, but it has proven itself to be a valuable medium for commercial enterprise. In any situation where there's money to be made, there will be abuses of the system. Your role as a legitimate e-mail marketer is to take the time to learn the ropes and play by the rules. Your role, too, is to be a proponent of opt-in, permission-first e-mail marketing programs.

Here's one caveat: As you build a relationship with your subscribers, be sure to build one with your ISP as well. Because of the spam backlash, many ISPs will close you down first and ask questions later if you're accused of spamming through their system. To ensure that your e-mail practices are perceived by others to be as legitimate as they are, incorporate the following procedures:

- Do not let anyone onto your mailing list without making them opt-in. Even customers should have the choice to add themselves (but you can certainly thank them for their purchase and offer them the option).

- Do not associate yourself with anyone who uses spam. This goes back to your duty to be a proponent of legitimate practice. Become part of the legitimate e-mail marketing community (by joining lists that discuss these topics, for example).

- Give recipients a way to unsubscribe. Make this option available when they subscribe and with every e-mail you send to them. Make the directions for unsubscribing as clear and prominent as the directions for subscribing. Honor these requests immediately. Many people get nervous when they can't find unsubscribe instructions alongside the subscribe instructions.

Opt-Out Is Just Another Word for Unsolicited Commercial E-Mail

Even tricking people into subscribing, known as opt-out, is a bad idea. For example, you might have at the bottom of your purchase confirmation page a prechecked box that subscribes customers automatically to your list, like the example in Figure 10.1. Instead of them making the effort to join, they have to make an effort *not* to join. They have to choose the option not to be on your list.

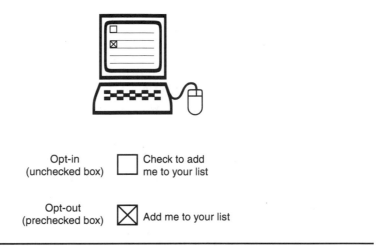

Figure 10.1.   Opt-in vs. opt-out.

If you add people without their explicit permission and give them the opportunity to opt-out, three negative things will occur. First, you'll have an inflated subscriber number that isn't a true reflection of interest in your list. Many people trash unwanted messages using the filter feature on their e-mail program. As you send unwanted messages, they may get trashed unopened, which does no one any good. Second, you'll have higher list attrition (the number of people who subsequently unsubscribe). If a list has high turnover, your marketing impact is greatly diminished and your community of users is weaker. Third, you'll annoy people. Perhaps not as much as if you were a true spammer, but you'll get flack from recipients who feel tricked.

Derek Scruggs holds the title of Permission Advocate for his company, MessageMedia. While working with clients, partners and consumers to ensure the best practices in permission relationships, Scruggs has developed an informative document titled "Ten Rules for Successful Permission-based E-mail Marketing," which is available at *http://www.messagemedia.com/rc/ten_guides.shtml*. This document specifies the importance of sending e-mail only to consumers who have opted in to receive it, using a two-pronged confirmation message in which the recipient has to actually reply to a confirmation to be added to the list. "Consumer trust is something you have to earn," writes Scruggs. "One of the best ways is to respect their wishes when it comes to e-mail." The document also includes the advice to always honor opt-out requests, confirm opt-in and orders via e-mail, let users specify their preferences, and never sell or rent your list to another. His final word of warning is to develop a privacy policy on your site and never violate it.

The Oxygen Network, produced by Oprah Winfrey's company, states in its privacy policy that it protects its users' privacy by keeping personal information volunteered during registration private and secure. They do reserve the right to use personal information for marketing purposes, but they explicitly state this during their registration process. Registrants are warned: "If you give us your permission, we may also use personal identification information for internal or external marketing and promotional purposes. On occasion, for example, we may send you e-mails to introduce a product or service that we think might be of interest to the users of our sites." Their wording for this explicitly states that they will get members' permission through and "opt-in" NOT an "opt-out" practice.

Legal Problems

According to a recent issue of the Association for Interactive Media's e-mail newsletter, the Internet Politics Insider, The Virginia state legislature passed a bill, which Gov. James Gilmore has promised to sign into law, to criminalize mass, unsolicited e-mail. This makes Virginia the first state in the United States to create a criminal cause of action for spam. Because AOL is located in Virginia, the bill has tremendous impact on the practice. Nearly half of the nation's Internet infrastructure is routed through Virginia. The law makes spamming a misdemeanor punishable by fines of up to $500. "Malicious" spamming that causes more than $2,500 in losses for the victim could be prosecuted as a felony.

This issue is the core of a raging debate on how and if spam should be legislated. The ACLU says that putting restrictions on spam goes against freedom of speech, which needs no further constrictions. Support for this argument is the contention that if spam continues to be the serious annoyance it currently is, then the backlash alone will snuff it out. The fact is that it doesn't work. As soon as everyone realizes this, perhaps it will go away.

Others, such as John Mozena, who is the cofounder and vice president of the Coalition Against Unsolicited Commercial E-mail, says that spam is a property rights issue, since someone sending spam takes up the recipient's system resources. Mozena believes that the best anti-spam law would be an amendment of an existing law prohibiting junk faxes, which has already survived a free speech challenge in the Supreme Court.

A technological solution, such as SpamCop (Figure 10.2), might be the best solution. According to Julian Haight of SpamCop, anti-spam legislation moves too slowly for the quickly moving world of the Internet. His solution is to have resources set in place to yank the spammer's Internet accounts right away. Legislation would be counterproductive, possibly legitimizing spam altogether. Additionally, it would be impossible to enact a global law for this global problem.

According to a recent CNET News article by writer Lisa M. Bowman, California could be the first to arrest two San Diego men on felony charges related to spam. The article stated that the spam allegedly crashed a company's computer system by rerouting tens of thousands of unsolicited e-mails through the company's servers. If convicted, the men could face up to four years and four months in

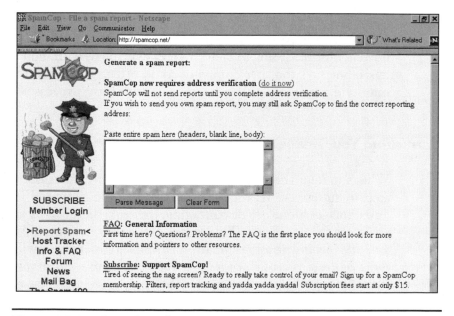

Figure 10.2. SpamCop's home page.

jail. The article continues that while many states have enacted legislation against spam, interstate commerce laws make it difficult. "If they are found guilty, it would be at least the second criminal conviction for a spammer in the United States. In December, an Orange County, Calif., man pleaded guilty in New York to sending millions of porn and get-rich-quick spam," according to the article.

The impact of spam is causing several more policy organizations to call for government intervention. In a white paper from the Internet Alliance, titled "Building Consumer Trust and Confidence in the Internet Age," consumer trust and confidence are cited as essentials to make the Internet work as a consumer medium. "As the scope of the consumer Internet broadens," said Jeff Richards, Executive Director of the Internet Alliance, "it becomes increasingly important for policy makers to be fully informed when it comes to important online issues, such as privacy and unsolicited commercial e-mail."

The Drag on Resources

Spam serves to drag down the speed of the Internet, clogging up the bandwidth with an enormous amount of e-mails, bounces, and flames. In 1999, eMarketer reported that almost 20% of all e-mail received in the United States was commercial, split almost evenly between spam and permission e-mail. The cost of spam in terms of system resources, bandwidth, and time spent by system administrators is horrendous, according to Sharon Tucci, who deals with it on an hourly basis. She says that her company could offer another 100 free community discussion lists if her server weren't busy processing spam.

Tarnishing Your Image

What's unique about this medium is that it only takes one tiny misstep to suffer serious repercussions. While the potential legal fines and damages alone are discouraging, the real risk faced by those who spam are the negative publicity, the loss of your community relationship, ISP penalties, and retaliation by spam-fighters who will do technical damage to your account, if they can figure out a way, or will blacklist you.

As a way to track where spam is coming from, Tom Geller of SueSpammers.org uses the domain name tgeller.com. "For example," he says, "I used 'rockstar@tgeller.com' on press releases when I did work for software company Rockstar Studios; that address is now highly spammed-to, telling me that spammers are scraping press releases and putting the addresses on bulk e-mail CD-ROMs." Geller named a major news organization that now uses his address to send constant, untargeted announcements... announcements that he has not asked for and has not given them permission to send.

Permission Is *Good*

Permission marketing, or opt-in e-mail, is a technique whereby consumers give their consent to receive information from a company. They choose the *opt*ion to be included *in* your list of subscribers. They give you permission to contact them. WebPromote, whose home page is shown in Figure 10.3, calls permission marketing on the Web "simply the best way to build relationships with your site visitors and turn them into your clients." In the white paper "Turning Online Strangers into Loyal Clients," WebPromote defines the difference between opt-in e-mail and spam: "Spam is unsolicited e-mail, whereas opt-in e-mail is requested by a subscriber based on a value proposition to fulfill a specific need or desire."

An opt-in e-mail list is a database of e-mail addresses that have been willingly submitted as a request to receive information. Each time you contact the recipient of an opt-in e-mail list, you must do three important things, according to Rosalind Resnick, president and CEO of opt-in e-mail list brokerage NetCreations.

1. *Notice.* Give full disclosure of what data you are collecting from users and tell them how this information will be used.

2. *Choice.* List members who opt-in to receive commercial messages on targeted topics have the choice to easily opt-out of the lists at any time.

3. *Access.* List members can check, modify, or delete the data that you collect about them at any time.

Dusty Bleher of ISP Franklin Software, Inc. *(http://www.fsinc.com)* recently wrote to the discussion list SueSpammers to endorse the SpamCop program *(http://www.spamcop.net)*, which systematically

Figure 10.3. WebPromote.com's home page.

responds to spam and attempts to stop the practice. "As an ISP and avowed spam hunter, I make heavy daily use of SpamCop," Bleher writes. "It automates and simplifies the spam hunting/killing process to probably its simplest evolution to date. Like any weapon, it's only as good as the user who wields it." Use this program wisely and thoughtfully, as the potential exists to target the wrong ISP, such as a non-spamming domain co-located with a spamming domain. Use the program, but use your manners as well, which leads us to the next topic...Netiquette.

Netiquette—It's All About Sincerity

Netiquette rhymes with etiquette, and it's the online version of minding your p's and q's. The important thing to remember is that you should err on the side of being overly polite, because it just takes one curt e-mail to a prospect to turn them off and send their business elsewhere. Here are some guidelines to follow:

- Buy your domain name so that your e-mail addresses come from you@your company name. It's more professional than, for example, an AOL account (unless, of course, you work for AOL!).

- Set your e-mail program up correctly so that it is addressed from *Your Name <Your address>*.

- Don't assume that, just because you've exchanged e-mail with someone before, that person automatically knows who you are. Introduce yourself the first few times you e-mail someone (even if they contacted you).

- Don't assume either that, in an ongoing e-mail conversation, the person at the other end remembers the last exchange. I field over 300 e-mails a day. I do research for books, magazine articles, and client publications online, moderate two lists, and handle various partners, employees, and customers. I'm often working on several projects at once. It's frustrating to receive an e-mail from someone who simply says, "Yes, that's correct." I rarely remember what I originally asked!

- Cut the hype! Sincerity goes a long way with virtual communications, but overzealous exaggeration and superfluous language fall flat.

- Write well. In a recent column in Earthlink's member magazine, tech support representative Lindsey Milton-Schoke ad-

---

SueSpammer's Stance on Spam

1. Spam is an problem that requires a combination of technical, social, and legal solutions.
2. Laws are useless without active, intelligent litigation.
3. SueSpammers addresses both legal and social needs. It provides legal information, and gives people a place to hone their arguments and strengthen their resolve to fight spam.

Reprinted with permission from Tom Geller.

vised readers using e-mail to mind their manners by using proper spelling and grammar.

- Consider the tone and quality of the tone of voice in your e-mails. Make an effort to be positive, encouraging, polite, and helpful.

- Don't use ALL CAPS. Readers perceive this as if someone is yelling at them. It isn't necessary to get your point across this way.

- Put a damper on your own emotions. Even if someone is extremely rude to you, wrong about their accusation, and just plain mean, don't stoop to their level. It's fine to respond and defend yourself (just keep it professional and gracious). Consider flamers (people who send obnoxious, rude, defamatory e-mails) as a test of your patience and eloquence. I've used this technique and received apologies, gained friends, and even gotten new business.

- Use the senders' names in the e-mail you send back to them. This is a Dale Carnegie trick from the book *How to Win Friends and Influence People*. People love to hear (in this case read) their own name, so use it liberally in your e-mails to them. It will keep their attention.

- Be concise. This is true in every single tactic listed in this book, from writing articles for your e-mail newsletter to online networking to customer service. Brevity is important and will ensure that your e-mail actually gets read by its intended audience. Plus, it shows that you value their time.

- Write e-mail as if it's intended for the whole wide world. While you may think that your e-mail is for the recipient's eyes only, it may end up in the e-mail box of your competitor (or their lawyer), so be cautious about what you say.

- Reply immediately to e-mails. This isn't always possible, but try to implement a policy that deals with e-mail as quickly as possible, or you risk missing out on opportunities.

- Above all, follow the Golden Rule: Treat others as you'd like to be treated. Don't assume you know what they want, even if you're 100% sure that they want to get information that you or an associate has to offer.

- There are plenty of legitimate ways to use e-mail to contact prospects, but they don't include abusing anyone with endless, unwanted communications.

Working for an e-marketing company, touchMarketing.com, corporate communications manager Stuart Hanson has seen a lot of good and bad e-mail marketing campaigns throughout the past year and says that there are some common traits of successful and unsuccessful examples. "Companies that think e-mail marketing is simply online direct marketing or 'sending catalogs via e-mail' are mistaken. Product-centric messages seem to be losing their effectiveness," says Hanson. "One of our clients, a computer distributor, has started segmenting their customer database and sending highly targeted and personalized customer-centric HTML e-mails." They send targeted offers to iMac users along with coupons for iMac software, a $100 coupon, and tips on using the products. "This approach focuses less on the product and more on providing useful and pertinent value that the customer can use, to learn and save money. In turn, this value instills a closer customer relationship—leading to higher customer retention (which is becoming highly important with the recent influx of online businesses). This value and relationship will hopefully turn into a two-way dialog of information between customers and businesses— where each depend on one another for information and products and services," says Hanson.

Keep in mind, as you launch your e-mail marketing program, that it's better to have a list of 1,000 subscribers, each of whom is interested in your message, than a list of 10,000 recipients who resent you for invading their e-mail accounts.

Another word of warning comes from a former spammer (name omitted to protect the not-so-innocent-yet-reformed), who wrote on a popular Internet marketing discussion list about her experience after sending out a batch of spam to the Internet community: "We had fake orders placed for millions of U.S. dollars, only to discover to our utter non-amazement that the credit card numbers weren't real, and about 15% returned mail."

Case Study: How Spam Affects All E-Mail Marketers

George Matyjewicz tells the story of how spammers can have an effect on you, even if you are a responsible e-mail marketer, as Matyjewicz is through his online marketing firm, GAP Enterprises, Ltd. He checked his e-mail one morning to discover 441 messages, up from his normal 75 to 100. Suspicious, he looked at some of the e-mails, which appeared to be undeliverable e-mails sent from his server, to find that they were messages he never actually sent, but that used his domain name.

"Obviously somebody blasted out a spam and used our post office as return address." He also contacted spam buster Jacques Chevron, who advised him to identify the source of the spam or the ISP or server that it came from and notify them. Chevron also wrote, "Call your ISP for help in tracking the offender. You may also want to contact the FBI. Fraudulent use of someone else's address so that a third party will receive tons of messages and not be able to use his e-mail is known as a 'denial of service attack' and is illegal."

Throughout the course of the day Matyjewicz's firm received responses to the offending spam, undeliverable e-mails, and offers from

---

Guarantee a Spammer-Free Reputation

Here are the steps to take to make sure that you're not labeled a spammer:
- *Step 1: Get permission.* Offer contests and ask entrants if they'd like to sign up for ongoing information. Ask customers if you can use their e-mail address to communicate with them. Whenever you receive an inquiry about your product or service, follow up with an offer to add the inquirer's e-mail address to your database. Save copies of all e-mails that grant you permission for further communications.
- *Step 2: Deliver on your promise.* Provide the information that you describe in your original offer. Keep tabs on the actions of your recipients. If you send content that results in a bunch of unsubscribes, consider changing your editorial strategy.
- *Step 3: Get personal.* If you receive an e-mail from a recipient of your e-mail marketing activities, respond to it. Match your editorial content to the types of products and purchases that you're sending. Provide tools for ongoing one-to-one interaction with your audience. Use a database to keep track of your audience, their preferences and their activities.

other spammers...a total of more than 1,000 messages related to the incident. He is working with the authorities on the matter.

Resources

- The Coalition Against Unsolicited Commercial E-mail (CAUCE), at *http://www.cauce.org*, is an ad hoc, all-volunteer organization, created by Netizens to advocate for a legislative solution to the problem of unsolicited commercial e-mail or spam.

- Esearch.com, at *http://www.esearch.com/studies/studies.htm*, is doing a series of surveys studying the trend of unsolicited and commercial bulk e-mail.

- The governor of Virginia *(http://www.state.va.us/governor/)* offers resources about the state's technology legislation, including their approach to spam.

- SueSpammers Digest *(http://www.suespammers.org/)* is a discussion list in which members search for ways to find a solution that ends the practice of spam. They also offer SueSpammers e-mail accounts at *http://www.suespammers.org/pop3*.

- The Hyper, at *http://www.thehyper.com*, frequently writes articles with solutions to the problem of spam.

- David Sorkin, at *http://www.spamlaws.com*, compiled a list of spam-related lawsuits for reference about ongoing legal activities surrounding this issue.

- America Online has a list of their outstanding lawsuits against those who use AOL's systems to spam AOL members. You can get the list at *http://legal.web.aol.com/email/*.

- SpamCop (*http://spamcop.net*) sends spam back to the sender by figuring out which ISP is responsible for sending and which ISP hosts associated Web sites, then notifying those organizations.

Take the Spam Challenge

If you're thinking about e-mailing, we invite you to take the Spam Challenge. Use the following questions as a guide to separate potential junk from unsolicited—but not unwelcome—e-mail. Answer each question as accurately as possible. Total the number for each question and review the scoring at the end of the page.

Question 1: How familiar is the recipient with my organization?

1	2	3	4	5
Not at all		Somewhat		Very familiar

Question 2: How great is the affinity between my organization and the recipient?

1	2	3	4	5
No Affinity		Somewhat		Complete Affinity

Question 3: Have I given recipients an easy way to opt out of future mailings?

1	2	3	4	5
No opt-out capabilities		Somewhat		A one-step process to opt out

Question 4: Is my message of value to the recipient?

1	2	3	4	5
Not at all		Somewhat		Very valuable

Question 5: Am I ready to adequately handle replies in a timely manner?

1	2	3	4	5
Not at all		Somewhat		Completely ready

Question 6: Am I using a list generated in-house?

No = 1	In-house & purchased = 3	Yes = 5

The Spam Challenge Scoring

Total: 20–25: Begin e-mailing today! Your e-mail is targeted, valuable, and has a high chance of success. But don't forget to keep track of those names!

Total: 15–20 You're on the right track, but your e-mail efforts may still be interpreted as spam. Identify the weaker components (affinity, value, etc.), then work toward bolstering them. For example, if you're mailing to a purchased list, think about implementing a system that captures all incoming e-mail addresses. Future mailings will be better received since their recipients voluntarily gave you a way in which to contact them.

Total: 5–15 Halt the (virtual) presses and slowly step away from your computer! Your e-mail efforts have a great potential to damage relationships and a small chance of success. An e-mail campaign may be low in cost but it is not without effort. Re-evaluate your efforts from the standpoint of your recipients. Can you more narrowly target your audience and your message? Do you have an e-mail infrastructure that lets you easily capture ad track those who contact your organization? Is that same infrastructure flexible enough to create an opt-in/opt-out system that's easy for your customers to use? Think before you mail.

Cheat Sheet: Do's and Don'ts of Spam

1. Be sincere. Don't lie or mislead your audience before or during your relationship with them. Stick closely to the content you outline in your mission statement.

2. Let people come to you. Don't make them choose not to be on your list (opt-out); let them request to be included (opt-in).

3. To your opt-in database, write concisely and with new, valuable information (not "me too" or recycled articles). Don't waste their time or yours.

4. Back up your subscriber list on a regular basis. Don't let anyone else send a message to your list or retrieve a list of your subscribers.

5. Offer forms on every page of your Web site to let subscribers sign up to your e-mail newsletter. Don't add the e-mail addresses of people you know to your list without their consent. Instead, if they request a sample, send them a copy and directions for subscribing.

6. Be thorough in your new-subscriber welcome message, including details about how to subscribe and unsubscribe.

7. Be clear about what you will send once people give you their e-mail addresses.

8. Be professional and businesslike in your e-mail communications. Don't post to discussion lists or send e-mail with grammar or spelling errors.

11

Technical Know-How

Now that you know *what* to send, this chapter will teach you *how* to send. To turn your plans into reality you need to know how to gather hundreds, thousands, or (dream big!) millions of people to sign up for your e-mail. Then you have to distribute your message to each and every one of them. And, don't forget, then you have to manage the responses.

Fear not, sending your mass mailing to subscribers doesn't have to be a difficult endeavor. In this chapter, we'll go over several of the different options that are available to you. Be warned, though, software is one of the most rapidly changing and improving areas of industry. It is impossible to present a book with a current list of products because it would be out of date before it was even in the stores! But the major players in this industry are here to stay, and they offer plenty of tools and information for you. Be sure to check with the additional resources listed at the end of the chapter.

First, you should understand the three hats you wear as an official e-mail marketer, as shown in Figure 11.1. You are the technical whiz, who has to handle holding the list of names and get each message delivered to each one of the names on your list. You are the customer service representative, who has to be polite to and considerate of each recipient (you know, the guy who subscribes, doesn't bother learning how to unsubscribe, and then gets mad at you for

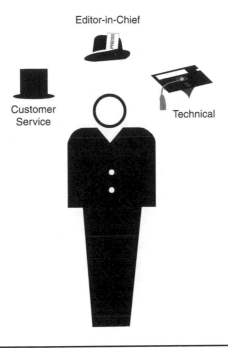

Figure 11.1.   The three hats of an e-mail marketer.

sending him an e-mail message). And you are the editor, figuring out what content and message to send to your recipients.

Hat #1: You, The Technical Whiz

Rather than go over products on the market at the time this is being written, we'll talk about the technical back end and the concept of mass distribution. When you sit down to send an e-mail program, you type in one e-mail address, which represents the intended recipient. Similarly, when you send to your subscriber base, you type in one e-mail address that acts as an alias to represent a *group* (hundreds to thousands) of recipients. To do this, you can set up a distribution list using your e-mail program or list hosting software, use a free or fee list service, or outsource to a company that will handle the whole shebang for you.

The full process should go something like this, as shown in Figure 11.2. You put out your message somewhere (perhaps in your sig file), inviting people to subscribe. People see it and follow the directions you've given for subscribing. Their e-mail addresses are added to your database. You send them a welcome message. When the time comes to send an issue, it goes out to an alias that represents all the names in your database or (through an automated process) goes out to each address individually.

When subscribers want to be removed, they'll e-mail a request to unsubscribe or they'll follow the directions that you've given them to unsubscribe (in the welcome message, among other places). Then you will remove their address from your database and send an exit note (often it just asks for their reasons).

The whole shebang is a simple process when you have a few hundred subscribers and add a few per week. But when your list starts growing rapidly, with fifty to a hundred new addresses every day, au-

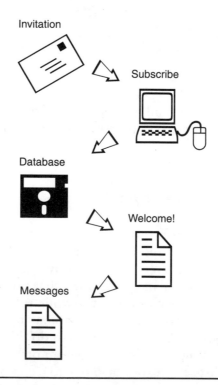

Figure 11.2. Sign up!

tomation will look pretty good. There are three ways to automate: Buy software and load it on your computer (like a distribution list in Microsoft's Oulook); use a company that offers list hosting (e.g., Exactis.com, Slingshot Media, or the free service Topica); or completely outsource the whole shebang to someone else. The first two options will have their own set of technical instructions for managing your list.

However, if you choose to outsource the task of automation, pay close attention to both their technological capabilities and their customer service. Using a company that's not there for you when you send out your first issue at 4 A.M. is extremely frustrating. You want to be assured that you'll get help when you need it. Find out their customer service process and policies, their response record, and full contact information to reach them by phone, fax, or e-mail. Find out specific names for accounting as well as tech support.

Internet Wire, the first and largest Internet-based distributor of company news, uses a program by the e-mail distribution company Commtouch to distribute Internet Wire's news feed to more than 12 million daily e-mail subscribers, including 26,000 individual editors and reporters worldwide. Internet Wire's chairman and CEO Michael Terpin cited the vendor's commitment to customizing their product for their members needs as the top reason for choosing their technology. As part of the partnership, new Commtouch users will be prompted to receive Internet Wire's daily technology news, increasing Internet Wire's reach.

Building this list of users is a tremendous value to your company. Your database is an asset that you've worked hard to obtain, and your outsourcing partner must absolutely respect this fact. At a minimum, look for 24-hour-a-day, 7-day-a-week tech support, personal contacts for tech support, full offsite backup, security, and regular reporting of your statistics. At a minimum, statistics should include your current number of subscribers, the number of new subscribers since the last report, and your most recent attrition number (unsubscribes).

Along those lines, be cautious when switching services. Should you decide to upgrade or change vendors for any reason, guard your list carefully. One publisher, Daryl Clark, says that when he changed over to an automated system, he lost nearly half of his subscriber base during the import. Still, he says that the free list hosting company he uses, Topica.com, was easy to set up and operate. "Their system is also designed to allow me to post my previous newsletters as an archive." The archive and subscribe button for his free monthly newsletter, "What's The Word," are available at his home page at *http://www.emarketingman.com.*

If you work with an opt-in list broker such as NetCreations (see "Resources"), who will build lists and rent one-time use to you, you will not have access to the recipient list, so they'll send it for you. But if you're building your own opt-in list (called a house list), you will want access to your own database, even if it's kept on the vendor's server. It's a good idea, even if you use an opt-in list broker, to simultaneously build your own list.

Statistical reporting from third-party list brokers should be held to a higher standard for reporting results than your own house list. Because they rent use, rather than turning over names and e-mail addresses to you, you should require them to trace URLs within your message (to see how many recipients clicked through) or to set up an autoresponder that measures response.

Manual Distribution

As you start your list, it might not be the best use of marketing dollars to pay for an outsourced vendor. Instead, you might want to run your list off your existing software program. In this case, you will either set up a distribution list, as shown in Figure 11.3, or use the BCC (blind carbon copy) feature so that you don't send your mailing list addresses to each member of your list. Each time you send your message, simply add the names from your list to the BCC field in your e-mail program (make sure that they are divided by commas, semicolons, or spaces to delineate between addresses) and press go. Be warned that any number over about 150 in this field could get you labeled a spammer and put you into hot water with your ISP (see Chapter 10).

Another method is to set up distribution lists. If the program that you use isn't listed here, use the help feature to search for distribution lists and learn how to send your e-mails this way.

To Set Up Distribution Using Pegasus

1. Pressing "F6," go to the Addresses menu and choose "Distribution lists."

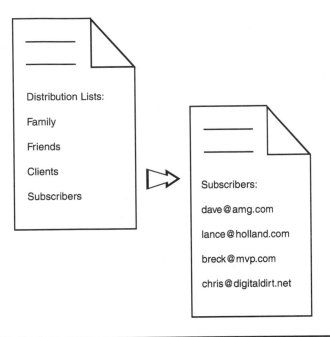

Figure 11.3. How a distribution list works.

2. Click on the New button.

3. Name your list in the dialog box that appears. Click "OK."

4. In the selector window, highlight the list you created and click on "Edit."

5. In the window that appears, you'll see the title you gave your list in the title field.

6. Click in the address list area and enter the addresses of your subscribers, one per line.

To Set Up Distribution Using Outlook

1. First, create your personal address book in the user profile.

2. On the Tools menu, click on "Address book."

3. Click on "New entry."

4. Select "Personal distribution list" in the Select Entry Type box. Click "OK."

5. Name your subscriber list.

6. Click "Add/remove members."

7. In the Type name/Select from list box, type the e-mail addresses that you'd like to add.

To Set Up Distribution Using Eudora

1. Setting up distribution lists in Eudora is done the same way as setting up an individual name. Open the address book.

2. Click on the New button or right-click on the entry list and choose "New."

3. In the dialog box, type the name of your subscriber list.

4. Enter a name and choose "Make it an Address Book." Click "OK." This creates the entry for this book. Now you have to enter names into it.

5. To add or remove entries, click "New."

6. In the dialog box that appears, enter a nickname for your entry and make sure that the name of your subscriber list appears as the file you're adding this name to.

7. Select "Put it on the recipient list."

8. Click "OK." Then you can enter the information for that entry. Type the e-mail addresses of your list into the address tab, separating each address with commas or returns.

9. Eudora recommends that each file contain under 2,500 entries.

10. Go to the File menu and click on "Save."

To Set Up Distribution Using Netscape Communicator

1. Go to the Address Book window and click on "New list."

2. Into the mailing List dialog box, enter your list name, list nickname, and description.

3. To add or delete addresses, simply type them in or delete them from the Address Book window and click "OK."

A Nasty Little Thing Called An "E-Mail Virus"

An e-mail virus is code that runs when an e-mail is opened. According to Nagaraja Srivatsan, Vice President at Digital Vision Labs at SeraNova, Inc., these codes do one or all of the following: replicate to all contacts in your address book, install in your system so that they can send themselves to future contacts, delete files, crash the system, and install date-related trojan horses (such as files that will open on a certain holiday.) He is careful to mark the difference between spam and viruses, "although sometimes as annoying as a virus, spam is not the same as a virus. Spam includes 'Get rich' schemes and others where the 'Spammer', after getting hold of your e-mail address, will send you stuff without your permission."

A famous virus that once made its way around the Internet was the 'Love Bug' or 'ILOVEYOU' virus. According to a May 22, 2000 Newsweek report, the code indicated that the virus was written by a Filipino computer student who was attempting to steal Internet passwords. Computer Economics estimated that $12.1 billion was lost last year as a result of Internet-borne viruses generated by hacker attacks.

The virus ended up doing damage to computers worldwide, including the National Security Agency and the Pentagon. The virus consisted of a small piece of code that would go into the recipient's e-mail program, replicate itself and send the program out to every address in the host computer's e-mail program. Steven Tool with W. Quinn *http://www.wquinn.com* explained exactly how viruses work:

> The "Love Bug" and all 29 of its variants were carried
> as Visual Basic script (*.vbs) e-mail attachments. Visual
> Basic is a programming language used by software

developers to string together several commands that execute successively when activated. For this reason, it's no wonder Visual Basic is the programming language of choice for virus authors as well, but the majority of typical Windows NT/2000 computer users are not software developers and do not need the ability to store Visual Basic files onto Windows NT/2000 servers. As long as users have the ability to involuntarily write Visual Basic scripts to file servers, the possibility exists for worm viruses to damage legitimate server files.

The other, less technical type of virus is the disruptive mass forwarding of e-mail jokes (especially the one that you get for the thirteenth time—after not laughing the first time), unwanted essays, and other types of chain mail ("forward this e-mail to ten of your friends and all of your wishes will come true!"). These e-mails promise everything from bad luck to financial ruin to granted wishes, depending on whether or not the recipient takes action to forward it to friends and associates.

These e-mails, often sent from personal accounts to others' work accounts are inappropriate to send to those using e-mail for business communications. These are not a virus in the traditional sense, but they are more of an emotional virus and should be avoided and discouraged—at least, in the business atmosphere (we wouldn't dream of stopping you from forwarding that great knock-knock joke to your dad's personal e-mail account!). If you were on your lunch break and a co-worker told you a funny joke, would you call a friend at their job to tell it to them? Probably not; use the same good judgment with e-mail.

Consider this: It might only take you a minute to forward a funny joke to fifteen friends at their work addresses. But imagine if fifteen friends all decide to forward the same joke to you, while you're at work trying to finish up a project on deadline. It's inappropriate and it's disruptive. For the same reason, your e-mail marketing messages shouldn't *only* be opt-in, meaning they have been specifically requested by the recipient, they should also be concise, helpful, and valuable to the recipient.

The Raging Debate: Graphic or Plain Text E-Mails

It used to be that if you wanted to send graphic e-mails, HTML was the way to do it. And while HTML e-mail is increasing in acceptance by e-mail clients, it's still not at 100%. It is a tough choice to determine whether or not, as a publisher, you should launch your publication in easy-to-format and universally accepted plain text or in visually appealing, high-impact richly formatted text. Both are tempting! But each has its pitfalls. Text can be boring. HTML can be messy, depending on what e-mail program a recipient is using.

One company has added another solution to the mix, creating a third type of solution for sending e-mail newsletters. OnMercial.com offers a product called MercialXpress, allowing users to design, package and deliver highly compressed files that support rich content, interactive links and do not require any reader software. Robert M. Caruso, CEO of OnMercial *(http://www.MercialXpress.com)* says that because the Internet is no longer made up of computer professionals, the largest and fastest-growing population on the Web is the new, novice, and beginner users. "This group has become extremely frustrated trying to download information, trying to find it once it is downloaded, and then understanding what software they need to have in order to read the information they have acquired." Their solution is to skip the risk of boring recipients with text or frustrating them with HTML that doesn't display properly. Their product, MercialXpress Builder Software, creates a proprietary file format that converts images into a tiny encapsulated file and sends to users.

Still, HTML can be a great alternative, depending on your market. In a recent issue of the LinkExchange Digest, Urban Weigl, the webmaster of *http://www.avara.org* calls HTML e-mail a pain to receive, writing that he only wanted clear information. He resents HTML in e-mail, writing that all he wants in e-mail is "clear, crisp information. What I don't want is ugly formatting and banner ads in my e-mail (text-based ads are okay though). Whenever I have a choice between HTML and ASCII, I always go for the later. Similarly, if an e-zine is offered only in HTML, I simply won't subscribe. No matter how interesting it appears to be." In the same issue, Andy Brock, President of Mrkt Inc: Integrated Marketing Strategy *(http://www.mrktinc.com)*, agrees, saying that he will delete HTML e-mails, especially when unsolicited. "I agree that HTML-enabled e-mail publications are attractive. However, I don't believe the Net Public are there yet in accepting it." He adds that the worldwide nature of the Net equals differences in bandwidth and capabilities for subscribers. Because it's a multimedia medium, HTML e-mail, such as the one shown in Figure 11.4, is more captivating, better as a brand-building tool, better as an advertising vehicle, and more robustly tracked. But it's also, unfortunately, ahead of many consumers' technologies.

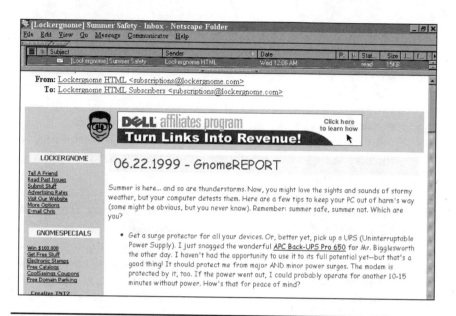

Figure 11.4. Sample HTML e-mail.

Is HTML for you? The applications are wonderful if you have a retail product, because you can show the recipient a picture of your product along with the forms to let them buy. You can send them everything that you would use on a Web page to convince people to buy. You can use different services that "sniff" out the recipient's e-mail client capabilities and send the appropriate format. You can also let recipients sign up for HTML or text and segment your market accordingly. Think about your audience: Are they a more technically savvy bunch, or are they hooking up mostly through America Online? If they have the capability, you will certainly have higher results through HTML. Think about your resources: Can you code HTML? Do you have someone who can create HTML for you? Do you have the desire to learn? This too should be weighed into your decision.

The difference is this: HTML is the coding language that allows you to see pictures, color, various fonts, hyperlinks, and layouts. Although HTML is normally used to create Web pages, many e-mail readers now support HTML-based e-mail messages. So when you send HTML in an e-mail to people set up to receive it as such, they'll get something formatted with text and graphics. Web-based e-mail accounts usually show HTML e-mail because they support standard mail protocols like POP (Post Office Protocol), IMAP (Internet Mail Access Protocol), SMTP (Simple-mail Transfer Protocol), and MIME (Multipurpose Internet Mail Extensions).

However, if you send HTML to people who can't read it, they'll either get a page of confusing coding or a link to go to their browser. For these people, you'd want to send text only, also referred to as ASCII. Text, like the e-mail shown in Figure 11.5, can either be plain text or it can be a link to a Web site. This link is a URL that users must click on to then open a browser. To avoid the download time problems associated with HTML messages, many e-mail marketers use clickable text, in which words within the message are hot-linked to a Web site.

The best decision? If you have the time and subscriber interest, offer two lists—one in plain text, one in HTML—and let your subscribers decide. The Internet-based printing shop iPrint says that they have experimented with sending messages in both HTML and plain text formats. Because HTML is richer format, iPrint found that they received a better response rate. However, fewer e-mail clients (and thus, fewer recipients) can support it. Still, they receive an overall

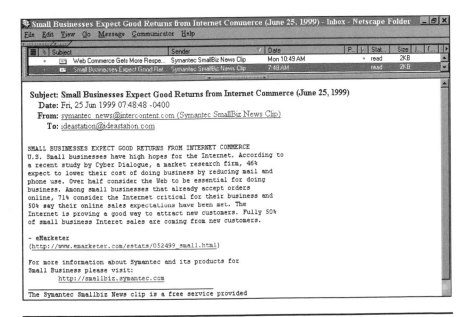

Figure 11.5. Sample plain text e-mail.

better response with HTML messages, although they aren't sure which customers can and cannot receive HTML. As you build your list, consider offering two versions with two different sets of members and subscribe instructions: one for HTML, one for plain text.

- *HTML.* Sending HTML e-mail means that either you have to know how to code HTML (like a Web page), or you have to create an e-mail in a program that can automatically convert your formatted text to the appropriate e-mail. Broadc@st HTML from MailWorkZ *(http://www.mailworkz.com)* is one product on the market that offers a cost-effective way of reaching your audience with HTML e-mail. They company has more than 1000 customers, including Novell and PriceWaterHouse Coopers.

- *Plain Text.* One concern with plain text is to add manual line breaks after approximately 60 lines. Because you don't know how the program on the receiving end will read your e-mail, if you leave this to chance, your newsletter may not look right. It may end up with line breaks in strange places, or worse, none at all!

The easiest way to achieve automatic, manual breaks is to create your e-mail newsletter in MS Word, using the following settings:

- Font: Courier New, size 11.5

- Margins, 1.5, left and right

- Then use "File" "Save as" "Text with line breaks." Close and reopen, then cut and paste it into your e-mail program or Web interface. This will eliminate any strange formatting codes that Word might insert and will automatically add the manual line breaks in your copy.

Hat #2: You, The Customer Service Representative

Keep in mind that you'll have to offer customer service not just to the actual recipients, but also to yourself. There's a large hands-on, manual work side to managing a list. If you send out bulk e-mail, be prepared to handle the response. You must have systems in place to process the technical and personal e-mails that will come back to you. You can do this through both automated systems and personal attention.

The bulk of your e-mails that come back in the first hour will have nothing to do with content, meaning it won't be letters to the editor about what a great job you did. Most of them will require management.

As part of your customer service helpfulness, consider telling your text subscribers that they can get a free e-mail account through which they can subscribe for the HTML version of your newsletter, if they are interested. Free e-mail accounts are available from services such as HotMail, MailExcite, RocketMail, netMessenger, iMailBox and more. (I personally use HotMail, and encourage your comments, advice and feedback for future editions of this book—send to shannard@hotmail.com.)

Bounce Management

It's inevitable that subscribers will change e-mail addresses and close accounts, servers will go down, the Net will get busy, and a computer glitch, virus, or bug somewhere along the line will prevent your message from going straight from you to the intended recipient. The result is a bounce. A bounce is what happens when you send a bulk e-mail out to a group of people and certain ones come back to you as undelivered. Bounces are either deemed "hard" or "soft."

A hard bounce is an undeliverable e-mail that will never, ever become deliverable. The address is just wrong. Hard bounces happen when a subscriber terminates an account, changes addresses, or does some other thing that makes the address cease to be valid. Addresses that result in a hard bounce need to be immediately unsubscribed from your list.

A soft bounce can again become valid and is only temporarily undeliverable. Occasions that might result in soft bounces include down Internet connections, random server problems, and blocked addresses. A soft bounce is a temporary situation that has to do more with the connection to your intended recipient. It will usually correct itself. If the same address keeps coming up as a soft bounce, it's usually best to unsubscribe it manually.

Idiot Management

There are people who, no matter how clear you make the unsubscribe instructions, will not be able to figure it out. They will first do it incorrectly, then they will send you a nasty note saying that you are spamming them. It often takes several attempts to unsubscribe them, because they never seem to be subscribed under the address that they think they are subscribed under.

There's another faction of people who will opt-in and then insist that they never did. Forrester Research recently reported that "this phenomenon will repeat itself over and over, leading to a new trend: non-repudiable marketing." The best solution is to unsubscribe them, then sweetly and immediately write back to tell them that you have manually handled the situation. Be polite, be immediate, and be done with them!

Mismanagement

Things can go wrong with the technical aspect of sending your e-mail to a list of recipients. Don't let this make you too afraid to send, but it does happen. It doesn't just happen to people new to this industry either! In the same report mentioned above, Forrester presented a story about how Netscape's server crashed while sending press releases to analysts, resulting in a 10% failure to reach their intended market (including Forrester).

Hat #3: You, The Editor-in-Chief

You're the head architect (plumber, accountant and dishwasher) of the building that is your e-mail publication. Managing writers, contributors, vendors, advertisers, schedules and policies is your job. If you keep on top of this role as the glue that holds your communications plan together, you'll end up in a routine that is streamlined for efficiency.

Determine an Editorial Calendar

- *How Much Will You Send?* What length is best for your audience? If you're selling a highly technical product with a high learning curve, perhaps longer is better. If you're entertaining, perhaps medium is best. If you're marketing an impulse or high-image product, shorter is better.

- *How Often?* If you have a lot of information to share, but don't want to send a lengthy e-mail all at once, consider upping your frequency and sending shorter messages.

- *Say What?* Your editorial strategy is very important. First, offer a well-versed description of your list before people sign up, to lower attrition and elicit more targeted subscribers. Second, your content strategy must feed off your subscribers' needs and preferences. Pay attention to the feedback that you receive from them. Be flexible and willing to adapt.

Dr. Ralph F. Wilson, in his article "Marketing via E-mail Newsletters and Mailing Lists" from Web Marketing Today, Issue 17, lists the purposes of the different types of lists as

- To *Remind* former visitors with brief information about new articles, products, and features on their Web site (e.g., CNET, Ziff-Davis, TechWeb, etc.).

- To *Inform* with a regular newsletter containing helpful content along with information about one's business. Often such newsletters are also archived on a Web site, creating an increasingly valuable information resource (e.g., Web Marketing Today, Web Digest for Marketers).

- To *Enhance* a reputation through occasional articles of interest. A weekly or monthly publishing cycle is not crucial.

- To *Nurture* potential customers during the gestation period until they are ready to purchase or sign a contract.

- To *Support* existing customers with ongoing information.

- To *Solicit* paid subscriptions for newsletters with proprietary information not readily available elsewhere.

- To *Earn* revenue from paid sponsors of the newsletter.

Putting It All Together

"Presentation is everything," says my brother, the weekend cook, when he serves up a beautiful meal. That's also true for the e-mail that leaves your company and ends up in the in-box of a potential or current customer. You'll want each issue to be recognizable, readable and anticipated. Use the following tips to ensure that the presentation of your e-mail publication is as welcome as Eggs Benedict on Saturday morning (David Kinnard's breakfast specialty).

Don't neglect visual appeal when you put together the editorial content of your e-mail publication. Even if you skip HTML or graphics (which I wholly recommend in the beginning) pay attention to the artistic layout and paragraph layout of the information that you send to subscribers.

Determine a Look and Feel

When designing the outgoing e-mails that compose your e-mail marketing program, whether you use HTML or ASCII text, and whether you send them on a regular basis, through special promotions, or with sporadic personal responses to inquiries, it's important to determine guidelines related to the look and feel of every piece sent from every employee in your company.

Be careful about publishing a text e-mail newsletter and carrying advertising. You don't want to turn subscribers off by straying too far from the promise of good editorial content. "With traditional text e-mail, it is getting more and more difficult to determine what in a newsletter is content and what is advertising," says Robert M. Caruso, CEO of OnMercial *(http://www.MercialXpress.com)*. "I am often frustrated when reading newsletters in this format because it takes much longer to soak in the information. Also, humans like visual things like images and color that make absorbing information more appealing. It must be understood that people do not buy a magazine because it is open to an article and sitting on a counter. People generally buy them due to the rich cover and exciting headlines."

Layout Guidelines

Are disclaimers necessary at the bottom of each e-mail message? This can influence your layouts. Most brokerage houses (such as Merrill

Lynch) and law firms, to name two examples of industries this applies to, are required to notify recipients about the security and liability associated with each e-mail. Does your company need guidelines about the format of the e-mails that you send?

Content Guidelines

Tone and voice, too, are important to decide early on. Ray Owens is the publisher of Joke A Day *(http://www.jokeaday.com)*, which, at more than 169,000 members, is the largest daily humor mailing list on the Internet. In an interview with Christopher Knight, publisher of SparkLIST's List-Tips, Owens said that the publisher's personality is the most important element contributing to a list's success. Think about a radio show that you enjoy in the morning or the evening news broadcast that you prefer: It's the deejays whom you know will make you laugh, or the news announcers whose personality you enjoy that you listen to or watch (or the stations with the fewest commercials). Your list should work in the same way by letting your own personality come through in every issue. This means not just talking about business, but sharing some personal tidbits at times.

Case Study: L-Soft International

L-Soft's LISTSERV, as shown in Figure 11.6, was the first program in e-mail list management, originally introduced in 1986. As the first, this program set the standard for administration of e-mail lists. In fact, *LISTSERV* is the term often misused to describe all e-mail list management software the way *Xerox* is misused to refer to all brands of photocopiers or *Kleenex* to refer to all brands of tissues.

As the creators of the first software for e-mail list management, L-Soft takes their leadership role seriously. For example, they recently issued a warning to educate companies about the difference between effective e-mail marketing based on opt-in lists, and spam (through the purchase or rental of mass e-mail lists). Harvard Business School recently found that companies can boost profits by more than 25% if they simply reduce customer defections by 5%. L-Soft's CEO Eric Thomas said, "It may take a little more time and effort to build your own lists, but the payback is a more discerning and more interested potential customer—and it is also cheaper in the long

Figure 11.6. Home page of L-Soft International, Inc., makers of LISTSERV software.

run. Given that it is estimated that 9 out of 10 customer interactions are not transactions, companies need to understand what information their customers want."

The latest version of the product offers database integration, mail merge, and a customizable Web interface. The software's database integration facility allows organizations to use it in conjunction with their central database for direct e-mail marketing campaigns. Customer demographics or sales history information stored in a database can then be selected for the creation of highly personalized and targeted messages. Mail merge enables users to deliver individually personalized messages to each member of a large number of recipients.

The Web interface lets subscribers join or leave lists, change their own delivery options, post new messages, and review archived list messages. It also allows list owners to completely manage their lists. More important, it is created for non technical and expert users alike.

LISTSERV delivers 30 million messages on an average weekday to the 100 million subscriptions of over 170,000 lists worldwide.

Clients of all sizes include IBM, AOL-Time Warner, Intel, Microsoft, ZDNET, AT&T, New York Times, Ask Jeeves, Lucent Technologies, Delta Airlines, CNET, Campbell's Soup, and Victoria's Secret.

A demonstration is available at *http://demo.lsoft.com/demo-intro.html*. An evaluation copy is available at *http://www.lsoft.com/evalkits.stm*. More information about these features is at *http://www.lsoft.com/dbms.html*.

Resources

- ListServ (*http://www.lsoft.com*) from L-Soft is a leader in software for e-mail marketing campaigns.

- MailKing *(http://www.mailking.com)* by MessageMedia is an e-mail list management program designed for smaller list owners to run off their desktop. For use on Windows PC, MailKing sends personalized e-mail to your visitors. Cost: $129

- Earthlink offers an excellent tutorial full of tips for using e-mail ethically and effectively at *http://www.earthlink.net/internet/email*.

- OakNet Publishing, at *http://www.oaknetpublishing.com*, from Phil Tanny, offers Web-based management and customer service for their list hosting services.

- Exactis, at *http://www.exactis.com*, offers list management, distribution, and reporting for high-volume lists, such as E-greetings (profiled in Chapter 1).

- Listhost.net, at *http://www.listhost.net,* offers list hosting, consulting, list promotion, customer support, and a comprehensive manual on the technical aspects of publishing lists.

- SparkLIST, at *http://SparkLIST.com*, provides e-mail list hosting, promotion, and management services for e-mail newsletters, announcement lists, and e-mail discussion lists.

- Coollist, at *http://www.coollist.com*, Topica, at *http:// www.topica.com*, and ONElist, at *http://www.onelist.com*, are free mailing list services that will distribute your newsletter for you, but will place an ad of their own in each issue.

- Slingshot Media, at *http://www.slingshotmedia.com*, is an e-mail marketing service bureau (meaning they'll host your names) with top-notch customer service and an excellent e-mail distribution product.

- eGroups Inc., at *http://www.egroups.com*, is a free service that lets users build community around a subject. They boast over 14 million members with more than 600,000 diverse groups. Polling features, group calendars, and file sharing take this product a step beyond simple distribution.

- Alerts.com, at *http://www.alerts.com*, lets you contact your users with HTML or plain text e-mail over any communication device—pager, wireless phone, palm devices, or a user's home page.

- Digital Impact, at *http://www.digitalimpact.com*, offers a full-service e-mail distribution hosting program. Run off their servers, it frees customers from having to invest in hardware, software or management. They handle both development and results reporting.

- @once, at *http://www.@once.com,* is a full-service e-mail campaign hosting company. They use individual profiling to customize e-mail campaigns and have the technology to send rich multimedia. On the other side, they have detailed Web-based reporting of user behavior, click-throughs, and conversions.

- ListBot Free and ListBot Gold, at *http://www.listbot.com*, offer easy-to-use, feature-rich Web-based e-mail newsletter distribution, including a submission button you can put on your own site.

- Mail-list.com, at *http://www.mail-list.com*, is an easy-to-use list management service that is ideal for new Internet users.

- SmartBounce, at *http://www.bsabio.com/SmartBounce*, is used in conjunction with a program like LISTSERV to purge bad addresses from your list.

- Gamesville, at *http://www.gamesville.com*, a developer of permission-based, one-to-one targeted Internet database marketing solutions, creates online entertainment to attract users for data acquisition and datamining. In addition, their registration database and permission system is set up with a proprietary "e-mail client sniffer" technology that ascertains what type of e-mail software each subscriber uses and sends the appropriately formatted e-mail message: plain text or e-mail.

- MasterClips E-mail Animator, at *http://www.imsisoft.com*, adds animation, sound effects, and personal voice greetings to normal text messages with the click of a button using a user-friendly drag-and-drop interface, predesigned messages, wizards, and a built-in auto-send feature that automatically mails messages at the click of the mouse button. The product is "platform blind," meaning that it works with any e-mail program capable of sending and receiving attachments.

Cheat Sheet: Technical 1-2-3

1. Find software, a vendor, or an outsourcing partner to distribute your e-mail newsletter, e-mail discussion list, or direct e-mail messages.

2. Decide if you will offer your publication as plain text, HTML, or both (two versions of each issue).

3. Set aside time to personally send feedback.

4 Set up systems to automate bounces and feedback.

5. Determine what editorial type of content you will send.

6. Determine *how much* (in terms of word count, per article, per issue) you will send.

6. Determine *how frequently* you will send.

7. Assemble each issue using predetermined layout guidelines.

Cheat Sheet: What to Ask Vendors

Suzi Sevcik of SparkLIST.com offers the following questions to help users determine the right e-mail distribution service company for them.

- What is your primary software platform?

- How many years have you been in business?

- How big is your maximum bandwidth pipe?

- What is your uptime for the past month?

- Do you have external third-party monitoring of your network?

- How many technicians are on your staff and what is their skill level?

- What is the size, power, CPU, OS, ram specs on your list servers?

- Are you on a 100 Mbps network internally or a 10 Mbps network?

- What are your list security capabilities? How will you protect my list of subscribers?

- What are your weaknesses?

- Can you customize my list? How extensively?

- Where is your list hosting service going over the next 12 months?

- What is the largest list you host?

- How long does it take you to deliver 100,000 or 1 million e-mails?

- Who owns the material you mail to your list? (Copyright issues)

The Hidden Privacy Hazards of HTML E-Mail

By David Strom, Web Informant, reprinted with permission. To subscribe to Web Informant, send a blank e-mail to *webinformant-subscribe@egroups.com*.

If you have enjoyed receiving HTML-formatted e-mail messages, this news might come as something of a shock to you: Hidden inside those fancy, fun-with-fonts and link-filled messages are some sly ways of keeping track of who you are and what you do with this information. Specifically, many mailing list companies can keep track of what links you click on inside the message, and sell this "clickstream" information to its clients.

For example, take a look at a recent e-mail I got from Netcentive's ClickRewards, a company that will give you frequent flyer miles for doing various activities. If you examine the message in a text editor to view the HTML, you can see many of the links are coded *http://p02.com/ t.d?LEBmCU1_=clickrewards/rewards/index.html.* According to company representatives, this code just keeps track of three specific actions: whether you open the e-mail message or not, whether you click on this specific link, and if you want to unsubscribe. They aggregate this information and pass it along to their customers, so that no individual data is transmitted outside their organization. Interestingly, the p02.com domain referenced in the link is owned by Post Communications, a customized mailing software company recently purchased by Netcentives.

Once I heard about this practice, I found many other examples in e-mail messages from numerous sources, including Nordstrom.com, Wine.com, Netscape's Netcenter, Reel.com, and even an Australian real estate company, www.property.com.au. This is a very widespread practice, and many mailing list management companies are making a good living with this kind of technology. Chances are that you have already received a similar coded message with some kind of database identifier —check your own in-box for HTML e-mail and examine some of the links in the message to see if they contain odd things such as a question mark or other coding.

In defense of this practice, there isn't much in terms of your own identity that is being captured here, other than whether or not you clicked on a particular link. But the issue is more of perception of privacy invasion, and the fact is that none of these companies is clear about what information is collected and how it is used. Sure, there are privacy statements galore on their various Web sites, but they contain so much mumbo-jumbo that it is hard to understand exactly what they mean.

Not all e-mail messages with HTML links inside them are evildoers. Some are quite innocent, and others are pure as the driven snow, including the wonderful Good Morning Silicon Valley (and other postings) from the *San Jose Mercury News* staff. They just contain the links you need to go directly from the information in the e-mail to the specific Web page that they are discussing. That is the way it is supposed to be, until the e-mail marketing community seized upon this method to do some of their dirty work.

You see, being in the e-mail newsletter business myself, it is hard to keep track of your subscribers. People change e-mail addresses quicker than they change their underwear sometimes. E-mail subscribers are also bad about notifying their list owners of the new address. Since the addresses go stale so easily, e-mail marketers want some way to verify that real live humans are responding to their missives. Or precise ways to track down someone who wishes to unsubscribe (as the folks at Netcentives do). Given how much time I have spent unsubbing some of my own subscribers, I can certainly understand this last point.

Ironically, these Web Informant messages began their life (almost five years ago!) with me sending out HTML-formatted e-mail messages to my list. Back in those dark days, it was rare to see anyone sending out such messages, and indeed I ran into a few problems with the primitive e-mail clients that we all used then. Now, my HTML coding wasn't too fancy: I put just enough that most readers could just ignore the codes and read the text if their e-mail software didn't recognize the codes. But still, I got enough complaints and enough trouble that eventually I stopped the practice, about a year after I began sending around the newsletters. (And of course, I never included tracking codes in my HTML!)

So, let's say you are ultraparanoid and want to eliminate these sneaky HTML messages. (Of course, you probably will still get the coded links in a plain text message, but at least you'll be able to spot them more easily.) Good luck. Indeed, I was chagrined to learn exactly how hard this is when I tried to turn off the flow of some of these messages.

As a user, you don't have a lot of choices when it comes to unwind some of your HTML e-mail subscriptions. If you still want to be on these mailing lists, see if you can convert your subscription from HTML to plain text messages. Many of the sites make it impossible to do this—for example, Nordstrom.com and Wine.com both have only one method of sending out subscriptions, and it is the HTML method. With ClickRewards, you have to send them an e-mail request to turn off the HTML, even though on their Web site you can set up your account to receive special offers and do all sorts of other sophisticated things—but not manage how these messages are sent to you. (To their credit, my request was satisfied quickly and with an apology along with a credit of some frequent flyer miles to my account. A nice touch.)

If you are an e-mail marketing company, here are a few suggestions. First, put the instructions in plain text at the top of the message on how to unsubscribe and how to convert your subscription from HTML to text. Also, have a clearly stated policy that indicates the kind of identifying information that is found in the HTML e-mail message on your Web site, as part of your privacy policy. Don't hide it or cover up the fact that if recipients click on the links, they are tying their IP address, e-mail address, or account to a particular action. Finally, you should make it obvious how to unsubscribe from the newsletter, including putting this information on your Web Site near the subscription information, as a link in each newsletter, and as plain text with the link included as well in both places.

12

Measuring Results

Measuring the results of your efforts is a critical part of the e-mail marketing plan. It allows e-mail marketers to evaluate performance of specific strategic executions, to improve the next execution by tailoring it to the results, and to set budgets based on actual results and break-even points. This allows campaigns to adapt, evolve and improve more quickly than with any other form of marketing.

The process, shown in Figure 12.1, is to create a series of offers that test a variable, name one as the control offer, and then measure against and try to beat that control offer. In addition, you can determine which responses different segments of your market will have and tailor subsequent efforts to them.

Test Variables

As you begin to plan your e-mail marketing campaign, you'll want to make the most of your expenditure by testing each tool thoroughly. To test each tool, consider a test in which you vary different components of your e-mail marketing program. For example, if you're sending a newsletter out to 50,000 recipients, you might want to consider a call to action that directs them to a different Web site. Divide the

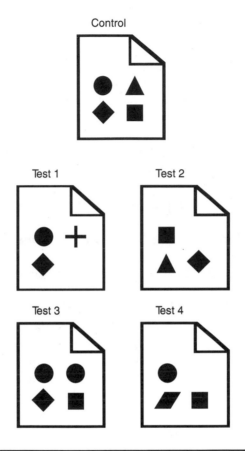

Figure 12.1. Creating a control group and testing variables.

list up into five 10,000-name lists. Send the same newsletter to each, varying just one of the variables. Measure the response to your message by using five different URLs, one for each strategy.

N2K's Music Boulevard recently ran a promotion that put this idea into action. They set up an identifying offer, or control group, that set the standard against which the rest were measured. Their control offer was a dollar-amount discount off a purchase. Then there were four test offers that included a different (lower) discount, the lower discount plus shipping and handling, a value-added buy, or a free compact disc with a qualifier. Following are some of the different variables that you can test in your campaigns.

Source

Whenever you send an e-mail, the first thing that the recipient sees is usually the line that says who the e-mail came from. Try varying this to determine if some approaches work better than others. There are many variations you can put on your "From" heading! For example, the e-mail discussion group from a fictitious organization called The Sample Company called "Sample News," an e-mail marketer could try the following executions:

- From: Sample President, *president@sample.com*

- From: Sample News, *news@sample.com*

- From: The Sample Company, *sample@sample.net*

Each one could be tagged to send a response when it is opened, as a way for a savvy e-mail marketer to gauge which executions don't even get read. Change the response addresses for each execution as well (for example, From: Sample Company is from a different address than the one coming from the company's president). This tells me whether people like to respond to a particular entity, such as one person (the company's president), versus a list (Sample News), versus a company (The Sample Company).

Subject

Likewise, you can vary the subject line. Try including or omitting the date, the issue/volume numbers, the name of the publication, the issue's featured article title, or whatever else you can think of. An example, taken from Online Publishers, might be this:

- Subject: Online Publishers, Issue 50

- Subject: Online Publishers, Issue 50: Measuring Response

- Subject: This Week In OP: Measuring Response

- Subject: "Personalized Name"'s Issue of OP

For the last execution, I would have to be using a personalization program matched with a database that held the first name of all my subscribers, which could be a required field in the signup form. Again, the message can be tagged to see how many (and which) recipients open it.

Keep in mind that one of the first things that your recipients see when they receive an e-mail from you is the subject line. For this reason, your subject line is very important. How will you use it to ensure that your e-mail gets opened? For starters, don't overuse the word that doesn't work anymore: *Free.* Because this used to be such a great word to use, it's been extremely overused. And now, it's totally ineffective. Donald Skarzenski, the VP of Interactive Marketing with CompuBank, N.A. *(http://www.compubank.com)* ran at least 10 split runs in a two-month period and says that "the creative that stresses 'FREE' in the subject line always loses." His specific advice is that bulleted lists work better than sentences, benefits are better than descriptions, short is better than long, and free is pretty "iffy" in the body, too.

Rob Frankel gives the following rules for subject lines:

1. Nothing in all caps

2. No use of off-topic ploys: "Free, $, Sex"

3. No abuse of a "re:" heading (a lame ploy to hoodwink the recipient into thinking the message is a reply. Junk ploys like these actually anger the recipient.)

4. Don't use obvious and meaningless mail merges ("Hello Rob Frankel! I thought this would interest you.")

He continues with the advice that the best success comes from subject lines that are honest and skip the hard sale. "I find that putting my intent in the header works well, for example, 'Rob Frankel's affiliate program proposal.' Boring, yes. But it is what it is and people respect you for it," says Frankel. "In that one subject heading, they know who I am and what's inside—and most importantly—that I'm not hyping them with a dopey header. Also, by not giving them the whole story in the Subject, they're more inclined to open it and read more." He finishes his advice by saying that you should make an introduction and an explanation in your commercial e-mails, not a hard sales proposition.

Header

Consider your opening. People don't read very far when it comes to e-mail that isn't personalized and customized to them, unless it's something that they've requested and are, therefore, anticipating. Create e-mail that your recipient looks forward to reading—not marketing text that just promotes your company. It's important to build a relationship with recipients. They'll decide in the first screen if they're going to continue reading, so make this screen count. Try sending with an opening personal note, versus starting with a table of contents, versus the featured article. Try listing all your automated instructions up front or pointing to them at the end of the issue.

Message

The message can be varied editorially by repackaging the content in different ways. If you have a four-section e-mail newsletter that goes out once a month, what about trying a shorter one-section newsletter four times a month, like the example shown in Figure 12.2? What about changing the format of an article and turning it into a checklist? Or turning an announcement of a new product into a product review? There are different ways to vary each component of your e-mail that goes out. Change the content of what you are saying and how you are saying it. Try writing the same content in a variety of different writing styles. Try one that's chatty versus one that's professional versus one that's comedic. Let your audience tell you by their response which one is their favorite.

Media

Using the same article, let your readers tell you how they want to read it. Try different variations: To one segment of your database, just send a URL that contains your entire message as a Web page. To another segment, send an autoresponder address and tell readers that

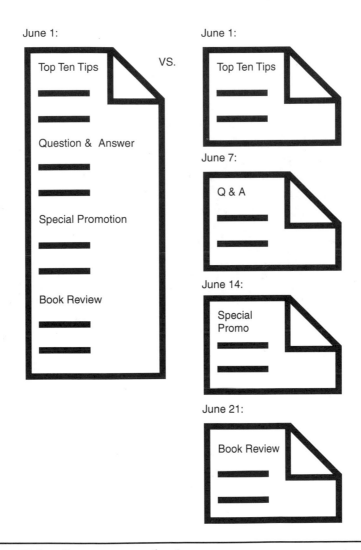

Figure 12.2. One message or four?

they have to request it to read the complete article. To another segment, send the entire article in the body of the message.

Try sending a full table of contents (such as the first paragraph of each article), then point to the full article through a variety of media, such as the Web or via autoresponder. Then you can measure which variation gets the most response.

Length

Try sending several versions of the same article as different length stories to find out which works best for your audience. At the end, give them a question that they can vote on simply (by sending an e-mail to a Vote Yes address or a Vote No address, for example). Test which length has the most response. A standard copy length might be a four-sentence paragraph. A short copy length might be one-liners. In one test (described in this chapter's Sharper Image case study) comparing the standard copy, explaining benefits, and short copy, getting right to the point, the testers found that the shorter copy pulled better results.

Format

Test several different layouts for your newsletter. Find out if your audience responds better to plain text, clickable text, or HTML. Test different levels of creativity as well: Do they like plain dividers between sections or fancy ASCII or graphic art? Try listing your articles and points as bulleted or numbered lists versus full paragraphs.

Call to Action

There are several ways to ask someone to do the same thing. If you want people to visit your Web site and download your software, try varying the invitation. Examples might be

- Enter our sweepstakes by downloading our software.

- Free software for the first fifty respondents.

- Take our quiz and win a free software program.

- Free software download for a limited time!

Timing

Different days of the week are important, for different reasons, for different segments, as is shown in Figure 12.3. An entertainment

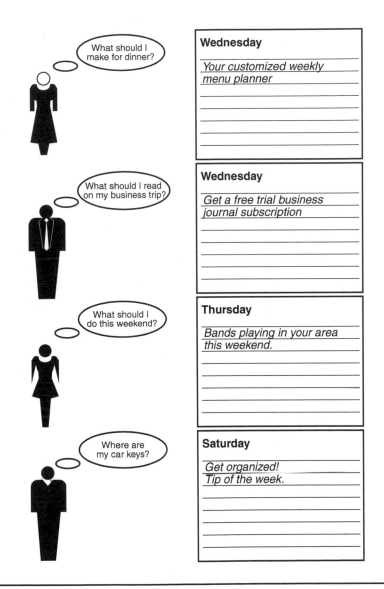

Figure 12.3. What day is best for your message and your audience?

site might do better sending an e-mail on the weekends, while a business e-mail might do better early in the morning. More specifically, an e-mail for flower delivery might do better the week before Easter versus the month before.

Response Mechanism

Some people like to respond simply by clicking the respond button. Some like to go to a Web site. Some like to order an autoresponder. Some like to fax. Some like to call. Some like to build a fire in the woods and send up smoke signals. Test your audience to see their preferred response method.

Setting Up Systems

If you don't put a system into place at the beginning of your program (before you press "Send"), don't expect to do so after. If you receive an overwhelming response, you might be okay with no system. If you receive no response, though, you'll want to know why, and you won't be able to tell unless you prepare for it ahead of time. Since there's no way of knowing if you'll be a success until you press "Send," set up a system beforehand, as shown in Figure 12.4.

Billi Perry is a consultant and the owner of Organizing Solutions, which works with small businesses to help them manage their time and money. She tells the story of a client who spent over half of his time on marketing endeavors that only produced a small fraction (7%) of his sales profit. Because the client wasn't tracking, there was no way of knowing about the wasted time and energy. Perry set up a tracking system and found that an area in which the client was only spending 10% of his time and money was producing 45% of his sales revenue. It's the only way to evaluate what is efficient from a time and cost perspective. Marketing efforts need to be tracked and evaluated repeatedly for success, advises Perry, and tactics need to be adjusted accordingly.

Have a Control Group

The first step in building your trackable, measurable e-mail marketing program is to set up a control group. This would be a core group of recipients that are interested in your general promotion, such as your e-mail newsletter. So, for example, you might send them a regular monthly broadcast that has a general promotional offer, builds

Figure 12.4.　Put systems in place at the start.

brand awareness for your company, and alerts customers to your latest activities and offers.

Within that market are subsets that have their own special niche interests. Finding these subsets of customers and speaking to them directly through special offers increases the relevance that your e-mail marketing communication has for them. This is one way to communicate with customers between monthly sends.

Tracking Users with URLs

Tracking users is the way to gauge the success of a campaign instantly. Tracking lets e-mail marketers use their efforts most effectively, focusing on the best-performing lists and adjusting or discontinuing the rest. E-mail marketing has always been about instant response according to Rosalind Resnick, CEO of NetCreations, which recently released TrackBot, a real-time e-mail-response tracking system that measures the action taken on an opt-in marketing campaign run by its parent company, NetCreations. (More about list broker NetCreations is in Chapter 14.) Using TrackBot or another unique URL tracking program, e-mail marketers follow a recipient from click-through all the way to the sale. TrackBot automatically generates dynamic URLs that are inserted into an e-mail message that is sent out. The clicks and sales produced by the campaign are then tracked and recorded by the company's servers.

MessageMedia offers tools to distribute to e-mail lists that e-mail marketers have built themselves (house lists). Like NetCreations, however, they offer trackable URLs so that an e-mail marketer can check on the dynamically updated statistics of a mailing to see which recipients clicked on a message, when they clicked, and if they bought. It also allows e-mail marketers to send follow-up messages to the parts of their recipient pool, based on whether they clicked or not. For example, you might want to send a special 24-hour-only promotion to your list. To act on the offer, a recipient has to click on a URL. Sixteen hours later, you might want to send a follow-up to all the recipients who didn't click that says, "Only eight hours left act now!"

Tracking Users with Aliases

An e-mail alias is an e-mail address that points to an active e-mail account. Mail addressed to such an alias is automatically forwarded to a specified e-mail account, as shown in Figure 12.5. This allows one e-mail address, the alias, to send e-mail to different e-mail accounts. For example, when I used to be the president of Idea Station, any e-mail sent to *sales@ideastation.com* (an alias) actually went to *shannon@ideastation.com* (my regular address). This allowed me to filter sales requests into a special folder, automatically, using the filter feature on my e-mail program. Similarly, you could have your company's e-mail addresses filter into an account (allowing you to track the number of responses), trigger an autoresponder (letting the user know their e-mail has been received), and forward automatically to the advertiser so that they can follow up on the lead.

Aliases are a good way to test the effectiveness of any (on- or offline) marketing tactic. Use unique e-mail addresses to test different vehicles, different creative executions, or different placements. Filters allow you to filter different aliases into different mailboxes. For example, if you advertise in publication A and publication B, all

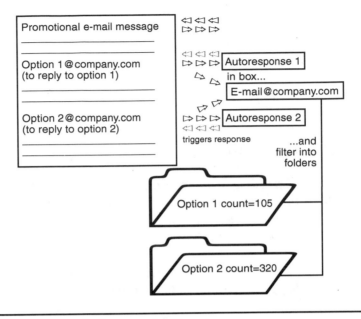

Figure 12.5. E-mail aliases can be filtered to measure response.

pub-a@yourdomain.com e-mail can be filtered in one-mailbox, *pub-b@yourdomain.com* e-mail can be filtered into a second mailbox, and *pub-c@yourdomain.com* can be filtered into a third. This lets you count which of the messages you send is the most effective.

Consider using a system of aliases to track responses to an offer that gives prospects a portfolio of client account work. When Idea Station used to market our e-mail marketing services, we used an "e-portfolio" to showcase our services for prospects in a unique way. This is an easy way to track which case studies draw the highest responses so that we can tailor our portfolio with the most appealing samples. When a prospect requested a copy of Idea Station's e-portfolio, they would automatically receive the following e-mail:

///

To: Recipient

From: Idea Station

Subject: Idea Station's e-portfolio

//

Client: Qwest Communications

Newsletter: "For Home"

Target Audience: Consumers of Qwest's telecommunications services

Marketing Strategy: To upsell current customers by building a better relationship with them through informative articles about products and services related to telecommunications.

Execution: Articles focus on new products, company happenings, and tactics for using the company's services.

Sample: "Introduction"

Do you ever wish you could explore the Internet as quickly and easily as you flip through channels on your television? Now you can. Read on to find out more.

To request the article in its entirety, send an e-mail to sample1@ideastation.com.

//

Client: Kinnard's Pharmacy

Newsletter: "The Balance"

Target Audience: Consumers of health products

Marketing Strategy: To inform patients of different options they have when using a pharmacy, and to make them aware of all their health options, from traditional prescription to alternative forms of therapy.

Execution: Articles focus on health news and information, unbiased, from both alternative and traditional fields.

Sample: "Back to Our Roots: Pharmaceutical Compounding" by Shannon Kinnard

You know that Burger King slogan: "Have it your way?"

That's the way compounding pharmacists feel about your prescriptions. While drug companies produce products that most of society can use, prescription compounding services, by a licensed professional, offer patients alternatives by altering the dose or dosage form of a medication.

To retrieve the article in its entirety, send an e-mail to sample2@ideastation.com.

//

Client: YesMail.com

Newsletter: "WebPromote Weekly"

Target Audience: Internet marketing professionals learning to do a better job with their interactive efforts.

Marketing Strategy: To build a relationship with their target audience with the side benefit of marketing Yesmail's other services.

Execution: Articles offer advice and tips for marketing on the Internet.

Sample: "Cause-Related Marketing" by Shannon Kinnard

To learn more, send an e-mail to sample3@ideastation.com.

//

In addition to triggering an autoresponder to automatically (and with no effort on anyone's part) send an e-mail with the full articles back to the recipient, each of the addresses listed earlier—

sample1@ideastation.com, *sample2@ideastation.com*, and *sample3@ideastation.com*—can be copied to a free Web-based e-mail account, which filters each alias into its own mailbox. At any time, we can go in and look at that account, tallying the number of inquiries we received per article. Then, as we find certain ones are not pulling responses, we update our portfolio to only include popular articles.

Using What Subscriber Data Tells You

At a minimum, your subscriber numbers let you know the reach of your e-mail publication. Taken a step further, they tell you when something receives a favorable or unfavorable response. If your subscriber numbers dip after an issue, you might want to check and see what part of your content wasn't targeted enough. List attrition refers to the number of subscribers who leave your list. The goal is to bring in targeted members so that your list attrition is low.

Remember that your subscriber number is important if you're selling advertising, but not as important as the focus of your audience demographic. You could have a lean subscriber base of 6,000 business owners, which is more valuable to someone trying to sell a service to business owners than a subscriber base of 10,000 students, some of whom might own their own business. But to truly use the datamining power of e-mail marketing, you have to aggregate and incorporate recipients' actions, responses, and activities *and then adjust accordingly!*

Track Media Efforts

Create special URLs or unique e-mail addresses (aliases or autoresponders) for each separate press release that you send. Then track the number of visits or requests that are recorded for each response mechanism. You can also keep tabs on the following online services that will track when and where your company is mentioned. Places to monitor when and where your company is mentioned:

- Excite News Tracker, at *http://nt.excite.com/*, offers free clippings for top news stories in business, sports, entertainment, technology, science, health, lifestyle, and national and world news. Users can enter specific topics to be tracked or choose to view top headlines.

- NewsPage, at *http://www.newspage.com*, is a free service that allows users to enter specific terms to search for related articles. If you want to subscribe, they'll send you personalized issues defined by your interest (such as your company name).

- NewsLinx, at *http://www.newslinx.com*, is a free service that clips online headlines for you.

- News Index, at *http://www.newsindex.com*, is a keyword-based search engine. Also free is a News Index Customizable Ticker.

- NewsHound, at *http://www.hound.com*, Knight Ridder's news and customized information delivery service, clips and sends articles using your choice of several delivery options, including electronically and via postal mail.

- Northern Light Search, at *http://www.northernlight.com*, is a search engine that searches over 54,000 news databases. If you want to pull an entire article from their Special Collection, it costs $1 to $4 per article.

- eWatch, at *http://www.ewatch.com*, monitors the Internet for information on your company or product.

- MarkWatch, at *http://www.markwatch.com*, is an automated system that follows your profile and continually monitors the Web for information about your product, reporting the results weekly. The annual fee is $1,195 per brand name, any additional mail fees extra.

- Luce Online, at *http://www.luceonline.com*, affiliated with Luce Press Clippings, monitors 3,000 sources for clippings and offers customers the option of only paying for clippings viewed in full text.

- Luce Press Clippings, at *http://www.lucepress.com*, is a clipping service that sends articles mentioning your company to you up to twice weekly.

- LEXIS-NEXIS, at *http://www.lexis-nexis.com*, is a database of 23,000 legal, government, and business sources that is available on a customized pricing basis, depending upon the particular plan that is chosen.

Case Study: The Sharper Image

The Sharper Image partnered with e-mail marketing firm Digital Impact to produce a one-to-one campaign that had built-in measurement tools. One-to-one, for them, meant that they needed to be able to target each customer and track results. Their tracking campaign included an e-mail audit that measured the response to different dates and times sent, different components of the message (subject, copy, and offers), and different types of e-mail formats (plain text, clickable text, HTML). They also integrated measurement by campaign, individual, and offer.

By customizing content to insert the name and other demographic information about each user into the message, they are able to make their outgoing e-mails more meaningful. Also, this demographic information helps them convert the data (how many people respond) into useful information (which segment responds). Overall, they increased the ROI (return on investment) of their e-mail marketing through measurement.

Some of the specific techniques used were the following:

- *Media Based.* They ran three different versions of the same content and compared results. One version was plain text. Another was clickable text, which is similar to plain text in appearance, except it includes a special code that turns links into familiar form (underlined, blue text) to encourage click-throughs. The third batch of e-mails were sent as HTML text.

- *Behavior Based.* This looked at how customers responded to e-mails and adjusted outgoing offers accordingly.

- *Customer Based.* Their database was segmented into different markets, and responses were used to indicate marketing preferences.

- *Pattern Based.* This method used a database to find subsets of consumers who would respond to segmented offers.

In one test, they compared e-mails with long copy to ones with shorter copy and found that the short copy "outpulled," meaning it elicited greater response from participants. For their varied message formats, they found that clickable text pulled a 92% higher response rate than plain text. They found that the HTML e-mails often pulled a click-through rate two to three times higher than clickable text.

They also ran a promotional campaign based on the one-to-one marketing concept, in which each participating consumer was tagged according to behavior and treated according to this tagging. For example, when they sent out a series of promotional e-mails, they eventually removed nonresponders. They personalized each message based on who they were sending to, with different copy and different offers. The goals were to reactivate old clients who hadn't purchased for a while and to push non-buyers into customers. They also targeted according to whether the recipient was a high spender, a low spender, or a seasonal or gift buyer.

One example was an introductory letter that went out from Richard Thalheimer, the founder of Sharper Image. Loyal customers received one letter, new customers another. Loyal customers received a special offer to reactivate their account by using clickable text in the message and the wording, "Thanks for being one of the first customers to shop The Sharper Image online. I'd like to offer you a gift for ordering again especially now that Father's Day is this Sunday."

Brand-new customers received a different message that sent them to the shopping window. The clickable text e-mail read, "Thanks for becoming a new Sharper Image customer. I'd like to offer a gift for ordering again especially now that Father's Day is this Sunday." This message was followed by targeted offers and discounts based on their shopping habits.

These types of behavior-based marketing tactics enabled The Sharper Image to take advantage of e-mail to build product affinity, build a history of their promotions (and the promotions' success), cross-sell and up-sell, track buyers vs. non-buyers and trace demographics, such as country, zip code, age, gender, and income.

The Sharper Image ran a test of length and format in which four messages went out: standard length in text, standard length in HTML, short length in text, and short length in HTML. Their observations were that the short copy in text was 26% more effective than the standard length copy and HTML was 93% more effective than text. Standard copy HTML was 7% more effective than short copy in HTML.

	Standard	Short
Text	1.00	1.26
HTML	1.93	1.80

They concluded that for text-e-mail customers, they would use short copy, but for HTML e-mail customers, they would use standard-length copy. Overall, they recommend using HTML whenever possible.

Resources

- TrackBot, at *http://www.postmasterdirect.com*, is for mailers who rent lists from NetCreations' PostMaster Direct Response e-mail marketing service. After orders are placed online, users can use the Web interface to automatically generate dynamic URLs for insertion into all the e-mail messages sent out. The clicks and sales produced by the campaign are then tracked and recorded by the PostMaster Direct Response servers.

- Digital Impact's Merchant Mail Service *(http://www.digital-impact.com)* uses a modular approach to integrate a database of customers with the different offers available for each e-mail (e.g., timing, format, etc.). Each e-mail is assembled and sent at the right time for each customer. Results are reported in real time, through the Web.

- EchoMail/Direct Marketing, at *http://www.echomail.com*, is a direct marketing platform for managing mailing lists and executing outbound e-mail campaigns. EchoMail/DM also receives and responds to inbound e-mail responses from promotions and campaigns via an Internet e-mail address.

- HitBOX Tracker, at *http://www.hitbox.com/tracker*, is a free program that tracks and analyzes traffic to your site by providing over 125 real-time statistics. It tells who is visiting your site, when they visit, their technical capabilities, and where they're coming from.

- eXTReMe Tracking, at *http://www.extreme-dm.com,* is similar to the HitBOX one and is also a free program. You can see a working demo and access statistics of the Idea Station site by going to *http://www.ideastation.com/* and scrolling down to the very bottom of the page. Click on the graphic of the globe and read the detailed statistics.

- WebTrends Reports, at *http://www.webtrends.com,* is used by ISPs and hosting companies to give you detailed statistics of who is visiting your site.

- NetMarquee, at *http://www.netmarquee.com,* is an Internet direct marketing agency that integrates interactive content and database technology with direct response marketing techniques to offer clients a high level of response measurement and campaign optimization.

Cheat Sheet: Measuring Your Success

1. Set up a measurement system for each tactic included in your e-mail marketing plan. For example, gauge which has better results: your e-mail newsletter or your media alert e-mail.

2. Set up measurement tactics for each e-mail message that goes out.

3. Use the systems you set up as a way to test variables against your control group.

4. Track users using unique URLs, aliases, subscriber data, and inbound traffic.

5. Optimize your actions based on measurement data.

6. Track media efforts and results to gauge the success of your media efforts.

13

Opt-In List Brokering

If the prospect of taking the time to build a list makes you feel a little impatient and frustrated, then this is the chapter for you! There are companies out there who are in the business of helping you with this little problem. Opt-in list brokers build lists for you by collecting the names and e-mail addresses of consumers giving their permission for targeted offers. Here's how it works: You define the great deal that you want to offer (such as your free newsletter, or a trial use of your product, or a freebie off your site, or a free hour of your consulting time). If you want to spend the money to get a quick hit that is both effective and ethical, where you can simply send a note out to thousands of recipients who are willing to receive and read your message, consider an opt-in broker. The broker you choose absolutely must be an opt-in broker because you are not allowed to spam. (If you only take away one lesson from this book let it be this: DON'T SPAM!)

Companies built around the practice of seducing online consumers to give up their e-mail address and demographic information in return for plentiful offers are building a careful business around the practice of not spamming, but still mass e-mailing. They have their reputation firmly built around keeping the promise of sending only information that meets the requests of the consumer. Trust is a sacred thing with these companies. If you sell blue paint and a consumer has indicated an interest in special offers on green paint, there's no way you're going to be allowed to send your special blue paint offer to the green paint opt-in consumers. That is the difference between spam and opt-in list brokering.

This practice is catching on. eMarketer reports that opt-in e-mail will increase in volume by 52.3%, growing from 61.1 billion messages by year-end 2000 to 240 billion messages by 2003. Opt-in list brokers are companies that gather information from Internet consumers who give permission and state preferences. The brokers make their money by renting usage of their lists. Rather than giving you the names, however, they send your message to the targeted segment of their database. They will only send to those people who have asked to receive the type of offer you're making.

Reputable opt-in e-mail list brokers have built their reputation on honoring the requests of the people who have given up their e-mail addresses, so they will not allow you to have the names yourself and they will not send a message that is inappropriate. Brokers charge per address. While this is more costly than building your own list (called a house list), it is less time-consuming and easier. Using an opt-in list broker is best suited for periodic promotional campaigns, such as a seasonal special promotion.

One piece of advice: If you use a list broker, do it in conjunction with your own house list (meaning a list that you keep in your own database). The problem with using brokers is that you don't get to own the list, you pay for the one-time rental use of the list. This is as it should be, but you'll get more bang for your buck if you use the responses to a brokered list as a way to fatten up your own list as shown in Figure 13.1. Consider it a jumpstart!

Set Reasonable Goals

The response you get is only going to be as good as the offer you make. Assuming you pick a broker who uses ethical practices and cleans the list on a regular basis, the essential elements to your success will be your ability to make an offer with a clear benefit to readers and your commitment to following through on the offer. The most reasonable goal, and one that every e-mail marketer should have, is to build a one-to-one relationship with every person who receives

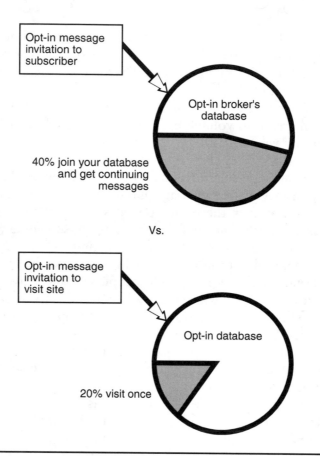

Figure 13.1. Drive opt-in e-mail customers to your database, not your site.

your message. The mechanisms to handle feedback are an essential tool for ensuring your success all the way through to the sale.

Measure your goal against your call to action and the worth of a new customer. For example, if your call to action is to encourage recipients to subscribe to your e-mail newsletter, consider what each subscriber is worth. One way to judge is if you sell advertising. If ads in your e-mail publication cost $80 CPM (which means you charge $80 for every 1,000 subscribers), then each subscriber is worth a total of $0.08 per issue. If you send 100 issues per year, each subscriber is worth $8 over the course of a year. So if you spend $1,600 for an opt-in list that goes to 8,000 people, at least 200 people need to subscribe for you to break even. This goal of a 2.5% response rate is where you should set your benchmark.

Opt-in e-mail tends to generate a better response than traditional direct mail. The reason is that list members are prequalified and self-selected. NetCreations estimates that a good response rate for a mailing is 2 to 5%, although they acknowledge that they've seen much higher.

Make Sure You Use a Reputable Broker

Pay close attention to what you're buying if you go to a list broker. The companies listed at the end of this chapter are a good place to start. All reputable brokers have the same characteristics in common: They can tell you where they got the names on the list, they won't actually hand the list over to you (they'll send on your behalf), and they'll monitor the messages that you send out to the list to ensure that you're complying with the wishes of the recipients.

One e-mail broker on the Internet even goes a step further, stating that they also fight spam in the courts. "Strike them hard and fast with no mercy, that's our method," boasts opt-in broker ReplyNet's Web site. "We are proud to be one of the handful of firms on the Internet that legally attacks any junk e-mailer that forges, performs any form of identity theft, or misuses any of our registered service or trade marks. We attack with lightening speed and powerful force to quickly put the offender into compliance or out of business."

If a company sells you a physical list of actual e-mail addresses and they relinquish these addresses to you for your use, it's different than renting a brokered list. If they give you a list of addresses and you e-mail all these people (regardless of what you send them or how long the message is), your message is spam, or at the very least unsolicited commercial e-mail (UCE). Don't work with firms that will give you the names. Only work with brokers that keep the names private and send the message for you.

Supposedly targeted lists of e-mail addresses are one of the Internet's biggest contributors to spam. Many of the e-mails sent to these list recipients are outright spam. However, many are innocent e-mail marketers uneducated in the rules of Netiquette who honestly bought lists thinking that the names on the list would welcome their message. They think they're e-mailing prospective customers. Instead, they're using a list built with harvesting software that strips addresses off Web sites, member directories, chat rooms, discussion list archives, and Usenet groups.

Don't buy lists based strictly on price. Reputable brokers might cost a little more in the beginning, but they will deliver more bang for your buck in the end. Spam lists are the most inexpensive ones on the Internet, but they're unethical and ineffective, so don't be tempted to run with what appears to be a great deal. These lists generate a hostile reaction that can be deadly to your company's online reputation. It can also cause severe technical problems for your servers.

The way it works is shown in Figure 13.2. Instead of honestly finding e-mail addresses of people who request to receive informa-

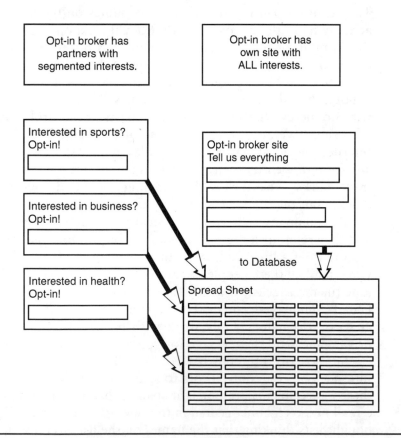

Figure 13.2. How opt-in brokers gather data.

tion, unethical bulk e-mail list builders go to a source such as a newsgroup about small business marketing strategies. They use software to strip the e-mail addresses automatically from every post (by taking every word with an "@" symbol in it) and add them to a list. Then these lists are sold. If you pay for one of these lists, you're probably under the impression that you're buying a list of names of people who are interested in products targeted at small business owners. This isn't necessarily true, and, regardless, these people haven't given you their permission to e-mail them.

Even if you were to manage to purchase a list that does truly include the names of people interested in your business opportunities, there's no way to verify this, given the growing numbers of people who aren't reputable and sell these harvested lists. The legitimate companies that offer opt-in lists don't give up that detailed information—ever! Instead, they send out the information on behalf of their clients. In essence, "renting" the list.

List brokers, such as PostMasterDirect.com (Figure 13.3), YesMail, and MyPoints, send your targeted e-mail for you. They won't give customers the opportunity to abuse the people whose e-mail

Figure 13.3. PostMasterDirect.com's home page.

addresses are contained in their databases. They don't sell the list, they rent a one-time use, ensuring quality control: Messages must fall within the confines of the information requested.

How Do Brokers Build a List?

The only legitimate e-mail lists are those that are generated when users choose to be included in a list on a particular topic and have the option of choosing to be excluded from the list at any time. Legitimate lists will fully disclose the list's commercial nature and where the information in the database was collected.

Brokers have a system of building lists that spreads their invitations far and wide. For a list to be truly opt-in, the subscriber has to ask to join. This means that opt-in brokers have to build a network that spreads across the entire Internet to bring users into their network of names. The invitation has to include full notification of what the subscriber is getting into when they hand over their address and permission. The invitation must include full disclosure of what data you are collecting from them and how you plan to use the information. For example, if the list broker asks them for their zip code and they request information on symphony concerts in their town, the broker will abuse that relationship by sending them announcements of rock concerts in neighboring cities or sales pitches for music stores in their town.

List brokers' subscribers will all have full choice about when and if they will start or stop receiving commercial messages. They can opt-out of the database at any time. Full access to their information will also be afforded to them, and they can check, modify, or delete their data at any time.

The process that an opt-in broker uses to get names into the database is this:

- List brokers set up a number of partner sites across the Web to invite new members into their opt-in database.

- A list member clicks through the partner site to go to the list broker's signup site.

- Members opt in to the list by going through a signup process and choosing which topics (what companies) they'd like to hear about.

- They continue the signup process, filling out demographic information that is of value to e-mail marketers.

- They receive a confirmation message via e-mail to authenticate their choice to join the list.

- They reply to the confirmation message, which officially adds their e-mail address to the broker's list.

Browse the Database and Target Your Message

Brokers don't just build one gigantic list. Instead, they build many small lists with specific opt-in offers. There may be two different lists under the Health category for alternative medicine. One, built by an opt-in broker site about special deals, may be specifically for offers of lower prices or freebies for alternative medicine-related products. The other might have been pulled from a medical information database, and these opt-in members just want targeted messages about alternative health news and developments. The broad categories are segmented into more specific subcategories. For example, list broker MatchLogic (Figure 13.4) offers "online shopping activities" through their DeliverE service. This means that the people who have filled out this form indicated that they were interested in messages related to online shopping activities. Further, within this category are subcategories that specify the types of online shopping activities the respondent is interested in. In this category are the following subcategories: insurance quotes, auctions, credit card rates, purchase gifts, grocery shopping, home insurance, life insurance, purchase books, purchase new or used computer equipment, purchase computer hardware, purchase computer software, purchase music, and purchase travel.

Some brokers, such as YesMail (Figure 13.5), will build the list for you and handle distribution and management of your campaign. Some, such as NetCreations, will let you do most of the work your-

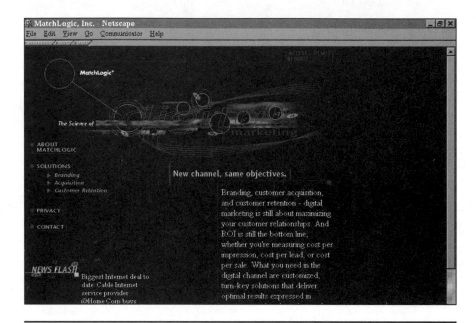

Figure 13.4. MatchLogic, Inc.'s home page.

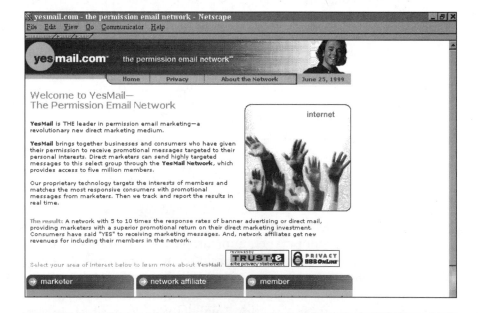

Figure 13.5. YesMail's home page.

self using their Web interface. Either way, the process is the same: You can choose certain categories based on the preferences of the people in the list and then send your message to them through the bulk e-mail program.

Focus on the quality, not the quantity, of the list that you send to. Target specialized groups and tailor your message to speak directly to them. Be careful about who you send to, defining the precise market that will respond to your offer. Remember that you just have one use of the opt-in broker's list, but once the recipient responds directly to you, you own their name. Keep track of which segments respond to you, and you'll be able to minimize your expenses while fattening up your database. Another list broker and one-to-one integrated marketing firm, Gamesville.com, offers direct e-mail to their very focused niche of entertainment-related products. Their niche contains 500,000 opt-in names and has been used for promotional mailings from companies like uBid (an auction site) and Music Boulevard/ CDNOW (an online CD retailer).

Your Offer

Consumers expect traditional direct mail and slick magazine advertisements to be colorful, entertaining, beautiful, and professional. On the Internet, consumers expect direct e-mail to be personal and customized. It's still important that your message focus on the benefits of your product, just as with traditional direct mail, and that a powerful call to action be included.

Short, quick messages are the most compelling. Your copy strategy should give a concise and clear pitch for your product. Keep your message under one screen of text or the end won't get read (there's actually less chance that the beginning will get read as well). Stick to one offer per e-mailing. Don't worry about giving people every last detail about your offer, because if they're interested in the surface offer, they'll contact you for the whole scoop.

But the message should not be too quick! While that call to action needs to be clear and direct, it needs to be thorough. Don't pussyfoot around with instructions for their next step or you might lose them. Don't be so vague with the first step, which might just be "Visit our site for details," that they never get to the second step, which might be instructions on the site saying, "Click this button to download our product." Instead, give them all the instructions they need in the e-mail: "Collect on this offer by going to our site, signing up for our program, and downloading your free copy of XYZ 2.0 today!"

Respect the fact that your recipients are busy and their time for your particular message is short. To get them to open your message, you want to hit them right away with your clear offer in a quick, understandable subject line. If your call to action includes a free, discount, or limited-time offer, it's more likely to generate response.

Not too long, not too short, not too much, not too little...writing the perfect offer is a little like Goldilocks trying to find a comfy bed at the three bears' house! Some more guidelines to follow are these:

- Make sure that the message you send out has substance. It must compel people to take action. Don't sound like a brochure!

- Don't recycle traditional direct marketing copy, such as the copy your ad agency produced for your last postal campaign, and use it again in your e-mail campaign. The Internet is a different medium, and the strategies that work offline don't necessarily work online.

- Time is precious, so get your important point in at the very beginning and then wrap it up right away. Several pages of text doesn't work in e-mail.

- Since there's some urgency about getting to the point, be upfront about what you're telling them. Don't make recipients have to figure out for themselves what you're talking about.

- Give people a reason to act on this very message. The reason must go above and beyond your everyday unique selling position (USP) to make something special about this message.

- End with a call to action.

The format of the message you send is an important component as well. There are several different pieces of your e-mail, and these should be tested and tracked after executions are carefully considered. First, your subject line is equivalent to your headline. Fill it with an enticing message that will encourage recipients to open it up. Second, the message itself can be tailored to different segments of your audience through split-run tests or tailored to split-run campaigns to pull the highest response.

Create Your Response System

You probably won't close the sale based on the-mailing alone. Be prepared to have the e-mail act as the first step in the sales process and the ongoing questions and answers as the rest of the steps. Be prepared to respond right away to leads generated by your mailing. Set up systems to prioritize leads and ensure *your* quick response to them (more about customer service automation systems is found in Chapter 6).

Be prepared to be flamed. Even with a 100% opt-in list, people forget what they've signed up for. It's just the nature of the Internet. Your offer might rub them the wrong way, even if they've chosen to receive offers just like yours. The percentage of people who will respond negatively will probably be very small, and it is up to you to be gracious and helpful in your response to them. Simply explain that they opted in, that you will take their name off the list, and that you apologize for the inconvenience.

Optimize

Keeping in mind reasonable expectations, e-mail marketing has the potential to deliver a higher ROI (return on investment) than any other medium. By measuring your results, you can continuously send test messages, measure results, analyze those results, focus on the most successful option, and re-send your message, tailoring your results to the most recent findings. Working in conjunction with your list broker, you can continue this process until you've come up with the most successful campaign possible.

For example, YesMail has a product called eCampaign that is designed to automate this optimization step of your e-mail marketing program. eCampaign works in conjunction with their proprietary tracking program to define a series of possible responses to an e-mail that is sent. Based on whether or not a recipient takes an action that is offered, a follow-up is triggered to send automatically. If a company sends an e-mail that encourages people to visit their site to learn about a new product, eCampaign sends an automatic thank you note to all those people who visit the site, excluding the people who ultimately bought the product on that first visit. Then, you want to send a message to the segment of the population who went for a second visit but still didn't buy, using a pricing strategy to send a special offer that offers a discount if they buy before a certain deadline.

Use the same decision trees and response mechanisms to follow through with your own list as a way to make the sale with interested prospects who just need a little extra handholding or a push to make the purchase.

Repeat the Offer

Be persistent. If you're on a tight budget, consider placing your e-mail marketing dollars somewhere else, because it takes several messages to pull results. As the number of messages sent out to opt-in lists increases, the effectiveness will decrease, although it will continue to deliver an excellent ROI, making a cost-effective tool. E-mail is only going to increase in popularity. As a result, consumers will have less time to open, read, and act on every offer.

This is why it's so important to send repeated offers to the same group, to ensure that they see and participate in the offer. You need to put your offer in front of recipients enough times that they will finally act on the offer.

Case Study: Holiday Inn (Bass Hotels)

Holiday Inn ran an opt-in e-mail campaign through YesMail.com during the fourth quarter of 1999. Their offers ran the gamut from "Get a Second Night Free" to "Save 40% off Rooms" to "Kids Stay/Eat Free." Their goals were simply to sell more rooms through their Web site.

On November 30, 1999, they sent 10,000 e-mails (costing $2,000) and achieved an 11.69% unique response, costing them $1.71 per click. The subject line read: "Free Second Night at Holiday Inn!"

Clever copy helped them get their message across. The Second Night Free message included the following wording: "They say the best things in life are free. At Holiday Inn® we agree, and in our attempt to continue that trend, we are giving away FREE nights at participating locations."

Derek Vannostran, the Internet marketing professional who worked on this campaign, gave his advice that it's important to "keep things simple when sending a message. The less options given to the recipient, the better results that were pulled." Holiday's Inn's first copy attempt stressed that recipients could get prices "as low as." The second copy attempt, which pulled better results, listed prices in several cities. The last, and best, copy attempt simply listed one city and one price, which drove recipients to the site to look up prices in the city they were interested in. "People saw a good deal in a major city," said Vannostran of the campaign, "and they want to look up pricing for the city that they're interested in."

Resources

- The Direct E-mail List Source, at *http://www.copywriter.com/lists*, develops lists that are compiled on a voluntary basis. Recipients of the e-mail messages must state that they are willing to receive commercial e-mail advertising messages.

- ReplyNet Solicited E-mailing Services, at *http://www.replynet.com/*, offers brokered list services for $59 per month that entitle you to 50,000 pieces per month. Customers can access and revise their lists via e-mail.

- NetCreations, at *http://www.netcreations.com*, is a network of sites that collects names and preferences from audiences on the Net. Their lists cover topics including Internet Business, Internet E-Commerce and Web Advertising. PostMasterDirect, at *http://www.postmasterdirect.com*, is a NetCreations service that rents use of the names on these lists for clients such as Cybershop, USWeb/CKS, O'Reilly, J. Crew, and Perseus. Lists cost $0.20 to $0.25 per name, with a $400 minimum purchase.

- DeliverE by MatchLogic, at *http://www.DeliverE.com*, rents opt-in lists and offers e-mail list management and database services.

Cheat Sheet: Using Opt-In Brokers to Reach a New Audience

1. Set goals for your opt-in campaign by first determining your break-even point. The offer you're going to make needs to elicit some measurable response from your audience. Your goal should include the number of people who have to act on your message in order for it to be effective. What response do you *have* to see to make the campaign cost-effective?

2. Do your homework to find a reputable list broker. Make sure that the list that you buy is 100% opt-in. Check first with other customers. Then decide if you want to write and send yourself, using a Web interface, or if you want to have the broker handle this for you. What level of marketing advice do you need?

3. Browse through the different categories and finely segmented lists to find which markets are available and how large the databases are. To ensure that you pinpoint the precise demographic audience you need to reach, be very thorough in checking out the sites that collected the data that fills the list you will send to. To ensure a high response rate, make sure to tailor the offering to the recipients.

4. Write a compelling offer. Make sure that you pay special attention to the subject line to make sure that they open the message. Then consider your copy strategy, making sure that it holds appeal. Keep your message format and length appropriate to the medium.

5. Get your customer service system in place to make sure that the respondents to your message are not left waiting and won-

dering if you really care to make a sale. Make them feel important and glad that they wrote to your company.

6. Segment your market to randomly test different executions. Track the results carefully.

7. Optimize your campaign based on what each test or each e-mailing tells you.

8. Repeat the offer as often as you can afford to.

14

Worksheets

Building a Plan...One Step at a Time

Planning is essential in all marketing endeavors, and e-mail marketing is no different. For a streamlined and effective use of e-mail marketing, build a plan that starts with an outline of what you'd like to happen (think in terms of how you would define the "perfect" subscriber.) How many subscribers do you plan to have? What is the dollar amount that you're expecting to make per issue? What exact action would you like your audience to take? These are the questions to address before you launch your email marketing publication.

Now you are in a position to plan your strategy, which integrates the tools at your disposal. The last step, which makes it possible to build constant improvement, is to measure your results. E-mail marketing adds immediacy to your plan by letting you tailor your tools as soon as you get results. An e-mail marketing plan serves several purposes:

1. It identifies where you are going. Your first step, making a list of what you want to accomplish, should be the heart and soul of your plan, which simply states the steps you'll take to get there. This plan serves as a beacon when you get off track, pulling you back on course.

2. It helps you communicate your goal and the path you're going to take to reach everyone involved. You'll undoubtedly have some help along the way from vendors, employees, technical gurus, and—never forget—your audience. Your plan helps them help you.

3. It motivates you to continue. Stopping a plan that isn't successful on step 2 never lets you see the big payoff after step 6. The plan will give you the roadmap and motivation to see it through to success.

The following steps will help you put together your plan using the worksheets at the end of the chapter. Throughout, we'll show you examples of a plan in action through a sample campaign for a company, The Inside Track, Inc. *(http://www.theinsidetrackinc.com)*, which facilitates and brokers the relationship between vendors and exhibitors in the trade show industry. The company works for exhibitors for free, earning a commission from vendors, who pay a commission for the role that The Inside Track plays to make a sale for them. Because The Inside Track has such an intimate knowledge of the needs of exhibitors, and such strong relationships with vendors (who appreciate their timely and no-maintenance service), they are a welcome partner to any overworked or understaffed company exhibiting at a trade show. Their challenge is to publicize the free service that they offer.

As you work through this chapter and write down ideas for your own e-mail marketing plan, follow along the development of The Inside Track's example e-mail marketing plan to see a viable implementation of the ideas presented in this book. Be thinking as you read this! How can you implement similar tools on your company's site? This step-by-step plan will get you off and running.

Step 1: Define Your Audience

Your first step is to make a list of the characteristics that describe your ideal customer. Be specific about this person's age range, gender, buying habits, income, education level, family, lifestyle, values, and whatever else is important for defining this individual. Then make a list of all the interests of a similar group of consumers who fall into that demographic. What are the topics that interest them? Are they frequent purchasers? Big purchasers? What events are happening in their lives?

Here's an example: The Inside Track's clients are trade show exhibitors and meeting planners of all sizes, from those that work for big corporations with million-dollar trade show budgets to smaller companies in which the trade show exhibit manager is also in charge of other marketing functions (such as Internet marketing, in which case they're sure to be online, subscribing to discussion lists). The following list describes this market:

- Middle- to upper-manager-level positions.

- They are sales and marketing savvy, although they're not as Internet-marketing savvy.

- Age is usually 30 and older.

- The group divided almost evenly between men and women, although leaning toward more women.

- They use computers, although only about 50% of their time is spent using one.

- A growing percentage are getting online every day.

- They travel frequently.

- They tend to be very budget conscious, although they need quality material.

- They expect results from a show and need to impact their bottom line with every marketing dollar spent.

- They work for larger organizations, with a minimum of 100 employees.

- They have a myriad of responsibilities. Managing a company's trade show efforts is often just a part of a trade show manager's larger role at their organization.

As a result of this analysis, The Inside Track has decided to target upper-level marketing and trade show executives at Fortune 1000 companies. They also see a secondary target market: exhibit houses. Exhibit houses are the companies that build custom displays and booths for companies that are going to exhibit at trade shows. They are often the first stop in an exhibit manager's process of putting together a program. Building a relationship with these companies would make them good sources of leads for The Inside Track. What is your secondary target market and how can you educate and build relationships with them?

Step 2: What Action Do You Want Your Audience To Take?

If you could ask them to do something, what would it be? Make a list of what you want them to do, starting with the obvious: to become your lifelong customer. Now take it further: to refer you to others, to subscribe to your e-mail newsletter, to download your software, to bookmark your site, to add a link from your site to theirs, to sell more to existing clients, to get more information about prospects.

For example, The Inside Track would like to create awareness across all their target audience categories in order to build a database, and then to build relationships with these groups so that when they're ready to plan for their next trade show, they will come to The Inside Track for help. On their site, The Inside Track will have one general signup that gets people logged into their database. The call will be to get great offers and valuable information. Prospects will self-select themselves as one of the following: exhibitor, exhibit house, trade show vendor, or trade show industry writer. The Inside Track will use this demographic information to create special targeted offers for different segments of their market. In addition, they will offer different options to their audience about what they would like to receive: e-mail newsletters, e-mail discussion lists, announcements, or press releases. Finally, users will have the option of self-selecting which shows they will be attending, allowing further customization of content.

Step 3: Develop a Strategy for Each Objective

Each of the different tools described in the previous chapters of this book can be tailored to fit the marketing needs of your company. Determining which strategies will be employed to meet your objective is the hardest and most important part of your e-mail marketing plan. While the objectives have described what you need to accomplish, these strategies explain how you're going to make things happen. This part of the plan requires good old brainstorming: tossing around and tossing out ideas and possibilities until the most feasible, logical, and workable strategies present themselves. Use the appendix to jog your creativity as you determine which strategies to employ.

As you consider what tools to employ, here are some different types of strategies that you might want to consider:

- *Market Share Strategy*. Will you go after a competitor or work to build the entire industry? The latter works best for new technology companies on the Internet, where the consumer market needs to be educated on a broad level before they start considering individual companies or vendors.

- *Geographic Strategies*. Can you go after a certain geographic segment of the market on a national, regional, or local level?

- *Seasonal Strategies*. Does your product or service have up and down times in the sales cycle? Are there opportunities to take advantage of holidays or other time-sensitive events?

- *Personality Strategies*. Are you your brand, or does your company have someone who represents the brand of your company?

- *Niche Strategies*. Does one segment of your market stand out as having a large possible user base for you? Can you exploit this opportunity?

Here's an example: The Inside Track will use the database on its site as a central part of its e-mail marketing plan. In addition, proprietor Dave Sterne has created a signature file that promotes his service and invites people to visit his site for free trade show services.

- Their primary goal will be to send regular monthly mailings of an e-mail newsletter covering all aspects of the market to everyone in the database. Members who indicate which shows they will attend will receive a customized article seamlessly inserted into each standard newsletter, but tailored to the show they will be attending. The show-centric e-mail marketing campaign continues with short "show alerts" sent during the following three weeks, leading up to a final one with a subject line that reads "See you on the show floor." To all of the people who receive this message who are currently clients, it will express The Inside Track's eagerness to have a successful show. For all others, the message will encourage them to set up a face-to-face appointment to meet with an Inside Track representative at the show, enabling them to make a pitch for the following show. Finally, every newsletter will include a feedback mechanism, whereby recipients are encouraged through incentives to respond to a demographic survey so that The Inside Track can learn more about their preferences.

- The company will focus on its exhibit house market with a second monthly e-mail, Trade Show Marketing, that includes statistics- and tips-filled professionally written articles intended to help the exhibit house market to exhibitors. The information will pull information from the demographic survey that goes out to the audience listed above. Other than the fact that the e-mail is generated by The Inside Track, each personalized piece will be free of blatant advertising messages. The goal is simply to solidify the trusting relationship that the company wishes to build with prospects.

- A weekly discussion list will be sent to vendors and exhibitors. The goal is to moderate a discussion between these two groups in order to position The Inside Track as a broker and as the expert insider. Both parties will come to recognize The Inside Track's very important and time-saving role as middleman.

- An autoresponder program will be set up to automate the following pieces of information:

  - Order forms for each vendor that The Inside Track uses.

    – A list of testimonials from satisfied customers. This will also include contact information for references so that interested prospects can contact existing clients.

    – A To-Do checklist for exhibitors. If exhibitors forget anything on the list, they can check what they still need and e-mail or fax it back to The Inside Track for a follow-up phone call.

- Since the business takes so much time and the owner of The Inside Track feels that the online networking component of the plan needs to be done personally, he has chosen to only participate in one list, and to do so on a limited basis. He has picked the list trade-show-international, sponsored by the Association for International Business (Figure 14.1). The list's purpose is given as "discussion, mentoring, sharing tips, tricks & solving problems, international trade show reports and co-

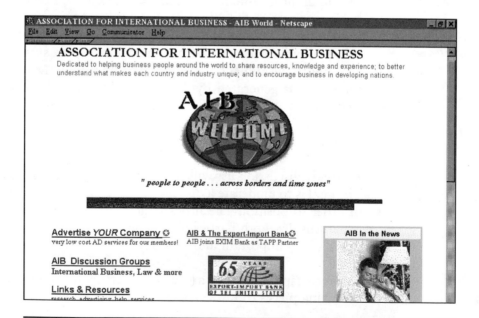

Figure 14.1. Association for International Business' discussion list.

operative collection of actual onsite catalogs/brochures at trade fairs around the world." His goal is to post two public message per month to the list and to make at least one private introduction per month.

- Sterne will have two different e-mail addresses so that tracking results will be easier (simple to do when you own your own domain): *dsterne@theinsidetrackinc.com* and *dave@theinsidetrackinc.com*. The first will be his public address, the second his private. His public address will actually be copied to a customer relations assistant, whose job it is to take care of every incoming e-mail that she can handle herself. Most of these are answering general questions about how the service works, directing prospects to the various e-mail resources available, scheduling meetings at upcoming shows between Sterne and prospects, and printing out hot leads for Sterne to use to make follow-up calls.

- The Inside Track will run a series of test ads in e-mail publications across a variety of subjects that could reach its target market to find out which markets are better fits for its e-mail offerings. Each ad will encourage respondents to enter their database. Ads will be placed in the following e-mail newsletters:

  - Marketing Tip of the Day (daily marketing instructional guide)

  - Event Management (special event and exhibit management)

  - Tradeshow Listserver (a list hosted by the UNLV Tourism and Convention Administration Department)

- After the trade show season ends, The Inside Track will look at results of its current e-mail marketing campaign. At this point, they'll reconsider using a brokered list to launch a direct e-mail campaign inviting people to join their discussion list and e-mail newsletter list. They'll also look into other e-mail publications and consider placing text ads in publications that reach their desired target audience.

Because the initial goal for this e-mail marketing campaign is simply to raise awareness and announce their service, they don't want to do too much at the beginning. Additionally, they don't have the customer service resources in place to handle the response that a full campaign will produce. Using the test—track—measure—optimize model, they will wait until the campaign is in progress for second-phase planning.

Step 4: Quantify Your Objectives

Step 4 takes step 2 further. For each objective, add a quantifiable objective. According to several experts, e-mail marketing should seek to achieve a 6% to 12% response rate. If your message is effectively targeted to the market you defined in step 1, you should expect even higher results.

For example, The Inside Track expects to see the following results:

- The e-mail newsletter should achieve a 10% click-through rate on each issue.

- The discussion list should achieve discussion of at least three questions a week from the audience of exhibitors, to be answered by vendors on the list.

- The exhibitor brief should generate at least three phone calls and new leads per month.

- The goal is to add 200 new names to the database each month.

Step 5: Write Copy

Copy is probably the single most important element of your campaign, because it is the way you communicate with potential or current consumers. Copy is also the easiest component to tailor.

Copywriting is what makes your offer soar or fall flat. Your creative strategy should include building a relationship, making your offer irresistible, and, of course, popping the question: Ask them to do something (the call to action). The offer must promise results: to make them more effective, smarter, faster, quicker, happier, richer, or whatever it is that your product does.

For example,

- The Inside Track will use a combination of in-house and outsourced writers for their tactics.

- The tone of the e-mail newsletter will be very professional and authoritative, but at the same time, friendly. Articles are going to be professionally produced by business writers and public relations departments at the vendor companies with whom The Inside Track does business. In addition, reviews of certain towns that will be hosting trade shows will be sent to the segments that indicate which shows they'll be attending.

- The exhibit house e-mail will be a brief, almost report-like article that summarizes results of the database marketing and survey endeavors, along with an analysis of the marketing activities that these results indicate exhibit houses should take to better serve their customers.

- The weekly discussion list will be friendly, informal and not at all threatening to the reader. The identity of participants can be cloaked or public, and vendors will be prohibited from

---

Time/Contact Management Trick—Use Filters

Use filters to automatically put e-mails into mailboxes. Don't put anything off, though. Create a system where you take care of the message when you receive it, delete the message, forward it on to someone else to take care of, or put it on your schedule.

selling through this vehicle. The overarching goal is to be helpful to exhibitors, solidifying the relationship between them and The Inside Track.

- The articles in the autoresponders will be outsourced to professional writers. The other information will be provided by vendors.

- The ads will focus on pulling traffic to the site based on a number of offers for free information and services from The Inside Track.

Step 6: Develop a Schedule

The timeline for your marketing plan should be set up on a calendar so that you can look at the entire campaign at a glance. This helps you visualize what activities will be taking place at one time, what audiences are being reached, and what seasonal opportunities you are taking advantage of.

For example, The Inside Track has set up a calendar to take advantage of downtime in the trade show industry and keeps a top-of-mind presence so that companies will remember to include The Inside Track in their planning. Their schedule is shown in Figure 14.2.

Step 7: Test

E-mail marketing can let you take baby steps for little cost. Remember to send several versions to smaller segments of your market, testing different variables with different versions. Use this data to figure out what works best for your market so that you can optimize activities in your e-mail marketing efforts when you run a particular strategy at full speed.

For example, for the advertising campaign that The Inside Track places in their three test e-mail publications, Marketing Tip of the Day, Event Management, and Tradeshow Listserver, the publishers will split their database and test different executions against each segment. The Inside Track will run a total of 12 ads across five months and three

	Jan	Feb	March	April	May	June	July	Aug	Sept	Oct	Nov	Dec
		Monthly Newsletter										
			Weekly Discussion List									
	Three special announcements for upcoming (March) show											
			Three special announcements for upcoming (May) show									
					Three special announcements for upcoming (June) show							
							Split-audience e-pub ad campaign runs in Pub. # 1					
								Split-audience e-pub ad campaign runs in Pub. # 2				
									Split-audience e-pub ad campaign runs in Pub. # 3			
												Full-scale e-pub ad campaign begins
	Press Release		Press Release		Press Release		Press Release		Press Release		Press Release	

Figure 14.2. Sample schedule for The Inside Track.

publications, with an offer and a different trackable URL in each. They will measure which three advertisements pull the highest results, then will run those ads in several more expensive e-mail newsletters.

Step 8: Measure

Measurement is an important element for determining the next steps to your campaign. It tells you if you were able to meet your objectives, if you were able to meet your budget, and if you exceeded the break-even point, and it lets you determine objectives for the next phase of the campaign.

In the end, Figure 14.3 shows what The Inside Track's entire year-long e-mail marketing campaign looked like. For each of the tools used and for each of the goals set, The Inside Track has set up both trackable URLs and autoresponders. They also will chart the increase in traffic to their site and the number of members in their database.

Questionnaire: Building Your Plan

1. Who are you targeting?

2. What benefit does your product offer to your audience?

3. Which media will you use to acquire the target niche's audience?

4. How much does it cost to acquire a customer (to determine your budget)?

5. What is your current business focus and overall strategy?

6. Who will be responsible for carrying out the execution of the plan?

Figures 14.4 and 14.5 on page 270–271 are provided for you to fill in the details of your own schedule and plan.

Tool	Goal	Frequency	Time	Actual Cost
E-mail newsletter	Regular communications with several audiences	Monthly	3 hours per issue (review, compile, send)	$1,600 per issue (writing & listhosting)
Discussion list	Facilitate discussion between vendors and exhibitors in order to brand trade show expertise	Compiled weekly, but messages go out post-by-post throughout the week	15 minutes per day	$100 per month hosting
Online networking	Build name recognition and personal relationships	Monthly	1 hour per week	$0
Special preshow announcements	Boost personal relationships through show opportunities	Prior to each show that The Inside Track attends	4 hours (write promo, buy list)	$3,000 opt-in list rental
Customer service	Make sure that each and every incoming e-mail is responded to	Daily	20 hours per week	$200 per week to part-time customer service represent-ative
Signature file	Sales opportunity	With every e-mail	0	$0

Figure 14.3. Overall plan for The Inside Track.

Jan	Feb	March	April	May	June	July	Aug	Sept	Oct	Nov	Dec

Figure 14.4. Blank schedule.

Tool	Goal	Frequency	Time	Actual Cost

Figure 14.5. Blank overall plan.

15

Top Twenty E-Mail Publications

Top Twenty...For Now!

It's hardly fair to compose a "Top Twenty" list with all the wonderful e-mail newsletters out there. Consider this a list of 20 leading favorites at press time. If you think your list (or a list that you subscribe to) is better, I encourage you to write to me at *shannard@hotmail.com* and see if the list you like makes it into the next edition of "Marketing With E-mail: A Spam-Free Guide." This interaction with you, the reader, is the very essence of what e-mail marketing is all about! Subscribe to these publications and use them as models for what might work in your own e-mail publication. Nominations from marketing experts, combined with my own suggestions of lists that are doing a really great job at e-mail marketing and e-mail publishing are included in the following list along with explanations of what and why these are the best e-mail publications on the market today.

Criteria

There are quite a few different qualities that make a list a "recommended" list. While the themes listed here were recurring for many of the lists that were chosen for this chapter—remember that rules can be broken. Take the following list and think about the creative ways that you can apply them to your list. Keep your audience in mind as you read this list.

Above all, focus on building a relationship with your audience. Each of these e-mail publications chosen for this recommended list focuses on the information needs of its audience. So, too, should the e-mail publication that you create. Focus on their desires (great information) and what follows will meet your own desires (more sales).

Personality

"Hiya! Howya doin' buddy? What's new with you? Oh, that's great! What's new with me, you ask? Oh, a few things. Didja see the new thingamabob out on the market? Oh, well here's the scoop! By the way, I saw an article that made me think of you! Here it is in my pocket. I clipped it for you."

Don't you just love those friends or business associates of yours who treat you like the center of the universe? They're considerate, compassionate, friendly, even a little self-effacing. But they're so darn knowledgeable about stuff! And to help you become smarter about your industry or hobby, they drill right down to the facts you need to know, then they tell you.

Publishers who put on a public face of gregarious expertise are wildly popular. They take to heart mass e-mail's ability to build a community between them and their readers. It's the number one thing that will keep readers interested in and subscribed to an e-mail newsletter.

Profitability

These publications might not be directly profitable, but that's because most of them don't exist in a vacuum. They're part of their parent organization or publisher's wider, grander picture of marketing. These publishers view their e-mail newsletters or discussion lists as the handshake component of their overall marketing plan.

Profitability, in this instance, means that the publications increase the overall profitability of the entire sales cycle: by encouraging purchase, branding a name, reminding a prospect, motivating an inactive customer to get active, reinforcing client purchase decisions, reducing the costs of customer relations, and other end results that contribute to the bottom line. Of course, they might also just be downright profitable: selling a ton of ad sponsorships and generating a steady stream of revenue.

Circulation

With discussion lists, the higher-circulation publications tend to have more active, more expert debates and discussions. This usually contributes to the value of the publication for recipients. Similarly, for e-mail newsletters, higher circulation can result in higher priority in the grand market in the e-mail marketer's mind. If you consider that your publication goes out to 2,000 vs. 600 subscribers, you might place more importance on it as a marketing tool.

However, since most publishers target a niche, some publications might have a maximum possible user base that is lower than a publication with a bigger user base. So a high circulation number is considered in the context of percentage of their possible market, not just straight numbers. One publication might target the wide universe of all mothers, while another might only target mothers of twins or of a certain age group.

Appeal

Some e-mail publications are just subscribed to by everyone. They appeal to a widely dispersed audience: business, personal, young, and old. Some e-mail publications appeal to a particular market segment, but they are useful (and therefore popular) with every consumer in that market segment. These publishers place a high priority on user feedback and use it to make adjustments and maintain their popularity among recipients.

The best lists available are popular because they focus on building relationships and they take their sweet time doing it. They work in over the long term, step-by-step, taking the time and making the effort to earn their popularity. They solve problems on a regular basis for subscribers.

Format

A publication can have great content and be really difficult to read. Great publishers take into account not just the HTML vs. text e-mail issue, but the actual layout, byte size, and presentation of their publication. Formatting can contribute to the response rates of a publication. It definitely contributes to whether or not these publications are recommended and forwarded to others.

Some publishers create three versions: text, HTML and America Online. Consider, instead, creating one text version with a useful table of contents and well-delineated sections.

Consistency

Being dependable is a big deal. Publishers that deliver information on a regular schedule, with a familiar voice, a predictable execution, and an uncomplicated call to action will find that users appreciate the publication and are more apt to recommend it to others.

Not all lists fall into all of these categories, they might just do one very well. Heck, they might even break a rule (well, not the sacred no-spam rule!) or buck a recommendation from this book. That might be what makes them so special. But something makes them stand out among the e-mail marketing crowd as being exemplary of doing it right—right in the minds of their subscribers, who anxiously await each issue.

The List

If you disagree with any of these listed, let me know! This is just a snapshot of what's available and in my circle of knowledge at the time of writing this book. The current, up-to-the-minute list is on the Web site. Nominate your favorite (but if it yours or a client's you'll have to be extra convincing) by writing to me at *shannard@hotmail.com.*

1. Sales Horror Stories

This newsletter of sales horror stories (see Figure 15.1) is written by a professional sales coach, Dan Seidman, who credits his newsletter with helping him gain publicity in such magazines as *Selling Power Magazine*, *Sales and Marketing Management*, and *Sales Force Automation*, as well as speaking engagements and a book deal.

To subscribe, send an e-mail to *salesautopsy@listhost.net* with "subscribe" in the body.

2. Internet-Sales

Internet-Sales (see Figure 15.2) stands out because it is one of the lists that set the standard for all other lists to follow. Since November 1995, the Internet-Sales Discussion List has been providing Internet professionals with a forum for meaningful and helpful discussion of online sales issues by those engaged in the online sale of products and

Figure 15.1. Sales horror stories.

Figure 15.2. Internet-Sales Discussion List's home page.

services. The list is moderated by John Audette, president of Multimedia Marketing Group, who strives to "keep the signal-to-noise ratio as high as possible," meaning that his moderating style weeds out anything promotional, to keep copy informative and helpful for subscribers.

The Internet-Sales community is currently comprised of over 13,000 subscribers from more than 70 countries. The Internet-Sales Digest is published daily, Monday through Friday, and has been one of the driving forces in building Multimedia Marketing Group over the years by building both credibility and visibility. To subscribe, send an e-mail to *join-i-sales@list.mmgco.com*.

3. Powerquotes

Get inspired every morning by Kevin Eikenberry of Discian Learning Services (Figure 15.3), who does more than simply send a powerful quote each day to his subscriber base. He follows up the quote with questions to help readers figure out how (and why) to improve their lives, their outlooks, and their inner spirits. To subscribe, go to *http://www.discian.com*.

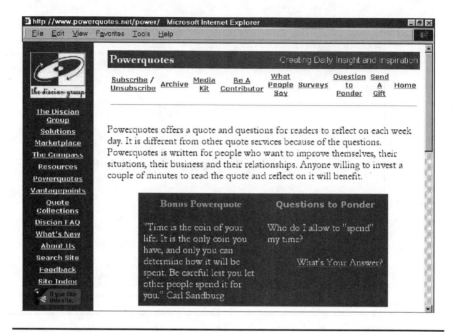

Figure 15.3. Discian Learning Services sends daily Powerquotes to help readers figure out how (and why) to improve.

4. Trivia Time

Shagmail, the groovy-baby e-mail publications featuring Austin Powers himself, offers one e-mail newsletter called Trivia Time (Figure 15.4). You'll be all prepped to be a contestant on "Jeopardy" or "Who Wants To Be a Millionaire" because, having subscribed to this newsletter, you'll know important things such as the fact that "chemist Earl D. Tupper invented Tupperware in 1942." Supported by advertisers, the flip side is a shagadelic affiliate program where you can earn $.07 for every subscriber you refer to the company. To subscribe, visit *http://www.shagmail.com/sample/trivia.html*.

5. LinkExchange Daily Digest, by MSN LinkExchange

MSN LinkExchange is one of the Internet's premiere resources for small business owners, offering their banner ad exchange network to help Web site owners increase traffic. Adam Audette expertly moder-

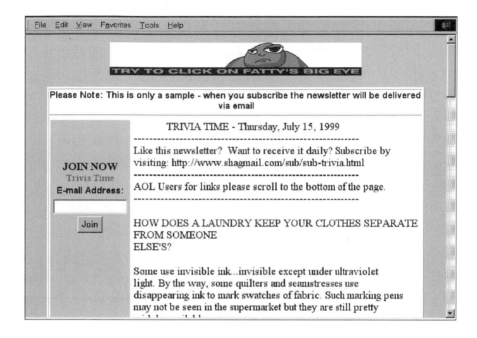

Figure 15.4.   Shagmail provides specialized sites like TriviaTime for the entertainment of its subscribers.

ates the company's daily e-mail discussion list (see Figure 15.5) with a large and active subscriber base. The novice- to expert-filled audience is tuned in to the rapid changes of business operations on the Internet. This discussion is the bulk of each publication.

Additionally, the regular sections "Geek Tips" and "Bulletin Board" offer technical advice and networking opportunities for members. The discussion list is so popular, with such exposure for participants who land just one post, that there is sometimes a backlog of over two weeks' worth of quality posts. To subscribe, send an e-mail to *mailto:subscribe-digest@le-digest.com*.

6. Virtual Promote Gazette

A top example of making your publication popular by infusing it with personality is the VirtualPromote Gazette, published by Jim Wilson (Figure 15.6). Crammed with tools and free advice for online marketing professionals, readers such as Shel Horowitz of Frugal Fun

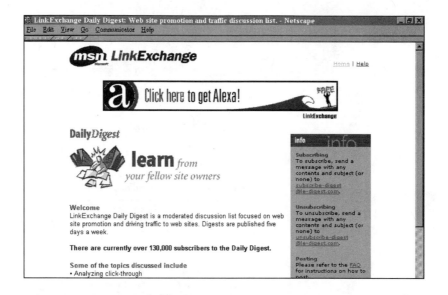

Figure 15.5.   LinkExchange Daily Digest's home page.

Figure 15.6.   VirtualPromote Gazette's home page.

(http://www.frugalfun.com) say that it's Jim's folksy opinions that make this publication one of the best on the Internet today. To subscribe, visit *http://www.virtualpromote.com.*

7. Web Informant by David Strom

If you're on the Web in any way—whether you're a marketing professional, politician, consumer, small business person, student or hobbyist, there's information in Web Informant that can help you be more efficient and effective in your online pursuits. Published almost weekly to 4,000 subscribers, this e-mail newsletter simply serves as a forum for the columnist's ideas. To subscribe, send a blank e-mail to *webinformant-subscribe@egroups.com.*

8. WebPromote Weekly, by WebPromote

A step above other online marketing newsletters, WebPromote Weekly (see Figure 15.7) offers professionally commissioned content from

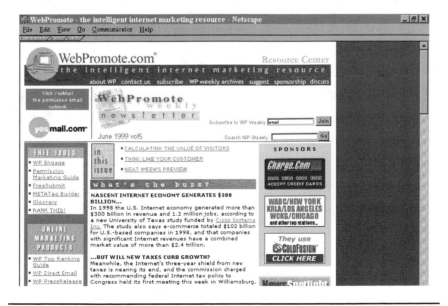

Figure 15.7. WebPromote's Weekly newsletter page.

contributing writers. It's chock-full of feature-length articles about all aspects of Internet marketing for businesses of all sizes, from one-man shops to Fortune 500 companies. This marketing newsletter has a subscriber base of over 400,000 Webmasters, Web publishers, marketing managers, and other Internet-savvy industry professionals who seek the pulse of Web site promotion. It is packed full of free information on the latest online promotion developments, opportunities, and tips to make your Web site more profitable and effective. Their searchable database of past issues is full of over two years' worth of articles. To subscribe, go to *http://www.webpromote.com*.

9. Dave's Daily Chuckle

Dave's Daily Chuckle by Dave Stone (Figure 15.8) currently boasts over 7,000 subscribers and generates advertising revenue for each issue. He says that his popular list, which sends subscribers a funny

Figure 15.8. Dave's Daily Chuckle home page.

(and clean) joke every day, is a hobby turned business, started one semester when he was still a college student. His hobby was to simply forward funny jokes to friends. The process turned into a time-consuming system of finding and forwarding jokes from a number of sources. He finally got organized and used eGroups to start his popular list, that started with only 150 subscribers. Growth, he says, required time and effort. He used ad swaps at first to grow subscriber numbers. Subscribe by sending a message to *daily_chuckle-subscribe@egroups.com.*

10. Geoff's Gems from Garage.com

This list (see Figure 15.9) is an excellent example of offering a downright valuable service that saves recipients a ton of time—Geoff does the work of sifting through publications for readers. He picks through the top online business publications and finds articles of interest to entrepreneurs and startups. Topics covered include stock market news, venture capital news, and technology business trends. Some recent

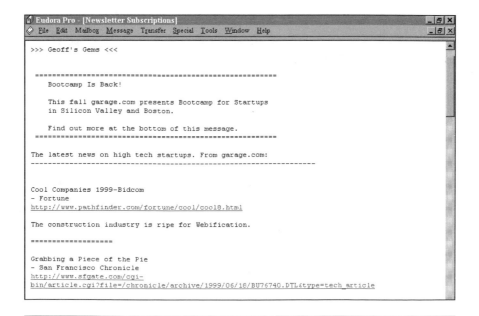

Figure 15.9.   Geoff's Gems from Garage.com.

articles were pulled from *Forbes ASAP*, *The Wall Street Journal*, *The Red Herring*, and *The San Jose Mercury News*. To subscribe, send a message to *geoffs_gems-on@lists.garage.com*.

11. Sparky's List-Tips

A comprehensive and valuable resource for e-mail marketers, Christopher "Sparky" Knight outlines instructions on running a discussion list or e-mail announcement, describing advanced issues with clarity that even the most novice list owner can understand (see Figure 15.10). The contents fall into the category of "tips, tricks, suggestions, secrets or resources that you can use to build, grow and maintain your list." To subscribe, send an e-mail to *join-list-tips@sparklist.com*.

12. What's the Word?

Look, there in your e-mail box, it's a bird, it's a plane, it's Emarketingman! Launched in May 2000 by an online marketing pro,

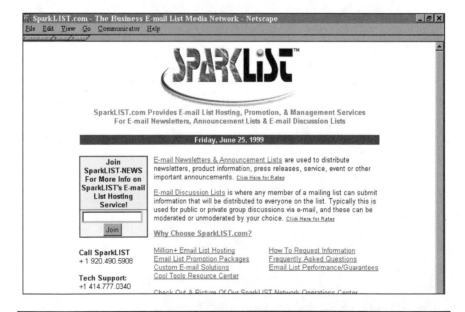

Figure 15.10. SparkLIST's home page.

Daryl Clark, the plain truth is that this monthly newsletter (Figure 15.11) covers all the things you need to know about marketing your online business and it does so clearly and concisely. Recent issues include search engines, tools for building a better Web site, marketing opportunities, affiliate programs and more (especially marketing with e-mail!). To subscribe, send an e-mail to *emarketingmansubscribe@topica.com*. This relatively new list doesn't boast a large number of subscribers at this time, but there is certainly a commitment to quality informative content. "My key focus for content has been to provide useful and current information that will excite others to take action to improve their online businesses," says Clark. "Part of that process is to continually improve my site and pass on what I learn to others. I like to call it excite, educate and entertain (not sell)."

13. SeraNova Perspectives

SeraNova Perspectives (Figure 15.12) is a useful combination of news from other sources, essays from in-house experts and information

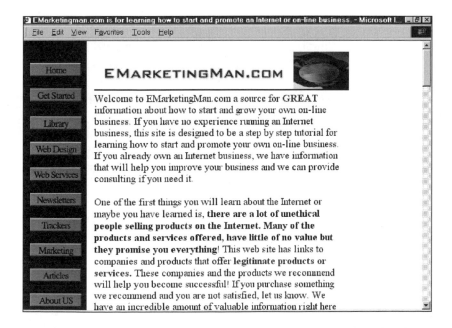

Figure 15.11. Emarketingman.com's home page.

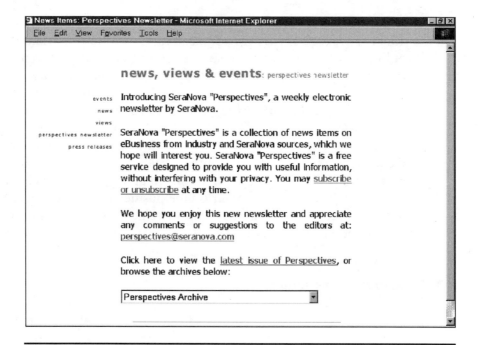

Figure 15.12. SeraNova Perspectives' home page.

about online business and e-commerce. Beyond presenting only technology industry news, this newsletter also takes a global approach to teaching readers about the broader reach of technology and how it can be used in a variety of industries. To subscribe, send an e-mail to *perspectives@seranova.com*.

14. I-ADVERTISING Discussion List, from Adam J. Boettiger, e/y/e/s/c/r/e/a/m Interactive, Inc.

Because it's true, this publication (see Figure 15.13) is billed as the Internet's definitive resource for information related to the Internet advertising industry. Another fine example of excellent moderation, this list manages to be a valuable resource for both the novice and the veteran advertising executive. Topics include news, resources, and information about the Internet advertising industry. In addition to the helpful discussion that Boettiger moderates, the list includes in-

Figure 15.13. I-Advertising's home page.

dustry job opportunities and announcements from list members. Subscribe at *http://www.internetadvertising.org*.

15. The MercialXpress Newsletter

It's time to learn about e-mail marketing from a technology standpoint, and this publication, while clearly marketing its own technology, will teach e-mail marketing newbies and experts alike about industry trends. They clearly cater to developers of their products, with software tips and information about rich content on the Internet. Their goal is to hit 30,000 subscribers by the end of the first year. To subscribe, go to *http://www.MercialXpress.com*.

16. List-Universe by SparkList

The dedication that the SparkLIST staff gives to it's List-Universe.com e-mail publishing industry daily newsletter (Figure 15.14) results in

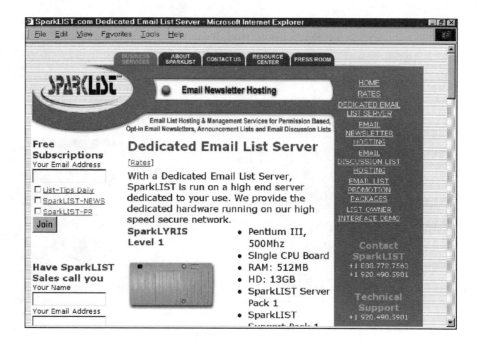

Figure 15.14. SparkLIST's dedicated e-mail list server.

one of the most robust and comprehensive newsletters in this industry. Topics in each information-filled issue include industry news, vendor reviews, helpful publishing tips, and list reviews (both consumer and business categories). To subscribe, send an e-mail to *join-list-universe@list-universe.com*.

17. Windough

This great customer-retention tool (see Figure 15.15) is used to pull online audiences back onto WinDough's Web site. As an advertiser-supported business, this is an effective strategy for WinDough, which runs contests on the Internet and has frequent prize giveaways. The brand personality behind the e-mail newsletters comes from Joe (or I should write "Joe, Joe, ba-boe, bananafana-fo-oh, me-my-ma-o, Joe," which is how he introduced himself in a recent issue). To subscribe, visit *http://www.windough.com*.

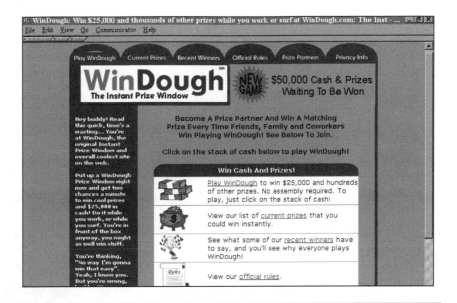

Figure 15.15.   Win at the Mailbucks! page from WinDough.

18. The Humor Network

This isn't just one e-mail publication, rather a whole family of publications under one roof. The Humor Network (Figure 15.16) calls itself one of the world's largest e-mail marketers. In just over one year, they've grown to more than 1.2 million subscribers (growing at a rate of 10 to 15% each month) to their lists, which include Joke-Of-The-Day.com, SportsJokes.com, Kids-Jokes.com, and CollegeJokes.com. Running on an advertising model, the jokes are delivered to subscribers on a daily schedule. To subscribe, visit *http://www.humornetwork.com* (and figure out why the chicken really crossed the road).

19. CRM Talk

The Customer Relationship Management Discussion Group (Figure 15.17) moderated by CRM guru Bob Thompson is your tool for learning when your company is ready to create a customer relationship management program and teaching you how to implement it. To subscribe, visit *http://www.crmguru.com*.

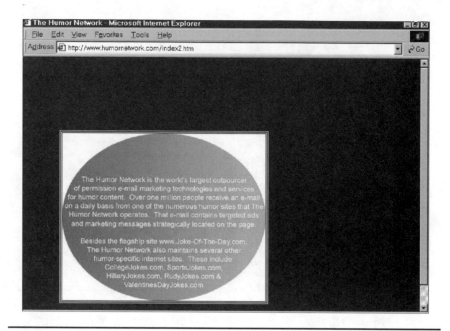

Figure 15.16. The Humor Network's home page.

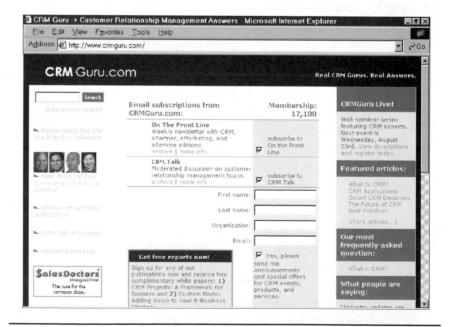

Figure 15.17. The Customer Relationship Management Discussion Group.

20. The Gnome Report, by Lockergnome

Is it fair to say one of these great publications is the best? I'm afraid so, when we're talking about The Gnome Report. Personality is the key to this useful compilation of computer-related information (see Figure 15.18). Publisher Chris Pirillo (and sometime-author Gretchen Pirillo, his wife, not to mention the occasional issue penned—or should it be "pawed"—by the family pooch) starts each issue with commentary. What follows the introduction is a list of useful tools that can be downloaded from the Internet: programs, utilities, and fonts. Pirillo follows each gem with a description of what it does, how he uses it, opinion about the quality of the program and tips for using it yourself. To subscribe, visit *http://www.lockergnome.com.*

Figure 15.18.   Lockergnome's free newsletter, The Gnome Report.

Index

Reader Feedback Sheet

Your comments and suggestions are very important in shaping future publications. Please email us at *moreinfo@maxpress.com* or photocopy this page, jot down your thoughts, and fax it to (850) 934-9981 or mail it to:

Maximum Press
Attn: Jim Hoskins
605 Silverthorn Road
Gulf Breeze, FL 32561

_____

_____

_____

_____

_____

_____

_____

_____

_____

_____

_____

_____

_____

_____

_____

_____

_____

_____

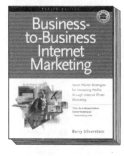

101 Internet Businesses
You Can Start
From Home
by Susan Sweeney, C.A.
520 pages
$29.95
ISBN: 1-885068-59-X

e-Business Formula
for Success
by Susan Sweeney, C.A.
360 pages
$34.95
ISBN: 1-885068-60-3

Exploring IBM
RS/6000 Computers,
Tenth Edition
by Jim Hoskins
and Doug Davies
440 pages
$39.95
ISBN: 1-885068-42-5

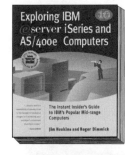

Exploring IBM @server
iSeries and AS/400
Computers,
Tenth Edition
by Jim Hoskins and
Roger Dimmick
560 pages
$39.95
ISBN: 1-885068-43-3

Exploring IBM @server
zSeries and
S/390 Servers,
Seventh Edition
by Jim Hoskins
and Bob Frank
432 pages
$59.95
ISBN: 1-885068-70-0

Exploring IBM
e-Business Software
by Casey Young
308 pages
$49.95
ISBN: 1-885068-58-1

Exploring IBM
@server xSeries
and PCs,
Eleventh Edition
by Jim Hoskins
and Bill Wilson
432 pages
$39.95
ISBN: 1-885068-39-5

Exploring IBM
Technology, Products
& Services,
Fourth Edition
edited by Jim Hoskins
256 pages
$54.95
ISBN: 1-885068-62-X

To purchase a Maximum Press book, visit your local bookstore
or call 1-800-989-6733 (US/Canada) or 1-850-934-4583 (International)
online ordering available at *www.maxpress.com*